The Subtle Subtext

The Subtle Subtext

Hidden Meanings in Literature and Life

Laurent Pernot
Translated by W. E. Higgins

The Pennsylvania State University Press
University Park, Pennsylvania

The translator would like to acknowledge the unstinting support of Professor Pernot in vetting this translation and clarifying certain references to contemporary France, the helpful suggestions of an anonymous reader for the Press, and the generous assistance and astute insights of Pierre Zoberman and Nathan Gross.

Library of Congress Cataloging-in-Publication Data

Names: Pernot, Laurent, author. | Higgins, W. E. (William Edward), 1945– translator.
Title: The subtle subtext : hidden meanings in literature and life / Laurent Pernot ; translated by W. E. Higgins.
Other titles: Art du sous-entendu. English
Description: University Park, Pennsylvania : The Pennsylvania State University Press, [2021] | "First published by Librarie Arthème Fayard, L'Art du sous-entendu … 2018." | Includes bibliographical references and index.
Summary: "Examines forms of double meaning, including allusion, ambiguity, innuendo, and courteous phrases used in daily life, politics, and literature. Draws on examples from across the human sciences, from Homer to Shakespeare, Molière, Proust, Foucault, and others"— Provided by publisher.
Identifiers: LCCN 2021038356 | ISBN 9780271091976 (hardback) | ISBN 9780271092171 (paperback)

Subjects: LCSH: Subtext (Drama, novel, etc.) | Connotation (Linguistics) | Allusions in literature.
Classification: LCC PN3383.S83 P4713 2021 | DDC 808.2/3—dc23
LC record available at https://lccn.loc.gov /2021038356

Copyright © 2021 The Pennsylvania State University
All rights reserved
Printed in the United States of America
Published by The Pennsylvania State University Press,
University Park, PA 16802–1003

First published by Librairie Arthème Fayard
L'Art du sous-entendu by Laurent Pernot
© Librairie Arthème Fayard, 2018.

The Pennsylvania State University Press is a member of the Association of University Presses.

It is the policy of The Pennsylvania State University Press to use acid-free paper. Publications on uncoated stock satisfy the minimum requirements of American National Standard for Information Sciences—Permanence of Paper for Printed Library Material, ANSI Z39.48–1992.

Contents

Preface vii

1 SUBTEXTS ALL AROUND US
1

2 THE RHETORIC OF
FIGURED SPEECH
15

3 THE HERMENEUTICS
OF SUSPICION
26

4 RISKS AND SAFEGUARDS
OF INTERPRETATION
37

5 GREEK PRETENSES
ABOUT ROME
52

6 AN OX ON THE TONGUE
70

7 SEXORAMA
92

8 WHAT ABOUT BEING FRANK?
108

9 CATALOG OF FURTHER
EXAMPLES AND PRACTICES
119

A FINAL WORD
141

*Translator's Note on
Citations* 145

Notes 147

Index 163

Preface

We live surrounded by subtexts and do not realize it. Like Molière's Monsieur Jourdain, who unwittingly spoke prose, we send messages with double meanings and decrypt those sent by someone else without even thinking about it.

Consider the following sentence, said to be written by General Charles de Gaulle on a photograph that Maréchal Alphonse Juin had asked him to autograph: "To Maréchal Juin, who knew how to seize victory when it presented itself."[1] With a cordiality befitting chums from the French military academy, St. Cyr, de Gaulle paid homage to the victor in the Tunisian and Italian campaigns. But that verb "to seize," not "to win," that additional "when it presented itself." . . . Instinctively, the reader of such a sentence senses some reservations, as if the author of the dedication, while writing "You won, my friend" (the two men used the familiar form of French address), was saying at the same time, "You were not *the* winner." Through words, no matter how ordinary, one picks up mixed emotions, the rift between the Free French Forces and the Vichy army in North Africa, and all the dynamics of two personal trajectories, close at their beginning and divergent at their end.

That is how subtexts function, making something more understood, or something other than what is expressly stated. Depending on the case, one speaks of allusion, the unspoken, ambiguity, equivocation, implicitness, innuendo, a second level: the richness of the terminology readily attests to the diversity and extent of the phenomenon. All these terms are not synonyms, but they do cluster around the idea of double meaning whenever two distinct yet inseparable senses are present in any given statement. This is not a matter of the opposition between signifier and signified but of a double signified in a single signifier. The most comprehensive designation, used for this reason in the title of the present work, is "subtext," because it focuses attention on one of the two meanings in the double sense, the more interesting of the two, the one that counts and is not obvious.

Certain subtexts are automatic and even inevitable, as when we say, "Jim has quit smoking," implying that he smoked previously, or "Considering your experience, you will surely succeed," which supposes that experience is a sufficient qualification. Other subtexts, however, are calculated, subtle, and pursue an agenda, like the dedication mentioned previously. The word "ambiguity" is itself ambiguous, because the plurality of meaning that it designates is, depending on the case, conscious or not.

Yet subtext is not to be confused with deceit or secrecy. Indeed, it is not at all about leading into error or hiding. The subtext is more paradoxical: it consists in saying without saying and in conveying a veiled content that is meant to be unveiled. There is the obvious, and "submerged" beneath this surface the subtext lies literally "understood." Similar dissonance between the stated and the suggested enables all sorts of subtleties, but it does arouse suspicion and uncertainty. How many times do we ask ourselves after an inconclusive meeting, "But what did he (or she) mean, precisely?" Or even "Did he (or she) want to tell me something?" That is why it is worth the effort to scrutinize a problem of considerable importance, one where it is useful to know how to get one's bearings when it confronts us.[2]

The following pages aim, therefore, to explore the world of the subtext, connecting areas that are ordinarily treated separately. Subjecting them to a global approach breaches the disciplinary boundaries that have weighed on consideration of the subject, the compartmentalizing of the various humane and social disciplines (e.g., linguistics, psychology, history, philosophy, and political science), each of which, as will become clear, has a contribution to make. There is also compartmentalizing among the different levels of subtexts, notably between the precautions inspired by politeness and the insinuations that spring from polemic. Certainly, there are subtexts that soothe and there are subtexts that sting, but they both follow the same fundamental process. Outlining this general picture is critical if we are to take in an entire panorama of our social conduct, our thought, and our literature.

By way of setting out lights to guide us through this field, it seemed expedient to offer conceptual tools and keys to reading, to evaluate the opinions of authors who have dealt with the question in different periods, and to provide examples, citations, and anecdotes, be they serious or funny, and sometimes daring; in this area, a telling word can be worth more than an entire speech. The material gathered is obviously not meant to be exhaustive, and bibliographical citations have been restricted to the most important. I have selected cases that seemed to me indicative and that reflect my tastes, reading, or experience. Moreover, since the subject has a long history, the approach must be historically broad. It would be different with other themes, and each period could involve an irreducible uniqueness. But the subtext belongs to all times. That is why it is permissible, and even desirable, to engage the periods in mutual dialogue without being either eclectic or cavalier, having due regard for their individual peculiarities while building on their actual structural and thematic similarities. Greco-Roman antiquity, in particular, emerges as an essential contributor, which one does not necessarily expect with this topic; to be sure, it is not the be-all and end-all, but it did lay down theoretical markers, and it has provided evergreen examples. Without wishing to elaborate on my personal history, I have to admit that my training does dispose me not to neglect this illuminating and often overlooked area.

My other point of reference in these pages is modern times, considered broadly from the nineteenth to the twenty-first century, since the reader has a right to expect results relevant to the world in which we live. That is why the investigation is organized around two poles, antiquity and modernity, the aim being not to trace a continuous history (that would be interminable) but to select instructive moments. This does not mean that intervening periods failed to offer useful areas of inquiry; simply put, one had to choose, and it seemed interesting to bring together the past and the present in a single echo chamber.

Nor will the space accorded here to rhetoric come as a surprise, in its meaning as "art of speaking" or "art of persuading." Rhetoric arose in antiquity as a technique at the service of courtroom and public speakers, and quite quickly evolved into a leading intellectual discipline. Finally, triumphant and taken up by the educated public, it reigned over the curriculum of a liberal education, a position it held for a long time, as even the names given to the grades in French *lycées* showed, "Rhetoric" and "Advanced Rhetoric." Rhetoric involves at the same time the education of elites, public instruction, and the history of *mentalités*. After abundant criticism, this discipline has currently been rehabilitated as a connecting thread in cultural history and a multifaceted methodology for thinking about the use of language in society. That is precisely its role in our study. The philosopher Leo Strauss, author of an outstanding contribution on allusive literature, noted this, writing about the expression "to write between the lines": "The expression is clearly metaphoric. Any attempt to express its meaning in unmetaphoric language would

Preface

lead to the discovery of a terra incognita, a field whose dimensions are as yet unexplored and which offers ample scope for highly intriguing work and even important investigations. One may say without fear of being presently convicted of grave exaggeration that almost the only preparatory work to guide the explorer in this field is buried in the writings of the rhetoricians of antiquity."[3]

My own studies on rhetoric have helped my awareness of the inexhaustible potentialities of language. Persuasion speaks to the mind and the heart: that is a first point. But a second is that one can also make oneself understood without speaking, thanks to the unspoken and speaking differently. This is where the realm of the subtext begins, to which the ancients cleared the path. To continue in this direction, antiquity and rhetoric, which were the point of departure, no longer sufficed. It was necessary to broaden the horizon, integrate other points of view, cross perspectives, and isolate problems. Those are some of the things ventured here.

Everyone perceives the art of the subtext intuitively. All readers are qualified, especially the French, since my nation has a reputation for being intellectual and particularly endowed in this regard. "This sudden coalescing between what one thinks and what one doesn't say, this genius for the subtext, is half of the French language," Balzac wrote.[4] If one may sometimes complain that, in the age of various media and the internet, cultural codes are changing and literature is less present, it nonetheless remains the case that the subtext is still here, whatever its mutations, because it is a constant given of the human intellect. So this is a question of taking the time to examine the inner workings of devices we already use. The task is to analyze a notion everyone knows, or thinks he knows, and to take seriously a universal mode of communication. The subtext does not amount merely to lewd allusions or vexing insinuations; it is omnipresent in daily exchanges, as it is in politics and literature. It lies beyond discursive logic. In exploring it, one turns oneself toward a less rational part of human communication.[5]

1

Subtexts All Around Us

The Niceties of Daily Life

To begin our reconnaissance, the rules of social life offer a choice terrain. Etiquette is definitely not limited to posture, proper dress, and table manners. It also includes a language, ways of speaking, which call for lowering the tone and occasionally saying just the opposite. Giovanni Della Casa, a master of the social graces, was a sixteenth-century Florentine and author of a standard reference work on the topic, the *Galateo*, which has become synonymous in Italy with etiquette itself (*galateo*, a common noun, designates any treatise or collection of rules on manners). He is careful not to omit among his recommendations what he calls "ceremonies," those hyperbolic and flattering formalities ("I am, Sir, your humble servant"), as well as courteous turns of phrase like "I have not been able to express myself clearly" instead of "You just don't get me," "Let's step back for a moment to determine if what we are saying is correct" instead of "You're wrong."[1]

Such sweetening even today is common currency in daily life. It is rare to blurt out "That's it, I'm outta here!" Better manners would be "Oh! I am afraid my train will be leaving soon." "Do you have a light?" is more polite than "Give me a match!"

In England, when your hosts offer you tea, all the nuances count. If someone says to you, "Would you like a cup of tea?" or "Can I get you some tea?," he probably is really offering you some tea. But if a somewhat old-fashioned sort asks, "Would you like a cup of tea, or would you rather not?," this way of posing the question suggests that it is time to leave, that is, "Please leave soon"—and maybe you were only waiting for the cue . . .[2]

Consider the following dialogue, which I personally overheard.

First Speaker: Hello! It's N. Forgive me for calling at this hour. I hope it's not too late.

Second Speaker: For you, it's never too late.

The person summoned to the phone at a late hour meant to say kindly, "When it's you calling, the hour is of no importance because it is always a pleasure to take your calls"—unless, that is, the answer is a bit ironic, even critical, meaning, "You're just not a person who observes normal hours."

All members of the French Academy, when considering a candidate, know that a formulaic expression like "He will be one of us one day" means "Do not count on my vote today."

If the expert charged with evaluating a project certifies that the file is OK, one must understand that it is not exceptional. The committee receiving the report will not be misled.

Politeness extends to saying the reverse of what one might expect. When we declare to someone who has given us a gift, "You shouldn't have," this sentence, taken literally, sounds like a reprimand. But in the majority of cases it is not taken that way; it obviously means the complete opposite and constitutes a stronger way of saying "Thank you."

During a group discussion, a participant begins to speak when his turn comes. He mentions how he agrees with previous speakers and praises their proposal. Then he lays out his own viewpoint, and the listeners gradually become aware that he is really voicing a different opinion from the others, that he is, in fact, totally opposed to them. His introduction said yes; he really meant no.

The implicit is thus an integral aspect of communication. It contributes to the smooth functioning of human relations, and it avoids giving offense among individuals or groups while maintaining hierarchical harmony. It is always a touchy business to confront an interlocutor directly: to rebut, dismiss, and contradict, some sweetening is called for to ease social interaction. This is not just another way of saying the same thing; it reveals a choice to say something else, showing that one does not mean to be aggressive and that one wants to meet the other halfway, or at least to take his or her viewpoint into consideration.

Beyond immediate utility, the politeness of the subtext contains an image of what ought to be the relationship among individuals in a civilized society. It reflects an ethical code. It also answers to a need for "distinction," according to a notion dear to anthropologist and theorist Pierre Bourdieu,[3] because someone who knows how to employ subtexts is refined and graceful. He is "distinguished" and thereby makes himself "distinct" from others. Even wicked digs are more graceful when allusive rather than blunt. Among the thousand "historical ripostes" Stéphane Bern has collected, here is the judgment that the eighteenth-century French epigrammatist Nicolas Chamfort rendered on a couplet its author had submitted to him: "Excellent, but you need to cut a couple of lines."[4]

Layered Novels

Moving on to literature, an entire book can contain two or even more levels of meaning. The reader sees the evident sense and makes out the hidden one, the two superimposed like interleaved layers of meaning. This is what critics call a coded work, a kind of cipher.

For example, *Penguin Island* by Anatole France traces the history of the Penguin people from their origins until his own time and even beyond (the book dates from 1908). The narrative begins with the evangelization of the community by St. Maël, an elderly noble as pious as he was poor-sighted, for he mistakenly baptizes these winged creatures, "having taken them to be humans small in stature but serious in bearing."[5] They go through ancient history, with the first clothing, the invention of private property, and the establishing of a body politic. They have a Middle Ages and a Renaissance, which are distinguished, among other things, by transference of relics and, in the arts, by "the Primitives of Penguin painting,"[6] arriving at modern times with wars, literary salons, trials, and scandals, and finally coming to the future, which will witness the development of technological progress as well as revolutions. Obviously such a chronicle operates entirely on two levels. It is a history of France under the guise of the Penguins' history. The Penguin people's fortunes and misfortunes have allowed the author, with a smile, to suggest ideas he wanted to promote concerning rationalism, social justice, and especially Dreyfusism.

The same process occurs in *Animal Farm*, the novel by George Orwell published in 1945, which deals ostensibly with animals but actually with human society, as it relates how the animals on the farm of Mr. Jones attacked and expelled him to take control of their own destiny. Founded originally on the principle of the strictest equality, the regime degenerates into a dictatorship in which the pigs, who exercise power, seize privileges and oppress the other animals, using the slogan "ALL ANIMALS ARE EQUAL BUT SOME ANIMALS ARE MORE EQUAL THAN OTHERS."[7] Manipulation of the masses, ideological indoctrination, broken alliances, denunciation of traitors, cult of personality: nothing is missing, and the enslaved animals finally declare that it has become impossible to distinguish the pigs, supposed liberators, from humans, their former masters. Throughout the narrative, the word "Communism" and the names "Russia" and "Stalin" are never uttered, and yet they impose themselves. Orwell confirmed this interpretation, writing in a letter that this work was "in the first place . . . a satire on the Russian Revolution," and that it had, moreover, "a broader application" and meant to call out the risks that every revolution entails when the masses lose control of the new regime, which "can only lead to a change of masters."[8] So there are three levels of meaning here, not just two: one consists of the apparent narrative content, with the two others as understood subtexts separated into a specific and a general message. The novel's subtitle, *A Fairy Story*, is itself designedly ambiguous and jarring, since it designates at once the narration, which is fairy tale–like in that it is not realistic (yet how dark!), and the content of the narrative, the lies and cock-and-bull stories dictators propagate. Such suggestions were so disconcerting at the time that the manuscript was repeatedly rejected before it found a publisher.

Orwell's masterpiece, *1984*, published in 1949, is likewise based on a double register of meanings. It tells the story of Winston and Julia, who, in a world divided up between the Big Powers, defy prohibitions and form a secret relationship under the eye, alas, of Big Brother. Their relationship, found out, will end tragically. Behind the work of imagination the reader perceives without difficulty the criticism of totalitarian regimes past and present and the revelation of future risks. Every utopia essentially associates on two levels the exposition of an ideal world and a lesson for the real world; this is even more so for dystopias, which invent terrifying universes for criticism and sounding the alarm.

Placing himself a century after Orwell, Boualem Sansal, in his work *2084: The End of the World*, describes the empire of Abistan, which takes its name from the prophet Abi, and which is forced into blind obedience and a monotheistic cult. The text comes with a categorical warning: "The reader will beware of thinking that this story is true or that it is based on any known reality. No, it is really all made up. . . . It is a work of pure invention."[9] Naturally, the more the author persists in his denials, the better we understand precisely the opposite, that we are being invited to look for resemblances, hardly accidental, with actual situations.

We cannot leave coded works without recalling the island of W described by Georges Perec in *W, or the Memory of Childhood*. It is a society, rigorously organized, devoted entirely to the ideals of competitive sports, selectivity, and masculinity. It conceals an image of the world of the concentration camps and also harks back to its author's biography, marked by the war and the Shoah that struck his family.

These few examples show the depth of coded works. Safety considerations are operative in certain cases, when an outright denunciation would be imprudent and would endanger the writer. But these precautions are not the whole story. Double meaning is sought out for its literary power, because it gives readers an active role, leading them to construct interpretations by themselves, thereby reinforcing their acceptance. We will have to return to these processes, which explain the subtext's effectiveness.

Role-Playing

In the theater, plays with a message are only a variation on the previous theme. The plot of Arthur Miller's *The Crucible* takes place in 1692, but the drama takes aim at McCarthyism. In *The Flies* of Jean-Paul Sartre, staged in 1943, the character Orestes poses the problem of resistance to the German occupation.

More profoundly, every play by definition elicits a double take. We see men and women acting and speaking on the stage, and we enter into their story, surrendering to the mechanism of comic illusion. But we are no less aware that the play is a game, that the characters are actors, that their deeds and actions exist only on our account, so as to move us, reform us, make us reflect, and so forth. By virtue of this shift, every spectator in the theater is, as such, a decoder of subtexts.

Things become complicated when distortions arise that expose the gap between the meaning as perceived by the characters and as understood by the audience. The extraordinarily various ways of address unique to the theater produce distancing effects. The plays of Molière are full of such asides, whose comic effect is guaranteed. How often does a servant mutter criticisms in his beard, making quite sure that his master hears him even as he refrains from direct address, like La Flèche insisting, "I am speaking to my cap"; or Dorine, "I am talking to myself"; or Sganarelle, "I am not speaking to you too"?[10] How many times does a character pretend to be addressing his interlocutor when he is really addressing a third party, like Elmire responding to the advances of Tartuffe with statements meant for her husband, Orgon, who is hiding under the table? Orgon's position physically translates the intended recipient lurking beneath Elmire's words.[11] Even today there is a proverb current in Italy, "Speak to the daughter-in-law so the mother-in-law understands," or "Speak to the daughter so the daughter-in-law understands" (the saying permits variations), which well depicts such a communication "triangulation" in a family context.[12]

Replies in the theater always pass through the speakers to address the spectators, as in expository scenes where one character explains the situation to another, such explanations being really intended for the audience. Cléante and Angélique exchange amatory couplets that only gradually awaken the suspicions of the young girl's father, while they are utterly clear to the outside observer.[13] The precious damsels, in turn, do not even recognize the import of what they are saying; their statements boomerang, and when they think they are praising refined Parisian sensibility, they unwittingly ridicule it.[14]

More serious are the ambiguities of tragedy. When Agamemnon in Racine warns Iphigénie that there is going to be a sacrificial offering, the innocent girl does not understand that she herself must be the victim. "Will I be permitted to join in your prayers?" she naively asks her father, who answers with atrocious duplicity, "You surely will, my girl."[15] Another monumental ambiguity occurs in Sophocles with the monologue of Ajax. Covered in shame after his mental breakdown, the hero has expressed his intention to commit suicide, but his concubine Tecmessa has tried mightily to dissuade him. That is why, in order to be left alone and free to act, he goes on a tirade implying that he has given up the idea of dying, when in truth his resolve is unchanged. He announces that he will go and purify himself, that he will bury his sword, and that people will soon be able to say he has been saved. Though the chorus may rejoice upon hearing these words, the spectator, who knows the rest of the story, can only tremble. Ajax means that death will be his salvation, that if he must bury his sword, it will be with its blade in the air so that he can throw himself upon it: tragic irony.[16]

Debates and Sound Bites

From the theater to politics is only a small step. Recently, former president and CEO of the *New York Times* Mark Thompson analyzed a debate between the Conservative Chancellor of the Exchequer in England and a Laborite opponent on the subject of state-supported social programs, following a news item involving multiple infanticides in a family living on public assistance. Thompson needed no less than four pages to bring to light the implicit conclusions and hasty generalizations used by each side in its arguments. The stark conclusion: in this important debate, all the critical points were subtexts.[17]

At the end of the nineteenth century, Theodor Herzl had a similar insight when, before becoming one of the founders of Zionism, he was in the early stages of his career as a Parisian journalist whose beat was the parliamentary debates in the Chamber of Deputies. One day, he was present at a particularly convoluted and engineered session that led to the fall of the government. He commented on the "hidden, second meaning" of the speeches, "the misleading statements and fakery," and drew an incontrovertible lesson: "Public debate constitutes the most accomplished form of secrecy."[18]

Yet, to be sure, all the dissimulations of politics do not come down to maneuverings. Some derive from carefully considered choices, when those in charge know that their words can have serious consequences. Officials of monetary policy, for example, aware of the importance of their statements and the repercussions they can have on the financial markets, have developed the art of expressing themselves in an oblique manner.[19] There is even the word "Fedspeak" to characterize the vague and obscure style used by the officials of the US Federal Reserve, the "Fed." One of the chairmen of this institution, Alan Greenspan, became a veritable theorist of deliberate obscurity and constructive ambiguity aimed at preventing any overly hasty reaction to his announcements. In the same vein, the former head of the European Central Bank, Mario Draghi, gave the impression of speaking with unaccustomed clarity when he affirmed in 2012, at a time of serious threats to the currency, that the bank was "ready to do whatever it takes to save the euro." This announcement had the immediate effect of reassuring the markets and improving the situation, and the expression "whatever it takes," while seemingly clear, if one wants it to be, but all the same susceptible to multiple interpretations, has passed into the historical record as a model of frankness. This goes to show that everything is relative in this area, and that there exist different levels of intensity in expressing oneself, be it directly or indirectly.

In today's democracies political expression is often reserved and subtle, because a sweeping statement could seem "impolitic" and prove counterproductive. Politicians have to promote themselves without seeming ambitious or overly aggressive. They must know how to suggest without going too far. Our newspapers and televisions are rife with coded statements that neither fool nor amaze us. Thus, in France a Socialist deputy declares: "I find that the Socialist Party, the Socialist community, does not measure up to the coming battle to provide direction." A magazine decrypted this into plain speech: "I warned you I was the better candidate to assume leadership of the Socialist Party. The current First Secretary is not doing the job."[20] Are the French government authorities paying homage in the excerpt below to a deceased former prime minister? The press had no hesitation in interpreting each sentence and commenting on "an encomium stuffed with current allusions":[21]

Subtexts All Around Us

"This man of compromise never hesitated to have recourse to article 49–3," François Hollande recalled at the end of a week marked by new confrontations in the Parliament among Socialists over the labor law. . . . "And since Michel Rocard respected the regulation in 1980, the victory of 1981 also occurred," Manuel Valls rejoined, a way for him, the Prime Minister, to vaunt the virtues of unity when strategies were being honed on the left, especially in Socialist ranks for 2017. . . . "He was never afraid to rock his political family," Manuel Valls also pointedly recalled, whose relations with the left wing of the Socialist Party have deteriorated because of his policy.

During the televised debate of the second round in the 1974 French presidential election, Valéry Giscard d'Estaing, the opponent of François Mitterrand, referred to the outcome of the first round, using Clermont-Ferrand as an example: "You have noticed the results in last Sunday's voting from the city of Clermont-Ferrand . . . a city which is intimately familiar to you and to me." Toward the end of the broadcast's first half hour, Mitterrand had just launched into a serious attack, charging his adversary with presenting a platform catering to the interests of a privileged "social class." Giscard knew he had to parry the blow, and he did so in a low-key and nasty manner. Clermont-Ferrand happened to be the family seat not only of Giscard but also of a lady who was "close" to Mitterrand. By emphatically citing the city as his first example, Giscard was alluding to Mitterrand's double life, a secret then unknown to the general public. He meant to rattle his adversary without risking criticism for being indiscreet or hitting below the belt, since he said nothing explicit. After this little detour through the capital of the Auvergne, candidate Giscard had the leeway to move on to the results from Paris and Lyons and to cast himself as the workingman's representative.

And since it seems in France that everything ends with a song, one will not forget, among the numerous episodes in the presidential wars of words, the *Little French Songs*, a 2013 collection from Carla Bruni, the first lady at the time. In a period when President Nicolas Sarkozy was the object of numerous attacks, this album seemed to defend and shed light on his presidency. Badgered with questions, the pop singer had to admit that "My Raymond" ("My Raymond, he's perfect") was a thinly disguised praise of her husband. As for the song called "The Penguin," some people need not have read Anatole France to suspect symbolic meaning. Nevertheless, the composer-lyricist denied having targeted anyone in this caustic text.

Fables, Enigmas, Proverbs

What has been said so far demonstrates the constant presence of subtext in the world we inhabit. One should likewise mention the legal domain, which distinguishes between the letter and the spirit; advertising, which uses and abuses double meanings and equivocations, and which continually regales us with mischievous and naughty messages; or the language of images, which would require another book all its own.[22] This presence has deep roots that we must now unearth. The basic procedures of the human mind and primordial forms of communication entail the double play of encryption and decryption, the hallmark of the subtext.

The fable, a universal genre, offers an example of a narrative containing a hidden meaning, which may remain implicit or, on the contrary, be revealed in the form of a moral. If the moral provides the narrative's meaning, the narrative, by being interactive, influences how the moral is received. From Aesop to Jean de La Fontaine to Ivan Krylov and the *Fables of Dictatorship* by Leonardo Sciascia, fables, by definition, have double meanings. "Fables are not what they seem to be."[23] They give lessons in morality, for example, or politics, with an apparent simplicity. "This fable is all about you" (*de te fabula narratur*) is the classic formulation.[24]

Akin to the fable is the enigma, which sets forth apparent impossibilities and poses a challenge to whoever must solve it. "What is the being that walks first on four feet, then on two, and finally on three, and is less quick when it has more feet?" the Sphinx asks Oedipus. "What is this ice that sets you on fire, that by enslaving you makes you king?" Princess Turandot in Puccini's opera asks the mysterious prince, who will realize that she is describing herself. All periods have adored these "bagatelles"[25] or trifles that stimulate the mind and pique the curiosity. Not only are they playful; they can be invested with magical, esoteric, poetic, and philosophic powers for "the enigma-intoxicated, the twilight-enjoyers."[26] Mottos and symbols are part of the same environment, even riddles: "What has teeth and doesn't bite? A comb." Enigmas, comic impersonations, and other types of charades were as much the rage in ancient Greek symposia as they are in modern European literary circles. The party game Taboo rests on this principle: it involves making other players guess a word without using certain forbidden words, or "taboos," because they are too close to the word to be guessed.

Jean Paulhan conducted original research in this area at the beginning of the twentieth century, and his name now appears for the first time, but not the last, in our inquiry. Paulhan spent several years of his youth on Madagascar,

Subtexts All Around Us

learned the local language, and upon returning to France made known poems he had collected called *Hain-teny*. "The Hain-teny are popular poems in use among the Malgaches . . . enigmatic poems, difficult in more ways than one and akin to those which literary historians call poetry of the obscure—medieval nonsense songs or troubadour lays."[27] Studying these poems' characteristics, the author examines in particular the use or creation of proverbs fraught with meaning. For example, "The ant who follows the dry wood finds itself at night in strange territory." Paulhan explains this pronouncement, which may seem cryptic at first glance, as follows: "It is about the ant that a gatherer of deadwood carries back in his bundle, in other words, the surprises to which an adventurous spirit exposes itself." The strength of such utterances resides in their opaqueness. They are used in ritualized disputes, and their sense is dictated by neighboring utterances and the general context of what is being said. There are, nonetheless, important variations in how they are received and understood, whether by a naive stranger, like Paulhan himself at the start of his investigation, or by a native speaker.

Paulhan followed up this study with *L'Expérience du proverbe* (The experience of the proverb), which started as a thesis project and led in 1925 to a first book.[28] Building on the Malgache collection he had assembled, Paulhan emphasizes the "mysterious authority" of proverbs and their complexity. For a proverb does not carry just one hidden meaning that would be constantly present behind the literal sense. It has multiple meanings, varying with the context, debatable, and endlessly susceptible to rejection or denial. When Paulhan himself tries to use proverbs with his friends and acquaintances from Madagascar, he winds up being surprised or rejected, and he needs a long apprenticeship to master their use so others listen.

Wisdom, real or supposed, readily expresses itself in the form of maxims and utterances, pithy but laden with meaning, which owe their stature to their adaptability and allusive character. It is up to the disciple to learn the lesson, to understand what the master meant, and to make the truth live in himself.

Deciphering the World

We now mount a step higher on the ladder of causality. The entire universe, according to some widely held ideas, is an enigma. Mankind traverses "forests of symbols"[29] that it must decipher. I am going to offer some different, occasionally daring, insights to shed light on what one might call subtext thinking, that is, ways of reasoning that are current in different areas and that all assume hidden contents and shrewd explanations. They create predispositions, visions of the world that are conducive to the recognition of multiple layers of meaning.

Belief in an underlying philosophical and religious framework finds expression in several interconnected themes that Pierre Hadot has studied, such as the aphorism of Heraclitus, "Nature loves to hide itself," the notion of the "secret of nature," and the image of the veiled goddess Artemis-Isis. These themes, going back to classical antiquity, have exerted a continuous influence down to modern times through the Middle Ages, the Renaissance, the Enlightenment, and German Romanticism. They imply that the world hides itself from man, an uncomfortable, even unbearable situation, which elicits varied reactions. While the learned struggled to wrest its secrets from nature and to dominate it through science and technology, poets and artists followed the path of empathy in approaching the unknown through ecstasy and contemplation.[30] From our point of view, it follows that the ancients and the moderns have habitually judged the world to contain mysterious features requiring personal efforts of comprehension. The movement of the stars, the laws of physics, and even our own psychology are all right before our eyes and yet everything eludes us, unless we discover the hidden explanations.

The philosophy of Plato, for example, rests on a distinction between physical appearances, or *phainomena*, and the intelligible forms, or "Ideas," the latter inaccessible to the senses and yet more true and real than the *phainomena* they produce and for whose existence they account. The famous image of the cave illustrates this opposition, drawing a contrast between the situation of the fettered prisoners, who contemplate the shadow theater projected on the cave's back wall, and the struggle of one, unfettered, who returns to the light and tries to see the upper world.[31] It is well known that Platonism has inundated Western art and thought. Its adherents had to ferret out Being from Becoming and pass beyond the gross pseudorealities that satisfy most people to gain access to a higher level and purer entities.

We come now to the most sensitive point: religions are the favorite realm of such conceptions. In religious matters, by definition, nothing is either simple or direct, since the faithful are summoned to turn themselves, against all logic, toward invisible supernatural powers. The vertical aspect of transcendence summons up a reading of the world on two levels, the quest for a truth truer than true, and faith in a nonrational Beyond that paradoxically explains the Here-Below. Whether they are pagan, Christian, or something else, religions entail a dimension of mystery not only in their ceremonies,

Subtexts All Around Us

rites, and sacraments but also in their theological content with its doctrines and dogmas. Religious mysteries create an expectation and call for revelation, more or less clearly, at the hands of intermediaries, priests, prophets, and exegetes. This dialectic of hiding and divulging arouses a propensity for decryption. Man is reduced to understanding imperfectly, to being the plaything of the gods, and to trying to make his way as best he can. Interpretation is required: "It is the glory of God to conceal a thing; but the honor of kings is to search out a matter."[32]

Sacred discourse is veiled discourse. The oracles given by the pagan gods were so ambiguous that their interpretation was entrusted to professionals. Even they were often mistaken. When Croesus, the king of Lydia, consulted the Delphic Oracle to know whether he should start a war against Persia, Apollo's priestess replied that, were he to do so, he would destroy a great empire. Nobody was able to warn Croesus that this great empire was his own and that the god was predicting his certain defeat.[33] The philosopher Heraclitus, previously mentioned, who had a gift for ambiguity (he was called "the Obscure"), stated that the god of Delphi "neither reveals nor conceals; he indicates."[34] In a different context, the parables in the gospels are a typical example of veiled discourse, familiar and concrete while being instructive, at once striking and vague, and commanding our attention, thanks to a symbolic narrative.

Allegory

Allegory, a complex concept, is here fundamental. *Allêgoria* is an Ancient Greek word compounded of two elements, one meaning "other," the second "speak." Etymologically, it means "to say something other." Something other than what? Something other than what one has said: the word "allegory" contains within itself the association of an obvious sense and an understood sense. In its first meaning, allegory is a stylistic device, a "type of continuous metaphor."[35] It is the suggestion that behind words' literal meaning lies a complementary sense enriching them or lending them nuance. For example, one may use the image of a ship to describe governing the state, storms to deplore political troubles, a port to arouse a desire for social peace. When joined with personification, allegory allows the presentation of an abstract idea or moral concept in the concrete form of an individual, like Discord in Vergil,[36] or "Liberty leading the People" in Eugène Delacroix's painting. Even more so, in the vocabulary of theology, allegory carries a religious message hidden behind Scripture's literal meaning.

The Subtle Subtext

Allegory implies allegorical interpretation—that is, making a methodical effort to search out the deeper meaning that does not give itself up immediately. The ancients practiced the allegorical interpretation of myths in the hope of detecting philosophical and moral truths in the legends about the gods and in the poetic and artistic works reflecting those legends. Thus, the labors of Hercules represented for some the triumph of courage over the passions, and the erect phallus of Hermes symbolized generative power. One of the oldest known Greek papyri, the Derveni Papyrus (fourth century BC), discovered in 1962 in a tomb in northern Greece, despite its fragmentary and charred condition offers a particularly precious example of ancient allegorical interpretation.[37] Commenting on verses attributed to the legendary hero Orpheus, the anonymous author begins by assuming that this poet speaks "in riddles," and his entire effort consists of uncovering a teaching about man and the universe from behind rituals and myths. If the faithful offer innumerable votive cakes, it is because the souls of the dead are also innumerable: the rite is a symbol. Likewise, the tales relating to Zeus and his forebears Cronus and Ouranos conceal lessons in physics: theogony is cosmogony. And so he continues.

The Bible underwent allegorical interpretation as well. The Old Testament, taken literally, seemed full of unacceptable or uninteresting narratives, leading Philo of Alexandria, a Greek philosopher inspired by both Judaism and Platonism (first century AD), to deploy the riches of his ingenuity by investing each detail with an edifying meaning. For example, if Joseph in Genesis is presented with the characteristics of a shepherd it is in order to symbolize political man, since politicians are "shepherds of men"; if he wears a many-colored coat, it is because politics is something wavering and various; if his brothers sell him into slavery, it is because the politician is the slave of the people.[38] After Philo comes St. Paul, who explains that the Old Testament is covered with a veil and that it prefigures the New Testament as an "allegory."[39] The deeper meaning of the Old Testament's message was addressed to Christians, who alone were capable of understanding it, and therefore it had to remain hidden until the coming of Christ. From then on, the interpretation of the Old Testament could be renewed in light of the Gospels' message, and the Fathers of the Church or the theologians of the Middle Ages were able time and again to elaborate allegorical approaches for explicating Scripture using multiple and highly specialized methods. Literal meaning covers a mystical meaning: "A cipher has two meanings."[40] The double movement of allegory, to envelop and develop, corresponds to a basic aspiration of art and thought.

Conspiracy Theories

Seen from a different angle, inquiry into the secrets of nature can lead to astrology, horoscopes, alchemy, and esotericism. A modern avatar of this propensity is rampant today in conspiracy theories. As we know, there are people who are persuaded that whenever some public figure dies, a government or some secret organization is responsible, whether it is President Kennedy, Martin Luther King Jr., the popular French comedian Coluche, or Princess Diana. They suspect ulterior motives in the manufacture of vaccines or in the white vapor trails, the "contrails," of flying aircraft, and they see Big Pharma, Monsanto, and the attendees of the Bilderberg Meeting at work everywhere. They think that the Apollo spacecraft never landed on the moon and that the whole truth has never been told about the disappearance of certain young girls in Normandy, or about Watergate, or 9/11. Best sellers like *The Da Vinci Code* or the TV series *The X-Files* play upon these inclinations. Somebody is pulling the strings, powerful interests are in play; there is no such thing as coincidence.

The idea of conspiracy, whose psychological mechanisms are highly interesting, is more pervasive than it might seem at first glance.[41] And it is spreading like a virus thanks to the internet. While it resembles obsession and madness when generalized, it can affect each of us individually to a lesser degree. Is there a reader of the list above who has not shaken his or her head at one or another of its items, saying that, at least in this case, there is some truth to the suspicions? After all, conspiracies are not all imaginary, and some had to have been real. According to a recent survey by the French pollster IFOP, 79 percent of the French believe in "at least one" conspiracy theory.[42] Be that as it may, those who detect a plot are proud of their distrust and their suspicions. They see themselves as justified, and they feel they have gained access to intelligence not available to all. They are convinced that their environment masks unacknowledged truths, according to a logic analogous to that dealing with the secrets of nature and transcendence, albeit under a depraved form.

With the different types of mystic thought, the anthropological and ideological bases for the subtext are in place. He who deciphers the world has all the more reason to decipher the world of words.

2

The Rhetoric of Figured Speech

In view of the subtext's actual range, a need arose for a method of describing and classifying it in order to understand and teach it better, distinct from a more or less haphazard treatment. The theoretical effort flourished especially in two periods, in antiquity with the construction of a precise and focused system, and in modern times with a proliferation of interpretative approaches. We start with antiquity.

The Invention of a Concept

About two thousand years ago, Greek and Latin theorists of rhetoric developed an original concept designed to handle situations in which an orator or a writer uses pretense to disguise his meaning by employing roundabout language to arrive obliquely at his desired point. This is why the old masters can claim the honor of having been the first theorists of the subtext. They called their concept "figured speech" (in Greek, *eskhêmatismenos logos*; in Latin, *figurata oratio*). The word "figure" (*skhêma* or *figura*) designates a shaping, an attitude, a posture; in language, it is applied to grammatical forms and stylistic figures. In the present case, it takes on the special meaning of a technical term designating the form given to a statement when one says one thing while meaning another. The translation "figured speech" is traditional and is taken to mean "disguised" or "made-up speech"—that is, "wearing cosmetic."

On the technique of figured speech (we will dispense with the quotation marks), we possess texts that date from apparently the end of the Hellenistic Age down through the Roman Empire until medieval times. Two authorities, the Roman Quintilian (first century AD) and the Greek Hermogenes (second to third century AD), comment extensively on the topic in their works, comments often repeated and discussed thereafter.[1] (Instead of

Hermogenes, one should say Pseudo-Hermogenes, the works at issue being today considered apocryphal after having long been thought authentic, but this scholarly issue has no further bearing on our investigation.) Before these two giants, a certain Demetrius, whose identity unfortunately eludes us (first century BC?), had raised the topic in his excellent Greek treatise *On Style*.[2] Two small works (ca. third century AD), erroneously transmitted under the name of the Greek historian and literary critic Dionysius of Halicarnassus, have the peculiarity of presenting themselves in parallel, probably reflecting two sets of notes taken by students in a course with the same professor.[3] In Latin, the theorist Fortunatianus and the encyclopedist Martianus Capella (fourth to fifth century AD) stand out for introducing the word *ductus* ("conduct" of the discourse), which includes the notion of figured speech, albeit with a larger sense covering all choices of expression, whether they proceed in a feigned or direct manner.[4]

These texts do not form a homogeneous whole. First, certain attributions, as we have seen, must be accepted with caution (as frequently happens in the world of ancient rhetoric). In addition, each has its own objective, its own method. The Romans mingle with the Greeks; a great imperial lawyer and teacher like Quintilian has much in common with the anonymous professor called "Pseudo-Dionysius." One writer focuses on teaching and courtroom eloquence, another philosophy, a third the mechanics of argumentation, while still another considers literary classics. They do not repeat so much as complement one another. They converge both in their overall doctrine and on many individual points, justifying our speaking of a coherent theory of figured speech in antiquity.

It is certain, moreover, that we do not have all that was written on this subject. Some significant works have been lost.[5] Already in ancient Athens, long before Demetrius, our first preserved source, there are instances of thinking about the topic. Take, for example, the startling conclusion to an encomium of Athens, where the great writer and political thinker Isocrates, nearly a hundred at the time, interspersed some ambiguous messages on the attitude to be adopted toward Sparta, portraying himself as if he were debating this very ambiguity with his students.[6]

And yet, for all its success, figured speech had no assigned place in the rhetorical system. One literally did not know where to put it. Sometimes, it was treated as a separate topic, unconnected to the other aspects of rhetoric. At other times, it was an appendage to oratorical tactics. In Quintilian and in the treatise of Pseudo-Hermogenes, *On Invention*, it occurs as a sort of afterthought to the study of the stylistic figures:[7] the relation with the

The Subtle Subtext

figures is, indeed, essential. Formally, the very name *figured* speech betrays its connection with the *figures* of style. Substantively, the figures (as well as the related "tropes") are defined in rhetoric as ways of transferring or deviating from a literal meaning; in other words, they introduce a supplementary level of import, which is what ties them to figured speech. Such is the case with enigma and allegory, among others, as discussed in the previous chapter, or even irony, along with the quantitative figures (which overstate or understate—namely, hyperbole and euphemism) and the figures of silence (which suggest without saying, like reticence and ellipsis). We will have occasion to meet all of these later on. The difference between figured speech and the figures of style is that the latter are generally specific and circumscribed, while figured speech encompasses both isolated expressions and the tactics developed throughout an entire passage or an entire oration. The two notions overlap but do not mesh exactly. Another difference is that the theorists present the figures in lists, because the figures are meant to be a systematic matrix of meaningful effects, with an exhaustive nomenclature, whereas figured speech is treated as a procedure unique unto itself.

Figured speech is a floating rhetorical entity, and the reason is that it constitutes an extreme case, a pushing to the limit. Rhetoric's traditional objective is persuasion, achieved through sustaining a thesis by clear and pertinent argument. It seeks clarity as a condition for public exchange accessible to all. Figured speech, on the other hand, takes an opposite approach. Instead of pleading his case frankly, the speaker uses covertness. The obscurity is deliberate, a calculated breach of normal procedure. The theorists go on to emphasize the paradox: what is a flaw elsewhere here becomes a virtue.[8] The sophists and their ploys were already well known, but, in the case of figured speech, rhetoric goes further and envisions its own transgressing, turning figured speech into a sort of parallel rhetoric.

It is this parallel rhetoric's aims and functioning that the theoretical texts cited previously analyze in detail. Since they are only available in scholarly and hard-to-find editions, some still awaiting translation, our highlighting their major ideas will be worthwhile.

The Usefulness of the In-Between

In principle, figured speech is defined as "a maneuver mediating between silence and revelation"[9]—that is, a careful navigation that aims to pass between two reefs, either the silence born from fear of saying what one thinks, or frankness with all its attendant dangers. If silence is not possible, the first reef reconfigures without changing its nature: it is no longer a question of avoiding silence but of avoiding speaking contrary to one's mind. That would be just another kind of self-censorship, dictated by fear and analogous to the previous situation. For example, if someone has to deal with a superior, "flattery is shameful, open criticism is dangerous, and the best course lies in the middle, namely innuendo, the figured turn (*to eskhêmatismenon*)."[10] In short, it is a question of tacking artfully in all those circumstances where speech is not free.

To describe these circumstances, Quintilian is the best guide. He presents clearly and methodically three reasons for having recourse to figured speech. The first is safety: it is necessary to express oneself in veiled terms when frank expression endangers the speaker. In ancient societies, the risk attendant on an ill-taken speech was higher than it is in present-day democracies. Tyrants, emperors, and other monarchs pitilessly punished those who braved them; popular assemblies were prone to reactions as violent as they were unpredictable, and courts handed down heavy sentences. The difficulty of speaking to the powerful, not only to criticize but also to counsel, posed a crucial and constant problem throughout the entire history of figured speech and the subtext.

When the speaker was not afraid, he could still feel required to respect certain norms, or risk antagonizing or offending, and so failing. Such was the case, for example, of a courtroom pleader who, in order to defend himself, had to accuse a superior or a parent, well understanding that it would do him no good to do so openly. The criterion is no longer security but propriety, a key principle in highly hierarchical societies where social and familial bonds were regulated by norms of both personal dignity that had to be preserved and the respect that was owed to individuals because of their rank.

A third reason for figured speech lay in the quest for cleverness and flair. Figured speech was quite fashionable in the rhetorical schools, which cultivated finesse and subtlety. As a serious and responsible teacher, Quintilian does not dally over this use, of which he scarcely approves, but all the same, he does say enough to crack open a window onto gratuitous satisfaction and an occasionally humorous conception of the subtext.

Toward a Typology

After the *why* comes the *how*. Once it has defined the principal motives for using figured speech (and those Quintilian outlines cover, indeed, the majority of cases), rhetoric busies itself in distinguishing the best ways to use it.

Considering the multiple forms of figured discourse and the variation in authors' classification systems, one may depend, this time, on Pseudo-Hermogenes and his treatise *On Invention*, as well as on Pseudo-Dionysius of Halicarnassus, both of whom define essentially three broad categories:

1. *Attenuation*, or saying what one means, but in a reserved and moderate manner, through sugarcoating and considerateness.
2. *Hinting*, or slanting one's speech in a certain direction to obtain a different objective by expressing oneself allusively or indirectly, saying one thing while causing something else to be inferred.
3. *Inversion*, or speaking in a vein contrary to what one truly wants, acting so as to obtain the opposite of what one explicitly says.

Three scenes drawn from the Homeric account of the Trojan War illustrate this typology:

1. Since Poseidon, disobeying the warning of Zeus, had aided the Greek warriors (Zeus at this time siding with the Trojans), Zeus sends his messenger, the goddess Iris, to require him to desist from contravening Zeus's plans. Poseidon, angered, violently rejects this injunction, but Iris asks him: "Am I then to carry, O dark-haired, earth-encircler, this word, which is strong and steep, back to Zeus from you? Or will you change a little?"[11] In this way Iris gives Poseidon a lesson in attenuation, by inviting him to moderate his response. And she herself presents this lesson in an indirect way, beginning with complimentary epithets ("O dark-haired, earth-encircler") and by suggesting menace through the name "Zeus"; for Zeus, as the elder, could forcibly restrain his younger brother.
2. Achilles, feeling insulted, has withdrawn to his tent and threatens to leave the army and return home. Phoenix, his old tutor, is dispatched to calm him. Phoenix begins by observing that, should Achilles decide to depart, he himself would find it difficult to remain, and he recalls all that binds him to the hero, as well as all the attention he lavished on him long ago when Achilles was a child. First, these memories show why Phoenix would feel himself compelled to support the cause of Achilles, but at the same time, they suggest that Achilles ought to listen to his teacher and that he might consider, if not immediately reentering the battle, at least remaining in the camp awhile before withdrawing to his homeland. The reasons mentioned in one vein (Phoenix must follow

Achilles home) argue simultaneously for a different solution (Achilles should put off his departure).[12]

3. To incite his soldiers to engage in combat, Agamemnon decides, strangely it seems, to exhort them to fight by withdrawing. He explains this tactic to his counselors: "Come then, let us see if we can arm the sons of the Achaians. Yet first, since it is the right way, I will make trial of them by words, and tell them even to flee in their benched vessels. Do you take stations here and there, to check them with orders."[13]

The Greek rhetoricians saw in this passage an instance of figured speech, since it recommends something to obtain its exact opposite. Agamemnon says, "Let's flee!" to persuade the Achaeans not to flee. It is striking how this order commands such obedience that the Achaeans rush en masse toward the ships to set sail without delay, taking their general at his word and beginning to do just what he secretly wanted them not to do. It requires the aid of the other leaders and divine intervention to restrain them. The strategy, therefore, is shown to be risky. But after a few moments of confusion, all's well that ends well, and then (always so, according to the theorists), one sees the point of the maneuver. Agamemnon acts as he does because he knew the men would never follow his direct order. The length of the siege, which had been going on for nine years, had worn them out; they had only one desire, to flee. Moreover, they blamed their general for the situation occasioned by Achilles's withdrawal, and they were unwilling to resume combat in such circumstances. Agamemnon had to test them, to take the measure of their discouragement; he had to provoke them and give them a way out. Hence this last-ditch expedient, for figured speech is often apt in dangerous situations. Agamemnon gave his men the opportunity to express their angry feelings against him; he even pushed them to it, in such a way that they got rid of their rancor and returned to the fight with renewed vigor. His speech, which might seem clumsy, turns out to be a piece of consummate craft.

We note in passing that this paradoxical scene remained famous and inspired other versions, proving that it was not just an isolated curiosity. In the epic of the Argonauts' capture of the Golden Fleece, a moment occurs when the heroes, having put in at the Greek island of Lemnos, forget their mission in the arms of the island's women. Herakles plies the heroes with a speech *a contrario*, in effect saying, "Oh well, since this is the way it is, there's nothing to do but give up." "Let's go back, each to his own homeland!" Hearing this "Let's go back," the heroes catch his drift. They get control of themselves and resume their voyage toward the Fleece. Later, Jason is the one who will put the Argonauts to the test, feigning regret at having engaged them in this adventure, only to induce them to cry out "No!"[14]

In the sixteenth century, the Spanish poet Lasso de la Vega used a similar procedure in an epic celebrating the conquest of Mexico by Hernán Cortés. After Cortés arrived in Vera Cruz, his men were combat-fatigued, and some mutinied. He destroys his ships to force the army to carry on. Just at this point, the author gives Cortés an utterly surprising speech, in which he exhorts the army to flee.[15] As in the previous cases, the speaker wants to stir up pride, so that the men correct themselves. The method used consists in his pretending to give up, and in encouraging his men to give up, all the better to convince them to persevere. Such a ploy is not only a literary trapping but a procedure with wide application. It borrows from the tactics today called "pleading the false" and "playing the devil's advocate," where one mounts an argument that one does not believe, in order to test one's interlocutors and to lead them to the opposite conclusion.

These, then, are the three categories defined by Pseudo-Hermogenes and Pseudo-Dionysius of Halicarnassus. This tripartite theory is the most comprehensive advanced and also the most useful for appreciating the attraction of the rhetorical notion of figured speech. Since "figuration" involves the gap that exists between what the speaker explicitly says and what he wants to achieve, or have understood, without needing to say it, the classification amounts to the enumeration of the possible gaps, which extend from nuances and partial discrepancies all the way to radical differences and total opposition. Three types of deviation are set forth in stages, from the lightest to the most pronounced. That is why the tripartite division does not have internally rigid boundaries; it foresees a progression from one case to the other, as well areas of transition.

It is beside the point to criticize the Greek rhetoricians for confusing different realities.[16] On the contrary, the power of the theory of figured speech is that it subsumes apparently diverse phenomena under a single notion and shows how they fall under an identical problematic. Attenuations, allusive hinting, paradoxes: the subtext links all these strategies in a profound coherence. It will be useful to keep in mind this broad and comprehensive conception.

Exercising the Imagination

The theory of figurative speech rested on literary analysis, as we have just seen with three examples drawn from Homer. Rhetoric desired to be anchored in the past and looked for models among the classic authors, at the cost of occasionally convoluted textual commentary. But there was another way to study and teach figured speech: figured declamation. A "declamation" (in Greek, *meletê*; in Latin, *declamatio*) was a speech on a fictional subject, set as an exercise, to allow students to put to work the theoretical rules that had been drilled into them. Rhetoric is an art and a method—that is, a productive knowledge, and so it calls in the end for the composition of a speech. Declamation was a type of exercise so highly prized that it broke out of classroom confines and became a type of popular entertainment, when students and their professors went before large audiences of their relatives, friends, and the curious. Among declamations, the most sought after were figured declamations. Quantitatively, these constituted a significant percentage of declamations in general. Qualitatively, they occupied a privileged place because they required special virtuosity. The sources verify this, including not only the witness of the theoreticians mentioned earlier but also numerous collections of texts and citations.[17]

Shameful family secrets, for example, provided a treasure trove of topics. Suppose that there were rumors about a father having illicit relations with his daughter-in-law. The son, not daring to attack his father openly, has recourse to stratagems to reveal this personally intolerable situation publicly. Using as a pretext a law requiring madmen to be driven from the city, he argues against his own interest and asks to be condemned to exile, supposedly because he is crazy—crazy with rage against his father, one understands implicitly.[18] In another exercise on the same theme, the son proposes a law against adultery in general but is really aiming at his own father without saying so.[19] If, hypothetically, the woman is found pregnant, and the father presses her to get rid of the child by exposing it, the son sues to prevent this abandonment.[20] In all cases, the theorists think that the son cannot say publicly, "My father has committed adultery with my wife." Adhering to a strict protocol, which says a lot about the contemporary position of the unassailable father, the *pater familias*, the son has no other recourse than to argue obliquely and to stud his remarks with deliberately ambiguous sentences, such as: "I married the woman who pleased my father"; "[If I go into exile], my wife will suffice in caring for my father"; "Think, father, of this child as yours, not mine!"[21]

Another category of subjects rested on a judicial procedure called "denunciation" (in Greek, *prosangelia*), with the sense of "self-denunciation." It consisted of handing oneself over to the law, claiming the right to die. It does not seem that this procedure actually existed, or, if it did, it was quite rare.

Yet current debates, in our own twenty-first century, on legal recognition of assisted suicide show that this theme could have serious implications. Be that as it may, in the ancient schools of declamation, self-denunciation was all the rage. It was used to devise speeches with double meaning, in which the speaker confessed his own mistakes before the court . . . so that the judges might understand the opposite. Thus, one sees all manner of people indicting themselves and seeking execution: Themistocles, calling down upon himself all his grievous faults so as actually to remind his fellow citizens of the services he had rendered them and to convince them to follow his advice;[22] a long-serving soldier who deserted, because he wanted to whip up hatred against his son who had forced him to the front lines despite his age;[23] a poor man, who pretends, during a famine, to offer himself as a scapegoat, ostensibly satisfying the judgment secured against him by a hostile rich man, all to rouse the people against the latter, a hoarder responsible for the scarcity;[24] and finally, a parasite deprived of his dinner, someone envious of a neighbor suddenly become rich, or even the case of the husband of a chatterbox, who says he is weary of life, all in the hope of winning a divorce from his "eloquent" other half.[25] These speakers apparently plead their cases contrary to all good sense, but none of them truly wants to die. Each has a hidden goal, which can only be discerned thanks to the theory of figured speech.

School and Life

Rhetoric classes were certainly not boring, where figured speech offered a repertory of vivid and subtle exercises. It introduced some fun into the sharpening of rhetorical rapiers. But is that all? Is it plausible that no one dreamed of profiting from such weaponry in practical life?

Reading the treatises, one can get the impression that figured speech was a technique cut off from the world, feeding on itself and leading merely to academic grandstanding, as if only argumentative and stylistic agility mattered. The theorists are primarily responsible for creating this feeling in their writings, for they remain quiet about the reality of the stakes and refrain from insisting on concrete applications of rhetorical theory, claiming only to analyze declamations or selections from archaic and classical literature. A pedagogical philosophy anxious to keep reality at the classroom door and not to confuse school with life explains their reticence. They were also probably responding to prudent worries, since the professors had no interest in turning schools into hotbeds of sedition and their handbooks into polemical tracts. Many scholars have failed to notice this.[26]

Nevertheless, if one judges the texts without preconceptions, one sees that the effective use of eloquence was not absent from the authors' concerns. Here is some evidence for this lurking purpose.

All throughout his work, Demetrius keeps in mind the situation, perfectly plausible, of an orator who wishes to reproach some powerful listeners who are quick to take offence, notably a sovereign or a popular assembly. To illustrate his argument, he uses examples relating to Plato, Xenophon, the Athenian Assembly, and the tyrant Dionysius of Syracuse. These illustrations could not have been more classic or learned, as well as several centuries old, but they are still—and this is how the author presents them—tangible instances of persons who really lived. The anecdote about Demetrius of Phaleron rebuking Craterus, the Macedonian general, is mentioned as an actual event: when the Macedonian received the Greek ambassadors with arrogant aloofness, perched on a golden couch that loomed over the audience, Demetrius, head of the Greek delegation, said: "We ourselves once welcomed these men as envoys, including yonder Craterus."[27] Everything is in that "yonder." Moreover, Demetrius, even as he depends on tradition, enlarges the compass of his thought and suggests that figured speech can be used in numerous situations likely to arise in actual politics, not just in literature.

As for Quintilian, he writes that there is "similarity" between the use of figured speech in declamations and its use in real trials, giving as an example a case he himself argued using precisely this method. It was an inheritance case, very complicated, where the heirs had arranged among themselves a legally questionable settlement: "I therefore had to plead in such a way that the judges understood what had happened, but the informers could not seize on any explicit statement. I succeeded on both counts. I should not have put this in [Quintilian modestly continues], for fear of being thought to boast of it, if I had not been anxious to prove that there is a place for these Figures even in the courts."[28]

The Greek Libanius says something similar about declamations that instruct those who practice them in the art of speaking carefully to political authorities. It would be the height of folly, he writes, if we did not apply in real life the rules learned in school from oratorical exercises![29] Another theorist notes that figured speech is useful in lectures where one wishes either to criticize someone else or justify oneself.[30]

Pseudo-Dionysius of Halicarnassus refers to the practices of daily life and enumerates situations in which the manner of utterance is crucial and influences the meaning of the message. His list includes greetings, which can be welcoming, respectful, critical, and so forth; dinner invitations, which

The Subtle Subtext

have to be formulated in a way befitting the social status of each guest; and loan requests, in which it is essential to weigh one's words in view of the circumstances, or even those cases when someone is waiting for a token of gratitude for a service rendered or situations where one declines a gift, all the time wanting to accept it. Back-scratching and the formulaic "Oh, you shouldn't have," already discussed in chapter 1, were just as current among the ancient Greeks as they are today.[31]

Even literary criticism was not divorced from real life. Indeed, the literary patrimony of the ancients did not consist only of works of literature; it also included works written or delivered orally in situations that, even though set apart and hallowed by the prestige of their classic authors, focused squarely on actual events. Studying figured speech in the legal and deliberative orations of Demosthenes and Cicero amounted to more than drawing upon an array of literary masterpieces; it was to meditate upon the vicissitudes of history and politics. Specialists recognized, for example, cases of oblique expression in Cicero's most weighty addresses to the Roman Senate. In the *Fourth Oration Against Catiline*, the orator portrays himself as gentle and humane, yet that is only a pose; for he demands the death penalty against the conspirators, a sentence to be carried out that very evening.[32] In his *First Philippic*, he softens his attacks against Marc Antony, "speaking everything with an air of having said nothing unkind."[33] He will change his tone in the following *Philippics*, dropping the figured speech in a forthright expression of his enmity and contempt. He did so at the peril of his life, as succeeding events proved, since he wound up proscribed and executed. Antony ordered Cicero's head to be cut off, as well as the hands with which he had written the *Philippics*.

So there was undeniably a world beyond the school. In analyzing figured speech, the ancient rhetoricians did not only produce a remarkable and articulated intellectual construct. They uncovered a mainspring of politics and society.

3

The Hermeneutics of Suspicion

Leaping over the centuries, we come to modern times. They have made a major contribution to the social sciences and literary theory through an effort to achieve a better understanding of words and texts with their detours and hidden bends. Indeed, with modernity, "we have entered into the Age of Suspicion," according to the famous assertion of Nathalie Sarraute.[1] Confronting the growing subtlety of narrative techniques and psychological exploration, the novelist held that the observation of feelings as it had been practiced until the start of the twentieth century was no longer appropriate. It had become impossible to tell a story with characters, she maintained, because the introduction of interior monologue and the unconscious had complicated the conception of time, acts, and motives. Moreover, readers distrusted authors, whose role and personality had become problematic. Readers asked themselves, "Who is saying that?" This analysis, now more than seventy years old, was not a mere manifesto for the Nouveau Roman, the collective name given to the literary experiments conducted by a group of French novelists in the 1950s, but a pointed depiction of how psychology and art had evolved.

Aesthetic criteria changed when art began to offer works that shocked the, shall we say, classical canons of beauty. Smashed face? No, a cubist portrait! Limping, unmetered verse? No, a surrealist poem! Cats caterwauling? An atonal string quartet! Works such as these would have all been considered ugly according to earlier norms. But ugliness and beauty were no longer the issue; truth was. It was all about getting to the bottom of things to reveal their true nature. The representation of a beautiful face is, in one sense, a mask: it presents harmonious features, a settled composure for our consideration, without revealing the complex emotions, the ruinous passions, the dire calculations that are the lot of the human soul, and all of which will blaze forth in a modern painting. In the latter, there is apparently little resemblance to the original model, yet it is truer, perhaps, than an ostensibly representational portrait.

Similar judgment extends across multiple disciplines, if one of the characteristics of modernity is the revelation of the forces at work beneath reality's smooth surface. What one thought was the social order can be analyzed as injustice and disorder, what one thought was prudent conduct is really explained by irrational motivations, and so on. The names of Marx, Nietzsche, and Freud, "three masters of suspicion," are emblematic of such a mental attitude. As Paul Ricœur has remarked, these thinkers of modernity have, each in his own way, invented "an art of interpretation," carried out an effort of "decryption," in order to construct a meaning and to respond to "the 'unconscious' *effort* of encryption" operative in society and the individual.[2] They explored "the vast territory of double meaning,"[3] and that is why they are of interest to our topic. Befitting the "Age of Suspicion," a "hermeneutic of suspicion"[4] grew apace, rich with a history defined by great thinkers whose philosophies I will not venture to summarize. It suffices here to have set forth the basic insight.

Linguistic Connotation

Among the social sciences that have faced the problem of subtexts, linguistics is one of the most important contributors: more precisely, pragmatics, which is devoted to tackling the ploys of language. Whereas classical linguistics looks at the functioning of language in itself—fundamental structures, vocabulary, morphology, and syntax—pragmatics concentrates on the use of language in social life and on the meaning that utterances assume as a function of circumstances, groups, habits, or expectations. Among pragmatics' many concepts, implication and intention concern our discussion, as they have been elaborated in the works, among others, of the British linguist Paul Grice. A typical example is an exchange like the following: "Are you coming to the restaurant with us?—'I have already had lunch at my parents'.'" A direct question, calling for a yes or no answer, is followed by a response that, taken literally, could seem off-kilter, and that gets its meaning by virtue of the context and the presupposition that one normally does not have lunch twice.

The concept of "connotation," highlighted by Catherine Kerbrat-Orecchioni, merits detailed discussion.[5] Connotation is defined to include the semantic data that are added to denotated contents. "In denotation, the meaning is specified, in an unmistakable way; its decoding is universally accepted. ... In connotation, the meaning is suggested, and its decoding is left more to chance." With the latter, the meaning is multiple and constructed, and it obeys a hierarchy of levels: there are several informational strata, and the connotation is second from the logical point of view, which is not to say that it is unimportant. "Connotation is second, but not secondary."[6]

From this, it is possible to draw up an inventory of the means and functions of connotation. "Connotating aids" are the devices that make suggesting a supplementary sense possible, and they are quite varied in nature. They include phonetic material (the expressive value of sounds and letters), the way a sentence is pronounced (tone), syntactical construction, choice of words, and complex procedures like literary allusion or metaphor. Using the word "wheels" to designate a car confers on the utterance a popular character, while the old advertising slogan "Tender is the night on board the *France*" contains poetic and cultural connotations owing to inverted syntax and literary and artistic allusion. The latter, in turn, can be read on different levels, depending on whether one can recognize in the expression "Tender is the night" a verse by John Keats, the title of a novel by F. Scott Fitzgerald, a film by Henry King, or a song by Jackson Browne.

Thanks to these devices, connotation functions to create "connoted contents" or "connotative data," whose classification intersects with that of the aids without being identical to it. Stylistic connotations connect the utterance to a particular linguistic code, when, for example, a word carries an archaic or exotic aura in addition to its meaning. Affective connotations add to the utterance the emotions the speaker wishes to convey (indignation, gentleness, etc.). Axiological connotations reflect a positive or negative judgment on the denoted object. Still other, quite numerous connotations result from all sorts of associations, which lead Kerbrat-Orecchioni to conclude: "Implicit contents are thus omnipresent, and this is not necessarily anything to be alarmed at."[7]

Within these broad outlines, such a linguistic study arrives at results not all that different from those of the ancient rhetoricians who dealt with figured speech. In both cases, the analysis shows that two layers of meaning can be distinguished, and it itemizes the means and functions of the gap between these levels. We are not claiming a direct influence by one discipline on the other, for linguists have their own problems for study, and the ancient masters of rhetoric are not their inspiration.[8] When linguists use the word "rhetoric," it is in the linguistic sense of this term, to designate mechanisms of enunciation at work in verbal exchange that are not requirements, unlike syntactic and semantic mechanisms. If there is a meeting of the minds between linguists and the ancient rhetoricians, it is because their object of study imposes a similar parsing.

The Subtle Subtext

The linguistic approach, however, is broader than the rhetorical. The material it deals with also includes short utterances, belonging to everyday language or advertising, as well as much longer texts and literary examples. Above all, linguistics takes into account the inevitable implications language routinely or automatically employs, in addition to those that are consciously chosen. "He ate some eggs" naturally signifies, in the absence of further clarification, that the eggs are chicken eggs, not salmon eggs, for instance. "If Peter comes, James will leave" immediately seems to imply a certain amount of prior thought, leading one to understand that the arrival of Peter will cause James's departure, or even that if Peter does not come, James will not go.[9] Whereas the rhetoric of figured speech concentrated on deliberately chosen subtexts, linguistics adds those that are not.

"Tracking down the unspoken"[10] never ends. Pseudo-Hermogenes and Pseudo-Dionysius of Halicarnassus had already made a great advance in postulating the unity of the subtext as an intentional rhetorical tactic underneath its different forms; now, another level has opened up, leading to postulating the unity of both the consciously and the unconsciously chosen. In other words, the subtext, considered broadly,[11] is not limited to insinuation but extends to everything implicit in utterances, whether this implication is deliberate or not, with, between these two poles, all the intermediate nuances of "not truly" or "not consciously" meant. That is to say, the different forms and manifestations that all spring from the same source cohere.

The Impact of Psychoanalysis

In a review of hermeneutical approaches, it is impossible to avoid mentioning psychoanalysis, since it deals with the unspoken, the repressed, ambivalence, pretense, the approximations of language, in short, an entire dimension that has much to do with double meaning and subtext. What is more, it does not limit itself to remedying pathological states but offers itself as a means of knowing the human soul; it aims to explain how the psyche functions, as Freud does, for example, with dreams (the subject of *The Interpretation of Dreams*) and ordinary little "failures," like mental lapses, forgetting, so-called Freudian slips, or various forms of error (the subject of *The Psychopathology of Everyday Life*). In both cases, Freud deals with banal occurrences, subjecting them to scientific scrutiny. Behind the appearance of ineptness or insignificance, analysis reveals a meaning and intent, unspoken desires, and compulsions, and it offers an interpretation that unveils a latent content deviating from what is expressly said. Human truth exists simultaneously on different planes. Mechanisms put in motion, such as "condensation," "overdetermination," or "displacement," escape logical rules to admit the overlay of multiple meanings, contradictory dynamics, and conflicts.

These results assume a particular importance because psychoanalysis has become the science of Everyman, a cultural baggage for the educated and hung-up Westerners of the twentieth and twenty-first centuries. Owing to its popularization, it influences our perceptions and our interpretations even in daily life.

The Poetics of the "Grey Song"

Thanks to Nicolas Boileau's couplet, famous in French literature, many may know that:

> Ce que l'on conçoit bien s'énonce clairement,
> Et les mots pour le dire arrivent aisément.

> Clear thought is clearly uttered,
> The words to say it readily obtained.[12]

These verses lay down a rule of transparency, which stipulates the equivalence between a clear thought and an expression exactly translating this thought. The inverse, subject to considerable criticism, is that an unclear and confused idea can only end up in a hazy and scrambled formulation. In the Ancien Régime, "French clarity," then at its apogee, placed the highest value on reason and the geometric spirit, guarantors of truth.[13]

But here is another *Art of Poetry*, two hundred years after Boileau, and a counterweight to it. Paul Verlaine enjoins:

> Il faut aussi que tu n'ailles point
> Choisir tes mots sans quelque méprise:
> Rien de plus cher que la chanson grise
> Où l'Indécis au Précis se joint.

> Never set out to be too "nice,"
> Choosing your words without something wrong:
> Nothing more precious than the grey song
> Where the Indecisive meets the Precise.

And later, the same poet comments:

> J'adore, autrement, certain vague, non à l'âme,
> Bone Deus! mais dans les mots, et je l'ai dit.

> I adore, otherwise, a certain vagueness, not in the soul,
> Good God! but in words, and I have said so.[14]

Calculated mistakes and indecision are opposed to the classical ideal of clarity and transparency. To be sure, we are talking about poetry here. The singular aspects of the Verlaine experience, those toward which, as a prisoner in Mons, he mentally retreated to make a synthesis of them and draw some strength from them, are music, rhythm, the formal requirements of verse, symbolism, impressionism, the intuitive apprehension of feeling, and reverie's creative imprecision. I believe, however, that, in the beautiful expression "grey song," Verlaine hit on a larger idea, of universal import, by bringing to the fore the indecision and ambiguity words convey.

The aesthetic of allusion, as Stéphane Mallarmé cultivated it, continues this questioning of classic clarity: "The evoking, in deliberate shadow, of the unspoken object, by words allusive, never direct, reducing themselves essentially to silence, reveals the attempt that comes close to the creative act."[15] This famous formulation caught the attention of Jean-Paul Sartre and André Glucksmann.[16]

Mallarmé also wrote, "Le sens trop précis rature / Ta vague littérature." ("Meaning too precise is an erasure / Of your vague literature.")[17] He declared one day that he "looked at a poem as a *mystery* to which the reader must find the key,"[18] this esoteric conception one of the features of symbolism.

The Egg-Text

In the twentieth century, literary criticism thought of itself as "an activity of decoding the text," according to the formulation of Roland Barthes, resting on the idea—always the same, endlessly recurring in the present chapter in diverse forms—namely, that there exists in works, beyond the apparent meaning, a deeper sense, secret and true, waiting to be discovered.[19] One sense or several: Barthes insisted on the idea of textual "plurality," thinking that connotation is a useful but insufficient tool and that it is necessary to go further, even to notions of "starred" or "broken" text. "To interpret a text is not to give it a meaning (more or less established, more or less free); on the contrary, it is to appreciate the plurality of which it is compounded."[20] Barthes spoke further of "egg-text," "full of multiple meanings, discontinuous and piled up, and yet sanded down, smoothed by the 'natural' movement of its sentences."[21] From this arose all those "deconstructions."

The process is the same with the fashionable notion of "intertextuality." It implies that every text says more than it does because it evokes, refashions, refutes, or parodies other texts (both prior and contemporary), formulaic expressions, or hallowed sayings. Here is Barthes again: "Every text is an *intertext*; other texts are present within it, to varying degrees, under more or less recognizable forms, texts of an earlier time, and contemporary texts; every text is a new fabric of bygone citations."[22]

Some types of allusion follow from this, which are well known to philologists, experienced as they are in searching out the sources and influences at work in classical literature and who seek, more deeply, to elucidate the consequences inherent in a work's place within a genre, a social environment, and a tradition.[23] Highly refined shades of meaning can be endlessly amassed in writings dealing with characters like Odysseus, Faust, or Robinson Crusoe; Gérard Genette, for example, has systematized these "second degrees" of literature.[24]

Another notion, a little less well known, is "self-reflexivity," as developed by Luc Fraisse.[25] In its broadest application, it covers cases in which the text reflects on itself—that is, gives an image of itself, when an author within his work speaks about himself and his own creative process, whether directly, for example, in a preface or digression, or indirectly, in a symbolic or oblique manner, through characters standing in for him or through metaphors used to describe the work. The subtext belongs to the latter category, wherein the thrust of the passage is only suggested and has to be divined: literature comments on itself, and when this commentary is made in veiled terms, one enters into the zone of the subtext. This is really a quite ancient phenomenon, as old as literature itself, since Homer already in his epics portrayed bards who could be understood as images of the author (insofar as one may speak of "an" author with Homer), fair likenesses, yet different at the same time, because embellished and placed within dramatic contexts that lent them importance.

A particularly clear example is in André Gide's *Counterfeiters*, a novel in which Uncle Édouard, a writer, is shown working on a novel that he will entitle *The Counterfeiters*. The same Gide popularized the heraldic expression "mise en abyme," using it in his *Journal*: "I rather like how, in a work of

The Subtle Subtext

art, one finds thus transposed to the character level the very subject of this work. . . . It is rather like that procedure with a coat of arms, which superimposes on the shield's image a second heraldic image in the center [the "abyme"]."[26]

The mise en abyme is a kind of self-reflexivity when it inserts within the main work something that reflects elements of that work. It may be a novel in which one character is a novelist, a play within a play (as in *Hamlet*), a romantic drama whose protagonist is a Romantic poet (Alfred de Vigny's *Chatterton*), and so on. These increments of meaning, enriching the work, stimulate readers or spectators. They stimulate authors, too, allowing them to contemplate their own effort, even in an egocentric or autobiographical way.

Seven Types of Ambiguity

Here is yet another system of classification, by no means the least. Such is the richness of the subtext that one system does not suffice; to take its measure satisfactorily requires multiple hermeneutic approaches.

Seven Types of Ambiguity by William Empson, published in 1930, was its twenty-four-year-old author's master stroke. A student at Cambridge of the great philosopher of language and rhetoric I. A. Richards, Empson was destined to become a poet and famous critic, a friend of George Orwell, and die having been knighted by the queen. He found himself for the moment, however, in difficult circumstances, sent down from his college the previous year because he was caught possessing condoms.[27] *The Seven Types* served to get him out of this pickle, inaugurating his entry on the intellectual scene.

Dealing with English poetry from the Renaissance to modern times, Empson strives to show that many texts, even the most familiar, are carriers of ambiguity, and, more radically, that ambiguity is an essential attribute and one of the means of poetic expression. To do this, he distinguishes seven types of ambiguity, illustrating each with examples. The types are not sharply differentiated from one another, existing, rather, on a continuum of "advancing logical disorder."[28] By this he means that what is said is slightly disconcerting from a logical or grammatical point of view in the first type, a little more so in the second, and so on until the seventh. While it is not always easy to distinguish among the different cases, the list is basically as follows:

1. A metaphor evokes multiple contents (and not just one), which is vague and intriguing.

2. The words suggest multiple meanings.

3. Double meaning is inherent in the words and expressions used (for example, Walter Scott's "From the red gold keep thy finger" signifies simultaneously rejecting marriage and rejecting commerce).

4. A double meaning reflects a state of complex awareness.

5. A comparison is not right; the author discovers what he is thinking as he writes.

6. Apparent absurdity, contradiction, tautology.

7. Contradictory statement.

For its time, Empson's attempt was original and audacious, first, because it celebrated ambiguity, and second, because it set forth a method for analyzing poetry and deciphering meaning, beginning with words and syntax, in contrast to the reigning impressionistic critical approach that tried to gauge the beauties of a work, often lapsing into gushiness. But his effort is equally interesting because of the problems it raises. If one considers the act of writing, the classification of the seven types causes the opposition to jump out between what is consciously willed and what is not; Empson reaches, by another way, the same conclusion as the linguists cited earlier. Ambiguity often positions itself in "the in-between," along with the thoughts that one does not admit to oneself and the states of consciousness that betray layers of psychological complexity. Empson does not hide the fact that certain authors in his analysis did not mean to be ambiguous. They would not have approved the term "ambiguity," preferring to speak of "grace" or "generalization":[29] they were ambiguous in spite of themselves.

From a reader's point of view, Empson's work shows how difficult and indecisive reception is. Ambiguity covers all cases where there is any hesitation over an author's meaning, and those are numerous: "any verbal nuance, however slight, which gives room for alternative reactions to the same piece of language."[30] Understanding happens through time, where the discovery of ambiguity is progressive, and where one learns to read, in short, the complexities revealing themselves little by little during the reading process.

Finally, Empson exercises such subtlety that readers sometimes ask themselves if he is not exaggerating and if he does not run the risk of uncovering ambiguities where none exist. This impression must be corrected immediately, for, in defense of the author, the texts he analyzes are great works, some notoriously difficult to interpret (the poems of John Donne, for example), which makes it reasonable, a priori, that they have depths of meaning. There are serious issues here, to which we will have to return.

Diagonal Coherences

Roger Caillois, the twentieth-century French intellectual, has investigated our problem in turn, in *Au cœur du fantastique* (At the heart of the fantastic), a paper published in 1965 and subsequently reprinted in the book *Cohérences aventureuses* (Adventurous coherences). It is not surprising that Caillois, who always approached art and literature in an unconventional way, as passionate about surrealism itself as he was about the Argentine fantasist writer Jorge Luis Borges, should take an interest in less than straightforward forms of exchange and communication. He had explained the essential role of dissymmetry in nature, society, and artistic productions (*La Dissymétrie* is another effort, from 1973, reprinted in the *Cohérences* volume), and he especially stressed "diagonal" coherences.[31]

Concerning the fantastic in art, Caillois attempts a classification of four principal possibilities relative to communicating a message:[32]

1. "The message is clear both to the sender and to the receiver. This is the usual case."
2. "The message is clear to the sender but obscure to the recipient," either because the latter lacks some necessary information, or because the artist has deliberately concealed his work's meaning.
3. "The message is unclear to the author, but capable of being deciphered by an alerted observer." This is especially the case with works that reveal their creator's psychological state or obsessions.
4. "The message is obscure both to the sender and to the receiver." Prophecies and mysteries are examples.

There is certainly an element of humor, or of paradox, in pushing such rigorous classifications in an area that is naturally elusive. But Caillois's point is serious. It allows the entry of double meaning into the analysis of the creative process with full rights, devoting to it items 2 and 3 on his list, and it recognizes the importance of double meaning, showing that it is not a defect but an asset. Item 2 includes the tactics of deliberate subtexts, in which "the obscurity is calculated by design," out of elitism, or, additionally, "out of fear of persecution." Item 3, developed in the last chapter of the essay, under the eloquent title "The Fertility of the Ambiguous," uses the work of the nineteenth-century French poet Gérard de Nerval to study the situations in which artists, whether painters or poets, come to express themselves ambiguously, because they are not certain what they feel or want to express: "I suppose that he [Nerval] was not clear about what he wished to communicate and that he had recourse to a labyrinth of allegories, persuading himself that everyone could find his own satisfaction, provided that he was sufficiently lured by the subsurface coherence of a network of disconcerting images."[33]

"Disconcerting" is just the right word. In contrast to ancient rhetoric, which analyzed a controlled strategy, modern theories have shown that the subtext has complex roots, tied to the very functioning of the mind. They provide a critical panoply that allows us to identify the subtext better under its multiple and fluctuating guises.

4

Risks and Safeguards of Interpretation

Attention! Subtexting is not an exact science. Its inherent difficulty is not to be minimized, since its use of complicated mechanisms conceals even as it conveys. Problems arise, glimpsed previously in the work of Empson. There are any number of malfunctions about which to be anxious, originating either with the sender or the recipient.

Message Sent... But Not Received

A first risk, for the sender, is slipping in subtexts so subtle and veiled that the recipient misses them. This mistake can have several causes: excessive caution, when, out of fear of giving oneself away, one winds up preventing the point from dawning; pride, leading to defiance and the perverse satisfaction of intentionally making oneself misunderstood ("for those who get me, if they can"); or even extreme delicacy, as in this following scene from Proust.

Céline and Flora, "in their horror of vulgarity, had brought to such a fine art the concealment of a personal allusion in a wealth of ingenious circumlocution, that it would often pass unnoticed even by the person to whom it was addressed."[1] The day when Swann offers them a case of Asti, these persnickety old ladies, who are the sisters of the narrator's grandmother in *In Search of Lost Time*, take considerable care to avoid any overt expression of gratitude and limit themselves to generalities about nice neighbors and vintage bottles, to such an extent that Swann, "puzzled," asked himself what they were getting at, and their brother-in-law, at the evening's end, reproached them for not having said "thank you": "'What! We never thanked him? I think, between you and me, that I put it to him quite neatly,' replied my aunt Flora. 'Yes, you managed it very well; I admired you for it,' said my aunt Céline. 'But you did it very prettily, too.' 'Yes, I was rather proud about my remark about "nice neighbors.'" 'What! Do you call that thanking him?' shouted my grandfather . . . You may be quite sure he never noticed it."[2] This comic scene plays out against the agonies of little Marcel, who despairs of getting his mother's goodnight kiss. Diverting, amusing, it illustrates for us a risk in this type of communication.

Message Received . . . But Not Sent

A second danger, more serious than the first, occurs when the recipient discerns nonexistent subtexts. We all know those jolly kooks who see political or sexual innuendos everywhere. When they get warmed up and start laughing, their attitude becomes infectious and provokes a group effect, as in the scene from Émile Zola's novel *L'Assommoir*, where the working girls, "really into it, eyes crazed, becoming more and more so," twist the sense of words and give them "a dirty meaning," finding "unusual innuendos in simple statements."[3] One cannot dismiss these people just by saying that they are deranged and obsessed, whether from sexual indulgence or deprivation. Obsessed they may be, but they make your head spin; nothing can stop them from casting doubt on any seemingly innocent thing. Their impish behavior shows that the issue is not, or not only, knowing what words say but knowing how to interpret them. They pose the problem of overinterpretation.

Here again, the reasons are various, and of an especially psychological sort. One invests oneself in the meaning one invents. Overinterpretation responds to desires and fears, such as the taste for figuring things out, of feeling intelligent, of knowing or understanding more than other people do; to the need for feeling sought after, wanted; or to mistrust and suspicion of others.

This type of attitude has been exploited in the theater for comic effect, for example, with the Marquise Araminte in Molière, who became prudish with age and took offense at everything: "Her skilled scrupulosity discovers dirtiness where no one had ever seen it."[4] Recalling somewhat the remark of Jesus to his captors in Blaise Pascal's *Pensées*, "thou wouldst not seek Me, if thou hadst not found Me," or the saying that "it takes one to know one," the women in Molière's *Les Femmes Savantes* (*The Learned Ladies*) detect naughty subtexts in the sounds or syllables of certain words, as they might now with "Balzac" or "pussycat," and they conceive a reform program to rid the language of "dirty syllables / which make the most beautiful words scandalous."[5] After all, do not printing conventions, even today, require avoidance of unfortunately ill-sounding letters at the end of a line in word breaks?

Another example, in Shakespeare, is the mistake Benedick makes in interpreting Beatrice's words as an amorous advance when they mean precisely the opposite.[6] Beatrice spoke grudgingly, only inviting Benedick to dinner under compulsion. "Against my will I am sent to bid you come in to dinner," she fires off, but he strives to uncover a hidden graciousness, commenting, "There's a double meaning in that." As he thanks her for the invitation, she adds, "I took no more pains for those thanks than you take pains to thank me." He comments again, "That's as much as to say, Any pains that I take for you is as easy as thanks." The comedy of the scene derives from the fact that Beatrice's replies are not at all tender and that Benedick dreams up, without the least justification, his own interpretation to which he steadfastly adheres. If he succumbs to this madness, it is because Don Pedro, Claudio, and Leonato have persuaded him that Beatrice was in love with him. This assurance leads him to discover a secret intent where none exists.

In the same way, Bélise, in Molière's *The Learned Ladies*, persuaded that Clitandre and several other men are dying for her, rebuts each argument to the contrary with irrefutable proof. They have not said anything? That shows how much they respect her. They criticize her? That is only out of jealousy. They are married? That was out of despair. And so go the fantasies of this romantic soul.[7]

Yet overinterpretation is not always a laughing matter. It can betray an unhealthy distrust, as in the case of Cardinal Mazarin, who was the sort of man "who could not stop himself from thinking there was a back room wherever there was space to build one."[8] Strained relations can provoke it, as in the case of Admiral Tchichagov, when he meets the commander-in-chief Kutusov at the end of *War and Peace*:

> In conversation with Tchichagov Kutusov happened to mention that the vehicles packed with china that had been captured from him at Borisov had been recovered and would be restored to him.
>
> "You mean to imply that I have nothing to eat from. . . . On the contrary, I can supply you with everything you are likely to require, even if you should wish to give dinner-parties," replied Tchichagov hotly in French. . . .
>
> Shrugging his shoulders, Kutusov replied, also in French, with his subtle, shrewd smile: "I mean only what I say."[9]

The old general understood Tchichagov's misunderstanding was caused not by the words themselves but by a pride quick to take offense at anything, in a context of personal and political animosity, and that explains why he was content to smile rather than insist.

The psychopathology of the subtext gives rise to a sinister exchange between the suicidal painter Michael Krauss and a wino named "Half-Pint" in the film version of *Quai des ombres* (*Port of Shadows*), with a screenplay by Jacques Prévert:

> Painter: What's more simple than a tree? Yet when I paint a tree, I make everyone uneasy. That's because there's something, someone, lurking behind this tree! . . . I paint, I can't help it, the things behind things . . . A swimmer for me is already a drowning victim.
> Half-Pint: *Still* lifes, right![10]

Overinterpretation turns into obsession. The strangest manifestation (we come back again to love) is known as the "Clérambault syndrome," after Gaëtan Gatien de Clérambault (1872–1934), Jacques Lacan's teacher in psychiatry, who described the symptoms of "erotomania."[11] The afflicted individuals are convinced that someone loves them, and they ruminate: he (or she) loves me secretly, I am certain of it; he (or she) doesn't show it out of discretion and displays affection by roundabout means. Crazy, querulous, the patients suffer, feel spite and rancor, possibly becoming dangerous if they progress to harassment and jealousy, to an actual crime of passion.

Here is the first case Clérambault describes: Léa-Anna, fifty-three years old, is convinced the king of England is in love with her. She believes people she meets are emissaries of the king, the king's go-betweens, or indeed the king himself, appearing to her in different disguises (which she recognizes each time, only too late). This situation fills her with pride, but also with resentment; she winds up angry with the king and feeling he persecutes her. In another case, Clémentine D., who is fixated on a priest, a curate at the posh Parisian church Saint-Philippe-du-Roule, believes with all her heart that he is renting an apartment for her and that he wants to marry her.

The Clérambault syndrome has inspired novelists who have built plots of male and female homosexual love around this illness, for example, Ian McEwan's *Enduring Love* and Florence Noiville's *L'Illusion délirante d'être aimé* (*Attachment*). Each time, a character falls in love with someone and believes it is reciprocal, with the story ending tragically. These psychological disturbances are interesting because they rest upon a continuous effort of interpretation. All the actions of the Love-Object are seen in a favorable light. Every gesture, every piece of news is taken as positive evidence. The subtext is as broad as it is imaginary.

Hervé Le Tellier, in turn, exploits this mechanism at small book length in the spirit of Oulipo (the consortium of writers dedicated to writing under strict, self-imposed constraints). His *Moi et François Mitterrand* (Me and Mitterrand) is an inventive first-person narrative of the thoughts of a man writing to the president of the French Republic.[12] Each of his letters receives the same canned response:

Dear Sir:
Thank you for your letter of (such and such a date), which has just reached me. Be assured, kind sir, your remarks will receive all the attention they deserve and will be considered by our offices with the least possible delay, etc. etc.

Now, our correspondent interprets this unvarying letter differently each time, depending on his expectations, the circumstances of his personal life, and his prevailing judgments about the president's personality. The salutation "Dear Sir" is at first for him a mark of courtesy but then signals an affectionate intimacy when it is used in the second presidential missive. The phrase "your remarks will receive all the attention they deserve" sounds the first time like a promise, before taking on, he thinks, a tinge of sadness and shame one day, when the president answers some criticisms addressed to him in a previous letter. Then, when Jacques Chirac succeeds François Mitterrand (for after having written to the latter throughout his two, seven-year terms, our writer continues with his successors), the letter (still identical!) is understood to reveal the difference in style and personality between the two presidents. In a funny twist of the Clérambault syndrome, it is the emotional investment of the character that induces his overinterpreting each of the replies received, the same words taking on a different meaning as changes in his situation intervene.

On a different level, one must deal with deciphered, *though nonexistent*, allusions, when a text takes on, after the fact, a meaning its author never foresaw and never could have. Cicero recounts how, in Rome, comedies and tragedies more than a century old took on new political undertones in contemporary performance. When the actor declaimed, "To this it comes, from a life of vice," the entire audience turned toward the tribune Clodius, seated among them, a man the play's plot had nothing to do with but who, owing to his escapades and intrigues, was an unmistakable target. When, in contrast, the script mentioned one "who aided the Republic with steadfast heart" and "who hesitated not to risk his life," the crowd cheered Cicero (naturally) and called for an encore.[13] At Caesar's funeral in 44 BC, people sang verses, also from an ancient tragedy, dealing with a subject from Greek mythology but seeming to allude to the present context, like this sorrowful cry, denouncing the assassins' ingratitude: "What, did I save these men that they might murder me?"[14] In such cases, it is the audience's reaction that discovers a subtext after the fact.

Slippery Eels

A passage attributed to St. Jerome, concerning figured speech in the Greek rhetoricians, captures in one expressive image the difficulties of the subtext. "It is as if you wanted to hold an eel or a small moray tightly in your hands: the more you squeeze, the sooner it gets away."[15] Jerome knew what he was talking about, since, by his own acknowledgment, the learned doctor of the Church had practiced figured declamation quite often.[16] In all periods of history, listeners or readers have come to experience that uncomfortable feeling of sensing an eel under a rock without being certain of what they think they are catching. Here are some illustrations, ancient and modern.

A work, now lost, by the Socratic Aeschines of Sphettos and dedicated to the Pythagorean philosopher Telauges generated a feeling of being at a loss (*aporia*) because of its ambiguity, for nobody could figure out whether Aeschines was expressing admiration or mockery.[17]

The *Farewell Address* of the father of the Church Gregory of Nazianzus, written when he retired as bishop of Constantinople, provoked a debate between those commentators who took it literally and those who saw in it only an imaginary departure. In the course of this scholarly polemic, which lasted for centuries, name-calling was rampant, and certain interpreters considered their opponents "ignoramuses," "sacrilegious," or, referring to an Aesopian fable, "asses dressed in lion's skin."[18]

Does Niccolò Machiavelli's *The Mandrake*, a bawdy comedy and satire of civic and religious customs, also contain a reflection on the usefulness of ruses and a political lesson akin to that of *The Prince*? Must one go further, looking for original models and then connecting the dots, as we might say today, wondering whether the young Lucrezia represents the city of Florence and her lover, Callimaco, one of the Medici? Scholars are divided.

Is Molière's *Amphitryon*, which portrays Jupiter's adultery with Alcmene, an allusion to the fact that the king took the Marquise de Montespan as his mistress? Some commentators and scholars, beginning with the nineteenth-century French historian Jules Michelet, have thought so, while others, just as authoritative, shun such a hypothesis.

And what about *Tartuffe*? It is obviously an example of veiled criticism through a character, as happens in drama, but the target is not clear. People have looked everywhere. Was it the pious? Hypocrites (insofar as they differ from the previous category)? Spiritual directors? Jansenists, Jesuits, or some other order? Not to mention successive rewritings of the play, in the course of which the meaning could evolve. "*Grammatici certant,*" as Horace quipped: "PhDs disagree."

Lastly, Laurent Nunez, in *L'Énigme des premières phrases*, has offered a troubling panorama of the beauties and risks of interpretation, using the openings of literary works in verse and prose, where he methodically searches for various depths and cascades of subtexts. Often the argument is compelling, as with Jean-Jacques Rousseau's *Confessions* or with *In Search of Lost Time*, works carefully crafted, certainly, and rife with meaning. His effort is always imaginative, as in the case of Charles Baudelaire's poem "La servante au grand cœur dont vous étiez jalouse" (The big-hearted housemaid of whom you were jealous),[19] an opening verse, as Nunez points out, that none other than Paul Valéry said contained an entire novel of Honoré de Balzac in embryo. Sometimes, the analysis borders on the acrobatic (André Gide's *The Counterfeiters*, Raymond Queneau's *Zazie in the Métro*). The author is quite aware of this and intentionally explores this zone of uncertainty, with the idea not only of interpreting the works but of reflecting on interpretation itself, pushing it to the limit to demonstrate the risks and the richness.

Need another example? Jacques Chirac's eulogy of François Mitterrand, delivered on January 8, 1996, was greeted as a moving and sincerely felt homage, an act of Republican reconciliation postmortem.[20] Yet it contained some details that allowed a certain distancing to peek through. There was mention of Mitterrand's "complexity," of the relation with Chirac as one of "contrasts." Near the conclusion, a rhetorical balance expressed "respect for the Public Official and admiration for the Private Citizen." A fine eulogy. But these words, weighed in the balance, hold back as much as they give; notwithstanding the goodwill he felt or expressed for the dead president, the speaker still refrained from voicing admiration for his public policy or respect for the conduct of his private life.

Great, then, is the difficulty of the problem. The interpreter risks either breezing by the hidden meaning or sinking into arbitrariness and shaky analyses. The mathematical principle of indeterminacy or the uncertainty principle in physics have their equivalents in language. That is why safeguards are necessary. It is essential to try to define the conditions that make subtexts possible, as well as those that permit their comprehension. Such conditions cannot consist in a single, unvarying response, and they call for taking into account different parameters. I will propose three of them here: the paratext, the context, and the text.

Yet before examining them, a word of caution. This is because the conditions for interpreting texts bring up serious questions of literary theory that were bitterly debated in the past century and led to sharply divided stances, some of which were mentioned in the last chapter. So it is necessary to explain why furthering these debates is not germane here. On the one hand, the most radical ideas have become by now passé or have been transformed beyond recognition. The days of asserting that the text alone carries its own interpretation are over, that its interpretation is immanent and self-contained, with all other considerations to be tossed aside: the author, the genesis of the work, its historical and social context, linguistic pragmatics have all regained their rights. Gone, too, are the days of maintaining that the work of art is by nature unfinished, shifting, and open to all interpretations. In this regard, the progress of Umberto Eco is telling, who, after having championed *The Open Work* in 1962, admitted in 1990 the need to hedge with safeguards and erect *The Limits of Interpretation*.

On the other hand, the subtext, as I understand it, concerns not only literary works but also daily exchanges in which the importance of intent and interaction is neither questionable nor questioned. A proof of this importance is the oft-made observation that the same words take on different meanings depending on the circumstances. For example, Isocrates says, "The same words must not be understood in the same way, if not spoken with the same intention."[21] Again, Pascal: "Those of discerning mind know what a difference there is between two similar words, according to the places and circumstances surrounding them" and "Those who say the same things do not take them in the same way."[22] It does not follow that one must make the author's or speaker's intent the alpha and the omega of interpretation—a naive problematic; rather, one must mobilize all the means for framing and justifying proposed interpretations. The deciphering of subtexts is not limited to listing impersonal and abstract effects, or to the sudden discovery of a meaning supposedly put there for the interpreter. It often presumes some groundwork, depends on conditions, is hedged with safeguards, and can be subject to conjecture and hesitation. Incidentally, that explains the difficulty of translating the subtext, for codes and presuppositions may vary from one language to another.

Paratext and Correctives

The "paratext" includes the external elements and additions that introduce the text, orientating its reading and ensuring its proper reception. Gérard Genette, distancing himself from strict structuralism, draws up a mind-boggling list of them in *Seuils* (*Thresholds*): they include the name or pseudonym of the author, the work's title, its dedication, the preface, notes, and also the author's comments (Genette calls them "epitext") made in public interviews, in correspondence, or in spoken or written private communications. An example of this sort, cited earlier, is Orwell's letter concerning *Animal Farm*.[23]

In Sanskrit literature, where the use of double meaning and ambiguity was frequent, one notes, at the head of certain epics, introductions that set forth the "rules of the game" and ready the reader to decipher what follows correctly.[24]

The notion of paratext not only targets literary works but can also include those intonations, gestures, and asides in verbal exchange that guide interpretation. I have in mind the mimicry of depicting quotation marks with two raised hands, or comments like, "You see what I mean," "Let's say," or "Just joking." Since every assertion risks having an apparent subtext, it is often necessary to add a corrective to prevent mistake: "You look lovely this evening—as always, of course."

If you say to a father that his son Pierre is smart, your compliment, too neutral for it not to be ambiguous, requires what follows to allow him to grasp its meaning and to understand what you really meant, whether positively or negatively: "He will certainly succeed in life" or "It's curious that he doesn't have better grades" or "And he's athletic, too" or "He's not at all like his brother."

These accidentals, written and spoken, have no other objective than closing a kind of contract, an interpretative pact meant to ensure the message is correctly transmitted between sender and recipient. Often, the pact itself is formulated in a fine and allusive manner. Thus, in correspondence, Madame de Sévigné, writing to her daughter, took care to advise her: "You well understand all that I am saying, and not saying."[25] A woman writing to a lady friend to tell her a dirty secret begins by reflecting on "the words that are so difficult to find to say certain things." "Oh well, too bad if you don't understand me! And so, my dear, try a little to read between the lines."[26]

In Balzac, Madame de Beauséant has an envelope brought to Eugène de Rastignac containing an invitation addressed to M. and Mme. de Nucingen, with an additional note: "I am sending you the invitation you requested, and I will be delighted to make the acquaintance of the sister of Mme. de Restaud [that is, none other than Mme. de Nucingen]." The invitation is the text, the note the paratext.

"But," Eugène reflects in rereading the note, "Mme. de Beauséant is saying quite clearly to me that she doesn't want the Baron de Nucingen."

Rastignac is an intelligent man (which helps him get ahead), and he has understood that the note has a subtext. He not only read the note; he reread it, and so he perceived the hidden meaning, which social conventions prohibited expressing outright. Even though the invitation was addressed to Monsieur and Madame, the accompanying note, which only mentions the desire to see Madame, lets it be understood that there is no desire to see Monsieur.

A little later, Eugène expands on this interpretation to Mme. de Nucingen herself: "'Don't you think,' Eugène said, 'that Mme de Beauséant seems to be saying to us that she is not counting on seeing the Baron de Nucingen at her ball?'—'But of course,' said the baroness, handing back the letter to Eugène. 'Those women have a gift for impertinence. But no matter, I will go.'"[27]

When it comes to breaking the rules, the game consists in utilizing the paratext not to enlighten the recipient but to plot against him, indeed to throw him off, and to make him think again, like this preface Flaubert thought of giving to the *Dictionary of Received Ideas*: "a good preface where one would indicate how the work was made with the aim of reconnecting the public to tradition, order, prevailing convention, and arranged in such a manner that the reader does not know if one is screwing with him, yes or no."[28]

Context and Collusion

While there does not have to be a paratext, the context, on the other hand, is always present. The material, psychological, and sociological conditions are crucial. The subtext is grasped if the sender and the receiver belong to the same world, share the same culture, the same experiences, and the same assumptions, if they form, in short, an interpretative community.

Ancient rhetoric, proceeding along these lines, emphasized the importance of the listener: the orators were not speaking in the abstract but addressing publics they wanted to stir. This theme was already recurrent in Aristotle's *Rhetoric*. Examining it more closely, one can make a distinction between the actual audience, composed of the people physically listening to the speech, and the virtual or presumed audience, composed of targeted individuals, "the audience on the orator's mind."[29] These two audiences are not identical; out of their difference arise all sorts of distortions, some fruitful, some not. In the case of public addresses delivered before crowds and not a select group, the creation of a sense of community is especially difficult, since the audience is an aggregate of diverse types, each with its own ideas, goals, and understanding. Multiple levels of reception can coexist: some get the point; others do not. Jesus, in using parables, recognizes this situation and tries to remedy it with the famous injunction, "He that hath ears to hear, let him hear!"[30]

In literature, the so-called School of Constance has clarified the problematic relationship of author, text, and readers with its notion of the "horizon of expectation." The school's essential contribution was to establish that, contrary to appearances, the classic works are not really like an object created once and for all; rather, they obtain their meaning through the process of reading, thanks to the readers and critics who take them up. The horizon of expectation is conditioned, among other things, by the themes and literary genres in which the works are written. More precisely, one must speak of two horizons, "that which the text implies," as a function of its actual place in history, and "that which the reader brings to bear in his reading," as a function of the reader's own system of references, expectations, and subjective experience. The reader's horizon may be close to that of the text, especially in the case of the "original audience," contemporary with the book's appearance, or it may be quite distant. The "fusion of horizons," in other words, the ways of encountering a work, take on multiple forms ranging from aesthetic pleasure to disorientation and critical distancing.[31]

Such observations take on special importance with the subtext, which is necessarily enclosed within a relational context conditioned historically, politically, and rhetorically, and which depends on the dispositions and abilities the partners in the exchange possess. I know what you know. I suppose what you suppose. I suppose what you suppose I suppose, and so forth. By its nature, the subtext consists of actions, reactions, and alternating interactions, guided inferences that determine the meaning and true value of utterances. But this collusion is not a given. It is created and requires practice. Certain speakers, certain audiences have a penchant for sending and picking up subtexts, like those one might encounter in the ancient auditoriums for figured declamation, in royal courts, or in totalitarian regimes.

Classical philologists interested in the Greek Neoplatonists of late antiquity (fifth to sixth centuries AD) have discovered, or rather rediscovered, a curious instance of collusion (among thousands).[32] They have noted that these philosophers used turns of phrase like "the current situation," "the present confusion," "people today," "our contemporaries," "prevailing opinion," and "the authorities." Not much to comment on, so it would seem. Yet these colorless locutions, unremarkable in themselves, were perfectly understandable in the milieu where they were used. They were nothing less than coded expressions alluding to the fact that Christians were dominant and that paganism was just a tiny island threatened on all sides, at a time when an imperial decree would shut the Academy of Athens for good. In pagan intellectual circles, these expressions served as a rallying sign and voiced a mute protest against the omnipresence of Christianity. Their context dictated their meaning.

Textual Criteria

Moving on to textual criteria, these are internal. They consist of elements within a text (or spoken words) that tip off and create the impression that there is "a certain something" hidden somewhere.[33] Paradoxes and anomalies will arouse suspicion, as will discrepancies and questionings that possibly emerge. When words like "elm tree" and "acacia" crop up with unaccustomed frequency in the letters of two bankers, so writes Jean Paulhan, their exchanges probably have a hidden content.[34] Hence the need for discretion: handling the subtext successfully requires moderation and deftness in the execution. "*Intellegenti pauca*," goes the old Latin proverb: "A word to the wise is sufficient."

Leo Strauss has expressed what are, perhaps, the most profound thoughts on textual criteria. It is true that some of this philosopher's interpretations have been criticized, when he deals, for example, with ancient authors or Machiavelli, and one might find fault with his tendency to bow down before the works of great writers, holding that everything they say is significant, and with his rejection of the idea that certain oddities are explained by the conditions of textual transmission subsequent to the author, that Strauss is, in short, overly sophisticated or overly strict. Nonetheless, it remains true that Strauss perceived the reality of double meaning acutely. The historic events he experienced during his lifetime (1899–1973), in Germany, France, England, and the United States, left their mark on him and influenced the formulation of his theories, which rested on an immense philosophical and historical culture. He studied with Edmund Husserl, knew Hans-Georg Gadamer, Martin Heidegger, and the historian of Judaism Gershom Scholem.

For our purposes, his principal contribution is "Persecution and the Art of Writing," an article about fifteen pages long that appeared in the journal *Social Research* in 1941 (the date is important) and was then reprinted, with revisions and cuts, in a book with the same title in 1952.[35] The article's subject is the art "of writing between the lines" in an authoritarian regime, with risk of persecution, in order "to express one's views" without danger. According to Strauss, the art of writing is not addressed to all readers but to certain among them whom he portrays as "in love with thinking," "trustworthy and intelligent," "attentive." These individuals will know to ask themselves whether there are some hidden meanings in the works of the classic writers. Given that disagreements may arise over interpretation, criteria are necessary, among which are "obscurity of the work's plan, contradictions . . . , omission of important links in the argument," and even "pseudonyms" and "strange expressions." The method of deciphering will consist in grounding oneself on the text, as it is, in its totality, paying attention to all the fault lines and shunning the belief that the author's opinion coincides with any one character's (in the case of a play or dialogue) or even with the opinion the author expresses most often. This essay on the art of writing is thus tantamount to an art of reading.

Indeed, one of the most efficacious mechanisms of the subtext (we now take our leave of Strauss) is readers' or listeners' ability, assuming they are prepared and in the right frame of mind, to create hidden meaning themselves, through a personal and interior action. This is a major point, made independently of one another, by several authors ancient and modern.[36] Someone who wants to be understood has an interest in not saying everything, in not giving detailed explanations, but on the contrary in leaving room for figuring out and deducing. Thus, readers or listeners are not limited to a passive role as recipients. They cooperate in developing the meaning, are secretly flattered to assist, and, through a phenomenon of self-confidence joined to self-regard, cling more firmly to what has been *suggested* to them because they think they have discovered it through their own devices. "Speech is half the speaker's, half the hearer's," wrote Michel de Montaigne.[37]

Here is an example of the division of labor between author and reader, according to an ancient Greek rhetorician as he proposes a keen reading of a passage in Plato.[38] The philosopher, listing the faithful who gathered round Socrates at the time of his death, notes that Aristippus and Cleombrotus were not there. "They were on Aegina, people said." No need to add more; the facts speak for themselves. The alerted reader, who knows that Plato does not write haphazardly, and who has noted that this is a memorial passage, will understand that this observation is not gratuitous. He will be able to conclude that these two disciples did not think it worthwhile to cross from Aegina to Athens, despite the short distance, even though they had had time to make arrangements, since Socrates was imprisoned for many days. Such a reader will come independently to the conclusion that the ingrates deserve blame. (One nagging detail: Plato also was not present on this sad occasion, but he had the excuse of illness.)[39]

Persuasion rests in such a case on a kind of transfer of expertise, the sender letting go of what ultimately comes back to him, the fixing of meaning, to confer this responsibility on the receiver. If the latter takes over interpretation unawares, there is manipulation. If he is aware, he colludes. And between these two extremes many intermediate situations are feasible. In figuring out a subtext, more than one reader, or author, will be able to take to heart a saying that has become famous in France, provoking a smile, and is really more profound than it seems. It concerns a leading cyclist caught in a doping scandal, who laughably tried to beg off responsibility, insisting, "I did it, unwittingly, willingly."

One Word for Another

To conclude on a reassuring note, it is worth taking a look at a scene that shows to what heights interpretation can rise when the necessary safeguards are supplied. At the beginning of Jean Tardieu's comedy *Un mot pour un autre* (One word for another), the following dialogue occurs:

> The Maid, *entering (whispering, anxiously, in the ear of Madame)*: Madame, it's Madame de Pumperdime! I keen, Madame de Pumpernick; Madame (*she stresses "Madame"*), Madame de Pumperdime!
>
> Madame (*finger on her lips to shut Irma up, then aloud and joyfully*): What a cluster! Quick, shower her thin!
>
> *The maid leaves. Madame, awaiting her visitor, sits at the piano and plays. A tinkling tune, like a music box's, emerges.*
>
> *Reenter the maid, followed by Madame de Pumperdime.*
>
> The Maid, *announcing*: Madame la Comtesse de Pumperdime!
>
> Madame (*closing the piano and going to meet her friend*): Darling, darling teddy! For how many moles, for how many wheels has it been without the delight of sugaring you!
>
> Madame de Pumperdime, *quite overwhelmed*: Alas, Darling! I was myself very, very glassy! My three youngest cakes have had the lemonade,

one after the other. Throughout the first stages of its corsaire, I had to nest in my windmill, running to the drug dealer's or the stool store, I spent lights watching their carbonizing, giving them drips and monsoons. In short, I didn't have a momentous to myself.

Madame: Poor darling! And I didn't suspend a thing![40]

In this exchange, few words are right, and yet the reader follows it without difficulty. That is because all the other conditions are in place: the paratext (in the form of the stage directions), the context (the social call setting, prerequisite and shared knowledge, for which both the author and the reader already know the stereotypes and obligatory responses), and in the text itself, the syntactical construction of the sentences, which is rigorously correct, and the words, which present similarities with the expected right words ("momentous" with "moment," "suspend" with "suspect," and so on). All this results in permitting the immediate and intuitive construction of a sufficient meaning, even though the surface is perfectly hermetic. "Mean" is hidden behind "keen," "pleasure" behind "cluster," "show her in" behind "shower her thin." It is not by accident that the collection in which this play appears carries as an epigraph a quotation from Maurice Blanchot asserting that "ambiguity is everywhere."[41] The delicious ramblings of the playwright demonstrate that the sender and the receiver can go quite far together, provided they are on the same wavelength.[42]

5

Greek Pretenses About Rome

The following chapter offers interpretations using the subtext as a way to revitalize certain literary works that have not always been sufficiently understood and to expose the tensions they conceal. In confronting might, speakers and writers employed pretense to affirm convictions and convey messages within a context of control and domination.

Searching for Greek Identity

The orations of the Greek sophists and philosophers during the High Roman Empire are an area of special interest because the issue of the rapport between the Greek-speaking elites and Roman power recurs throughout the period. This was a sensitive matter that motivated toned-down ways of speaking and orations that tried to put on a good face. Since we are dealing with a distant era, a brief description may be in order.

During this time (second century AD), Rome's conquest of the Mediterranean Basin was essentially complete, the relentless warfare that secured it several centuries in the past. To ensure its mastery of these lands, Rome did not rely solely on its soldiers and bureaucrats but sought to win its subjects' cooperation by all means possible. It granted privileged status to certain cities and Roman citizenship to their leading individuals. It conceded some latitude to local authorities, creating provincial deliberative bodies as well as permitting the populace continued use of their native languages, with Latin only required in the army and imperial administration. Municipal leaders did not merely endure Rome's power but actively promoted it by erecting buildings, doling out public assistance, producing popular entertainments, and celebrating the imperial cult in return for honors and advancement. Constantly repeated slogans like "Pax Romana," "On land and sea,"

"The city and the world," and "Rome the eternal" recalled the empire's extent and sure foundation.

Naturally, such an idyllic picture did not suit everyone. Roman imperialism, violently imposed, sought to exploit the material and human wealth of the conquered lands, provoking opposition and resistance. The Roman system had to defend itself against not only foreign invaders but also internal opponents like magicians, astrologers, prophets, or agents provocateurs.[1] Pacified provinces did experience revolts, social upheavals, and attempts to usurp power. People had to bemoan avaricious and despotic emperors and provincial governors sent from Rome. But, all in all, the situation for most people was not worse, and was even better—in terms of law, stability, material prosperity—than what had previously prevailed. A centralized, authoritarian regime, the cult of personality, these were all known quantities from earlier monarchies. Slavery, torture, oppression, persecution of Jews and Christians were just the way of the world, and one considered himself lucky not to be a victim. More important, there was no political alternative, no program aiming to overthrow Roman sovereignty. Rome had no rival.

In the Greek-speaking world of that time (corresponding roughly to Greece, modern Turkey, and the Middle East), many texts and other sorts of documents celebrate the empire's advantages, and they rehearse a catalog that includes the invitation for provincial participation, the advantages of Roman law, political stability, military might, security, peace, improved travel conditions, water supply management, refound affluence. Yet here and there, one notes certain digs, certain recollections of a time when the Greek-speaking cities were independent, certain signs of antipathy toward the Romans, moral reflections on luxury and the wealth concentrated in the city of Rome, some criticism of the servility certain subjects display toward their masters.

One must not forget that the Greeks were proud of their race, their history, their culture, their gods, and their language to such a degree that they considered themselves one and the same people despite their differences, and that they divided the world in two: themselves, the Greeks, and everybody else, the non-Greeks, the "barbarians." Imbued with their superiority, they preserved their identity even within the Roman Empire. A happy, or a sad, identity? The recent debate over this issue of happiness within French society, between Alain Finkielkraut and Alain Juppé, not to mention within the United States, shows that the response to such a question cannot be unambiguous. Hellenic identity rested on a constructed or reconstructed past, anchored in a heritage, in landscapes, in pilgrimages. This memory was not a wishful abolition of the present but a sustained and shared knowledge, suitable for creating a feeling of Hellenic community, a channel of communication for promoting some rights amid the Romans.

The Weapon of Pretense

54 The subtext can prove to be a fruitful approach in confronting such a situation. Greek literature of the High Empire often startles with its atmosphere of archaism and apparent indifference or resignation toward current realities. It is surely appropriate to go beyond this appearance to discern contemporary allusions lurking in the ambient antiquarianism and to understand that loyalty was less resolute than advertised. This is not a matter of looking for pronounced opposition or overt criticism, as happened during the time when the Roman conquest was still underway, but of locating the more subtle cracks that betray a disabused, quietly protesting state of mind.

The texts that will be our guide are those orations of Dio Chrysostom, or Dio of Prusa (ca. 40–110 AD), and Aelius Aristides (117–after 180 AD) that deal with the Roman Empire and the emperor. These two authors were celebrated in their time. Holding important positions in their respective provinces, possessors of Roman citizenship, they accepted Rome's authority and cooperated with it. Yet they were Greeks by language, culture, and identity, prompting a distancing, an aloofness, that one must neither minimize nor fail to recognize in their works (as some have been tempted to do, who take the protestations of loyalty literally). Their ploys have a particular interest because they bear on a strategic issue that brought into play the period's political and cultural context.

The Sophistic Milieu

Dio and Aristides belonged to a milieu called the "Second Sophistic," one keenly interested in rhetoric and, particularly, figured speech in its specialized meaning defined earlier.[2] The famous sophists excelled in declamations of double meaning,[3] and Dio and Aristides both used the words "figure" and "to figure" (*skhêma, skhêmatizesthai*) with a technical sense, demonstrating their knowledge of the subtleties of pretense. Dio faults the approach that uses veiled criticisms,[4] preferring carefully couched statements that allow one to address the powerful without drawing their anger or groveling before them unbecomingly, a twin preoccupation corresponding exactly to the two pitfalls theory signaled.[5] Aristides alludes to the form of figured speech that sweetens a criticism with personal safety in mind,[6] and he singles out the practice of criticizing while seeming to praise.[7] The sophists deserve to be understood between the lines because rhetoric had shaped them to the rules of a coded discourse designed for a society sharing the same code.

Those rules were valued in direct proportion to the absence of free speech. The government kept watch; censorship existed, as did a secret police; and books were burned for political or religious reasons. Hence the usefulness of knowing how to express oneself vaguely, but skillfully, or watch out! Given the authorities' prickly scrutiny, one had to be prudent even in the use of subtexts. Recall the cases of the rhetor Carrinas Secundus and the sophist Maternus, the former of whom was exiled, the latter condemned to death, by Caligula and Domitian, respectively, for having declaimed school exercises with an anti-tyrannical theme[8] (even though this was a common topic[9]). The same Domitian executed Hermogenes of Tarsus (an earlier homonym of the theorist of rhetoric) "because of certain figurative uses contained in his history," and he crucified the scribes who had copied the work.[10] One could only consider oneself fortunate when the emperor showed forbearance in the matter, like Vespasian, who "endured his friends' flippancy, as well as lawyers' figurative usages and philosophers' contumacy with the utmost leniency."[11] Or like Marcus Aurelius: the sophist Herodes Atticus took issue with him in public, in no uncertain terms, something that might have earned him the death penalty, as the Praetorian Prefect observed to him, but he got away with it, thanks to the emperor's clemency.[12]

Dio Chrysostom, Philosopher *Engagé* in Politics

Dio, nicknamed Chrysostom or "golden-mouthed" for his eloquence, belonged to an influential family in Prusa, a city in Bithynia (present-day Bursa in northwest Turkey). When he was about forty, during the reign of the fearsome Domitian, his ties to a disgraced prominent individual earned him banishment. The penalty lasted until Domitian's assassination ended the emperor's reign in 96 AD, when Nerva, Domitian's successor, lifted it. He was, according to Dio's own words, an old friend. Under Nerva (96–98) and Trajan (98–117), Dio resumed his political activities in Prusa and various other cities of the empire as a politician, intellectual, and touring speaker.

It is then that he composed the four *Discourses on Kingship*.[13] At the height of his fame, he tackles a large subject, the definition of monarchy and the conditions necessary for its proper exercise, in support of the idea that power needs intelligent and wise counsel. In all times, the sovereign and the sage counselor have formed a couple, with their ups and downs, like most couples: Agamemnon and Nestor, Dionysius of Syracuse and Plato, Charlemagne and Alcuin, Queen Christina of Sweden and Descartes, Frederic II of Prussia and Voltaire, de Gaulle and Malraux; one could go on. Dio's initiative thus belongs to an ongoing investigation in political philosophy, already traditional by his own time, even as it examines the actual situation in the second century. Note that the concept of "kingship" could indeed be used of a Roman imperial regime; in the Greek of this period, the word *basileus*, meaning "king," was commonly employed to designate the "emperor." Furthermore, the first and third discourses of the series are explicitly addressed to the reigning emperor through using the second-person singular of verbs and the vocative case of nouns. This recipient, not mentioned by name, is Trajan in all likelihood, since the *Discourses on Kingship* probably date to the years 100–105 AD. The definition of the good king contained contemporary ramifications.

That made Dio's approach a sensitive matter, as Pliny the Younger's Latin panegyric of Trajan confirms. Just freed from Domitian's tyranny, the panegyrists drew sighs of relief but remained cautious. "I am not afraid to please or to displease," Pliny writes,[14] a denial that only proves the problem was not forgotten. The risks of angering the emperor or his entourage were not to be gainsaid. In these conditions, Pliny chose to review Trajan's great accomplishments, one by one and in detail. Dio followed a different path, a more roundabout way.

Critical and rebellious, Dio's was an independent spirit, one not to let established practices hem him in. His turbulent life, marked by exile and success, as well as his multifaceted personality as aristocrat, sophist, and philosopher, brought him diverse experiences and broadened his outlook. He had had complicated relationships with Rome. His approach could be neither bland nor conformist. We now undertake to follow him, step by step, as he subtly states his case.

Simplicity on Display

The *First Discourse on Kingship* contains a definition of the essential qualities of a good king (piety, humaneness, devotion to his task, etc.) and then argues that the ideal monarchy reflects the gods' governance, concluding, like Plato, with a myth, here concerning Herakles. All the time with tradition in mind, Dio describes his effort as an "exhortation," and he wishes to make his work useful in the hope that the emperor will subsequently remember his words.[15]

He slips in two remarks about his own discourse that are especially important: "For this discourse of mine, delivered in all simplicity without any flattery or abuse, of itself discerns the king that is like the good one, and commends him in so far as he is like him, while the one who is unlike him it exposes and rebukes. . . . In plain and simple language I have described the good king. If any of his attributes seem to belong to you, happy are you in your gracious and excellent nature, and happy are we who share its blessings with you."[16]

These comments signal that the text calls for a reading on two levels and that it contains, on the one hand, an abstract philosophical discourse and, on the other, an implied application to the current situation. If the emperor corresponds to the portrait of the ideal monarch, the meaning inferred from the text is an encomium; if he does not, it is a rejection and a criticism. One may well imagine that the first case applies to Trajan, the second to Domitian. But is Trajan good in every way? Are all the defects Domitian's? The philosopher provides no answer, being content to say to the emperor, "You resemble the ideal ruler, or you do not." This is slippery ground, and that is why Dio proceeds cautiously, insisting on the "simplicity" of his words (an insistence that inevitably arouses the listener's or reader's suspicion that things are not quite so simple). He emphasizes that the application to actual circumstances happens "of itself," that it is involuntary and automatic, and thus he begs off his responsibility.

The final words of the discourse, intentionally ambiguous, suggest possible outcomes: Herakles protects you, Dio says to the addressee, and will continue to do so "for as long as you reign." These good wishes for the future may conceal a condition at the same time. "For as long as you reign" means both "for as long as you are king" and "for as long as you are a true king, and not a tyrant," according to the distinction between king and tyrant that was an important theme throughout the discourse. It would not require much more to make this exhortation, written probably early in Trajan's reign, sound like a warning.

Speaking Generally

In the *Third Discourse*, an ample introduction functions as a paratext and orientates the reception. Dio launches into the task of praising Trajan's virtues in such a way that one might imagine the work was going to be a panegyric. But he quickly breaks off, announcing that he is going to leave the specific case of the current emperor to discuss the good king theoretically: "Accordingly, that I may not be open to the charge of flattery by my would-be detractors, and that you on your part may not be accused of wanting to be praised to your very face, I shall speak of the ideal king, of what sort he should be, and how he differs from the man who pretends to be a ruler but is in reality far from true dominion and kingship."[17]

Dio distrusts the flattery and rhetorical encomia that might do a disservice both to himself and to his audience. The position of the parrot that learned to say "Hail, Caesar!" and then taught it to the other birds[18] is not at all for him; he prefers to be more like the owl of Athena. The refusal to praise Trajan thus betrays hesitancy about encomium, but not about Trajan. This is a philosopher being scrupulous and explains why the expected encomium will not be forthcoming. In its place, the orator chooses generalization.

Generalization is a proven method used at different times to convey suggestions in a manner as prudent as it is efficacious. "There are those who deny themselves nothing," the envious individual lets fly at no one in particular, using the plural to avoid taking issue with a particular someone on his mind, or, as the popular locution has it, "Naming no names." An ancient theorist of the stylistic figures stresses that the act of speaking "in general" keeps one from upsetting those with whom he is talking: "Thanks to this figure, it is often possible, all the while preserving the efficacy of our thought, to guard us from giving offense."[19] Molière defines the procedure's salient traits in a few words: "These types of satires hit social customs directly, and specific individuals only with glancing blows. . . . They are public mirrors, where one never has to admit glimpsing oneself," and "they stick to generalization."[20] Generalization makes an indirect image visible and allows the inference of a specific application that it would be inadvisable to express frankly. Empson recalled this method in his analysis of ambiguity.[21]

In the *Third Discourse on Kingship*, the supplementary meanings that generalization covers up are encomium and counsel. Dio may protest in vain that he is avoiding encomium, for it is understood that he is praising all the same; as much as he vainly denies that he is counseling, it is clear that that is precisely what he is doing. Placed in a situation where praising was obligatory and counseling dangerous, Dio did not want to portray himself as a panegyrist and cheerleader. So he had recourse to generalization to achieve his purpose. Many themes of the discourse, apparently general and philosophic in nature, thus take their meaning through connection to the ideology of the reign and Trajan's conduct. These include references to Zeus and Herakles, the importance accorded to the ruler's "friends" or the taste for hunting, all of which are other ways of honoring and approving the reigning emperor. So, too, is the contrasting theme of the tyrant, an implicit criticism of his predecessor, Domitian.

Games of Disguise

The *Second* and *Fourth Discourses on Kinship* do not, in fact, present themselves as discourses, strictly speaking, though this is their traditional name; they are dialogues. The former is a conversation between Alexander the Great, when he was young and still a student of his teacher, Aristotle, and his father, Philip of Macedon. Responding to Philip's questions, Alexander expresses his total admiration for Homer and finds in the Homeric epics a model encapsulating the culture, the way of life, the virtues, and the principles of governance that befit a good king. Thus, Dio manages to express his own thoughts on kingship through the device of historical figures dating from the fourth century BC, more than four hundred years prior to his own time. The great names from the past serve to speak of the present while maintaining a certain separation. "Cultural memory" functions as an "art of distancing."[22]

This detour through characters remote in time from the author and his audience corresponds to two techniques found in the rhetorical treatises. Aristotle, the real Aristotle, that is, not Dio's, provided the theory for this procedure of putting words into the mouth of a third party ("as if quoting the opinion of others")[23] to avoid exposing oneself to criticism when maintaining proposals liable to offend, such as self-congratulation, accusations against another, and so forth. The rhetoric of figured speech adopted this advice and recommended "introducing ideas by letting someone else say them," in the manner of "Someone might have said . . . but I am not saying that."[24] Other authors envisage the substitution of characters, not for the speaker but for the recipients of the speech: "Since powerful men and women dislike hearing their own faults mentioned, we will not speak openly, if we are advising them against a fault, but we will either blame others who have acted in a similar way . . . or we will praise people who have acted in the opposite way."[25]

The rhetorician Tiberius reclassifies these two techniques under the heading "ethopoeia" (literally, "creating a character"), which he defines as a figure that places criticism in someone else's mouth, or addresses criticism to someone other than the listener, as a hedge against offending.[26] The intervention of third parties enables the orator to go undercover and avoid speaking in his own name. This is what Dio does. By portraying Alexander in conversation with Philip, he extricates himself from the risky situation of being personally involved in dispensing advice. The dialogue does indeed contain veiled recommendations and criticisms, especially against excessive warfare, a lively issue at the time. Disguises let it all get by, and what makes the comments sophisticated, in every sense of the word, is that the disguises are ambiguous.

Greek Pretenses About Rome

Indeed, the imaginary scene in the *Second Discourse* is such that neither of the characters in the dialogue can be taken to represent only one of the real individuals concerned. Looked at in some ways, Alexander is the author's spokesman, since it is he who is discoursing on kingship, but he is also necessarily a representative of the emperor because of the actual Alexander's role in history and because Trajan took Alexander the Great as a particularly admired role model. If Alexander associates wisdom with power, his father, Philip, switches the order, associating power with wisdom. He embodies a sovereign figure, since he is king, but the authority, paternal and smiling, that he has over Alexander, the questions he asks him, turn him into Alexander's instructor. Looming in the background are Aristotle, whose instruction, it is said, Alexander simply repeats, and the author himself, who breaks in from time to time with comments of his own. Instead of looking at a mirror of the prince, reflecting a unified picture, one perceives a multiplicity of splintered and shifting images.

To be even more circumspect, Dio presents his subject in a vague manner, surrounding it with a calculated haziness: "They say that one day Alexander, when he was still an adolescent, had a conversation with his father about Homer . . . ; at the same time, these remarks had a certain bearing on kingship."[27] Were someone to attack Dio for having touched on the empire, he could retort that he had merely written a dialogue about Greek poetry.

Alexander reappears in the *Fourth Discourse on Kingship* in conversation this time with the Cynic philosopher Diogenes, in an exchange that is, once more, ambiguous and disguised. The imaginary dialogue takes place in Corinth, at the time of the famous encounter when Diogenes is said to have yelled insolently at Alexander, "Get out of my sunlight!" Diogenes wants to instruct Alexander about the nature of the good king, and to this end he addresses him with a series of eloquent and allegorical admonitions especially directed against imperialism and the vanity of royal trappings. Compared to the *Second Discourse*, this new setting deepens the mystery further by switching the positions of the speakers. Alexander is no longer an adolescent but has succeeded his father as king; he is no longer the one doing the talking but is rebuffed by Diogenes, who is another, and still partial, substitute for the author. There is never a complete identification between the character in the scene and his supposed model. Thanks to these sleights of hand, one is no longer sure, finally, where Dio is, where Trajan is.

Taking the four discourses *On Kingship* as a whole, one may conclude that they employ all the devices of figured speech: "attenuation," in the passages where the author addresses himself directly but politely to the emperor; "hinting" or "slanting," thanks to generalization and the play of disguises; and probably "inversion," if the description of Alexander's bellicosity in the *Second Discourse* should be read *a contrario* as a warning against this type of enthusiasm. All ends are achieved: security, in view of the possible risks; well-being, in keeping a certain distance from the ruler; and virtuosity, because the author amply demonstrates his skill and, what is more, does so four times in succession on the same topic.

In a context of constant and required adulation for an all-powerful emperor, who lacked only death to become a god, Dio's audacity, for all its seeming modesty, was still audacity. If these discourses were really delivered in Trajan's presence, one can only imagine the monitoring and carping they had to endure at court. The Platonic expression "serious game," which Dio uses about his characters' exchanges,[28] in fact applies to the discourses themselves, which under cover of multiple feints set forth to the emperor, and all his subjects with him, a theological, political, and moral conception of monarchy.

This message should not be taken as a criticism. Dio had no ambition to reform the Roman Empire, which he saw was firmly entrenched, and he had no reason to quarrel with Trajan. This emperor's reign represented for him a government of genuine worth, exercised by a respected sovereign, who watched out for him, as his predecessor Nerva had done, in contrast to the reign of Domitian. The philosopher was not an opponent. But he did make suggestions, and consequently the discourses *On Kingship* are much less panegyrical than an oration unabashedly written to glorify the prince would have been. They are encomia only to the extent that one wishes to apply them to the reigning ruler. In essence they are chiefly philosophic lessons: the author sets forth learnedly, but obliquely, the duties of the sovereign, says what he thinks the latter should do, how he should control himself, and how he should respect the superiority of the gods. . . . Here and there, he slips in, with humor, some pointed allusions and warnings, appearing to target the mistakes of the ancient and more recent past (Alexander, Domitian) but seeking, at least on certain matters, to encourage contemporary connections. Among all the ideas advanced, it would be difficult to isolate those uniquely Dio's, those that reflected the interests of his milieu, and those mandated by official propaganda. Moreover, the discourses are loaded with nuances that vary by their recipient, the listeners to whom they were addressed; for their author declaimed them before Greek-speaking audiences.[29] Thus, what was compliment and advice in Trajan's presence became in front of Dio's compatriots an official report and reflection on relations with the central power.

We cannot know what the emperor himself thought of this string of recommendations, but we are certain that he maintained the utmost goodwill toward Dio. When the orator, several years later, was accused of embezzlement and treason, a charge drummed up by his political opponents, Trajan, informed by a report from Pliny about the case, ruled in Dio's favor—but not without first ordering an audit of the philosopher's accounts.[30]

Aelius Aristides, Pious Valetudinarian

We now come to Aelius Aristides. Like Dio, he was a unique personality, but for different reasons. His recurrent illness took center stage in his life; he suffered his first attack when he was twenty-six, in the middle of a trip to Rome, and from that time forward he was prey to all sorts of afflictions, acute and chronic, which handicapped his career as a sophist. His autobiography (the *Sacred Discourses*) is replete with respiratory and digestive troubles, tumors, abscesses, "plague," and "consumption." In this situation, he quickly despaired of human medicine, which had no success in soothing him, and he turned to the great god of healing, Asclepius, whose sanctuaries took in the sick. Asclepius appeared through signs, prophecies, and visions that brought healing prescriptions. Aristides received more than his fair share of them and convinced himself that he was a beneficiary of divine protection exceptional in its duration, its variety, and its efficacy. His daily communion with Asclepius did not limit itself to medical questions and included one-on-one conversations about different topics in dreams with this god and others, in addition to instances of inspiration from poetry and rhetoric, miracles, apparitions, ascetical practices, and trances.

The conviction of being a man set apart, living out a supernatural experience, made Aristides skittish and standoffish toward public life. In his dreams he saw himself proudly confronting emperors to their amazement, as he invoked his relations with Asclepius and drew upon the spiritual riches he contained within himself, his measure for all things.[31] In reality, he fought with his fellow citizens and the Roman authorities to win exemption from the official duties incumbent on him at Smyrna and in the province of Asia (western modern Turkey), citing, in justification of his refusal, the absence of an express command from the god whose humble servant he was.[32] All these things, which a self-satisfied Aristides narrates, give one a sense of the complexity and cracks behind the official persona of the Famous Greek Orator, who had strong local roots in Asia Minor and entrées to the imperial court.

If his oration in honor of Rome dates from the beginning of his career, many events in his biography were still to come, but the feeling of being religiously special was already brooding within him, as his composition of verses under Apollo's inspiration during his youthful stay in the city attests. This poem was to prove prophetic because Aristides will later assert not only that it coincided completely unexpectedly with the Apollonia, a Roman festival, but also that Apollo out of gratitude for it saved Aristides from shipwreck on his voyage home.[33] Moreover, the first lines of the oration to Rome show that this work itself was fulfillment of a promise made to a god. Such was the man who set himself the task of praising Rome.

Telling Omissions

To appreciate the *Encomium of Rome*, we have a rich context available that allows us to reconstitute its horizon of expectation precisely.[34] Indeed, this discourse belongs to the established genre of the rhetorical encomium, a genre that was part of the period's educational baggage, both Greek and Roman. The encomium belonged to the "preparatory exercises" taught in the schools through theory and practice. Students learned the list of items to be treated, as well as the way to deck them out and expand on them, and they were coached in how to deliver them aloud. For those who wanted to go further, treatises existed with detailed precepts, and reading past models imbued readers with ideas and formulaic turns of phrase, as did listening to the innumerable ceremonial speeches inevitably declaimed in the course of special occasions public and private.

Aristides mastered all that, and so did his audiences. So it is no surprise that in structure as in style his discourse in honor of Rome conforms to the rules of the rhetorical encomium. The orator begins by emphasizing the difficulty of the topic, then praises the city's physical location and geography. Next, he praises the civil administration of the empire and its military organization, before ending with a brilliant depiction of the order and beauty prevailing in the provinces thanks to the Pax Romana. The praise of the emperor, Antoninus Pius (138–161 AD), brief but heartfelt, is reserved for the conclusion, the place of honor. As for its style, the presentation relies heavily on comparisons, couched in a persistently admiring and hyperbolic tone. So far, there is nothing unexpected according to the prevailing norms. It is what he does *not* say that makes this oration interesting.

In more than thirty pages, representing about an hour of oral delivery, Aristides finds a way to say nothing about the origins of Rome, even though a city's foundation was considered to be an important chapter in civic encomia. Aristides is silent on Roman history, a subject that would occur in the section, deemed essential by the rules, dealing with the accomplishments exemplifying the qualities or virtues of the praiseworthy object. He passes over its public monuments, art, literature, language. He never mentions a single illustrious Roman, never utters a single Roman name or a single Latin word. Some encomium of Rome without Numa, without Augustus, without Cicero or Vergil! No Punic Wars, no Gallic campaigns, no Forum, no Coliseum! None of the basics!

How to explain these omissions? Clearly, it was not for want of material, and one should not suppose that they slipped the orator's mind, since they were very much standard and prescribed features. Authors of handbooks had no qualms citing Aeneas and Anchises, mentioning the childhood of Romulus, and recalling the battle of Actium or the sorrows of Hadrian at the death of his beloved, Antinous.[35] We are dealing here with a series of Aristides's own deliberate choices. The orator decided only to consider the current state of affairs, the actual functioning of the empire, and that led him to the resolute elimination of mythological and historical givens (insofar as it was Roman, since he evokes Greek mythology and history in abundance). As a corollary, he is completely silent on Rome's expansion and its wars of conquest at Greek expense. Rome, for Aristides, is the imperial capital, the contemporary center of power over the provinces, especially the Greek-speaking provinces, to which he belonged. The author's vantage is political; that is why Rome's artistic and intellectual grandeur, as well as its local color, remain outside his field of vision. In this sense, his choice is similar to Dio's, with whose works he was most probably familiar.

But make no mistake: Aristides does not utter a word of criticism. On the contrary, he has nothing but praise for the way Rome governed its empire. He offers a carefully built demonstration full of personal observations, fair comments, and interesting historical reflections. But his admiration is anything but naive. With calm assurance, he decides what deserves attention and what does not, and he imposes a Hellenocentric perspective. Selectivity was normal in the genre of rhetorical encomium, choosing from among the theoretically possible ways of proceeding only those that suited the subject or the situation. But here that process is pushed to the limit. The omissions are so drastic that they become significant in themselves, and they have the effect of suggesting that Rome is essentially the empire, that its history and culture do not matter, and that the only things important in Greek eyes are the material benefits that derive from the Roman peace and the reality of the power to which the Greeks yield. Having judged it was risky, or churlish, to express this opinion openly (the oration was delivered before an audience of Romans whom the author addresses as "you"), Aristides makes it understood indirectly. His oration is therefore much less flattering than has been thought, and it makes a point both pragmatic and realistic.

What Is Rome the Name Of?

That is not all. The oration has another glaring omission: the absence of the name "Rome," although the adjective "Roman" is used of the subjects who possess Roman citizenship. Yet the name was expected. In his other works, he calls by name the cities whose praises he sings: Smyrna, Ephesus, Eleusis, Rhodes, Cyzicus, Athens. A formulaic turn of phrase in the *Panathenaic Oration* points up this difference in treatment: "The present Empire . . . does not refuse to honor Athens."[36] The name of the Greek city echoes proudly, the name of Rome not at all.

The use of the name is an important moment in the process of communication, especially for praising while glorifying, and for fixing blame while attacking, since that is when one touches the subject intimately. Conversely, passing over a name in silence is a symbolic annihilation of what it designates. The name is a synecdoche; it represents, like a fetish, the person or object mentioned.[37] Psychoanalysis has amply demonstrated the depth of these phenomena. In the Roman Empire, measures to erase the memory of important men after they were condemned to death (*damnatio memoriae*, to use a Latin term coined in modern times) included obliterating their names on public monuments. Aristides used a similar procedure as a method of attack in another work where he pretends to have forgotten the name of the individual he disdains; at first he uses the contemptuous "what's his name," only recalling the actual name some fifty pages later (it was a wine merchant, Sarambos).[38]

Avoiding proper names can sometimes be elegant, but, in the case of the *Encomium of Rome*, it is altogether something else: the name's absence betrays a reserve or unease, and all the more so since the absence is not total. For the orator plays on the word *rhômê*, which in Greek means both "might" and "Rome," when he says apropos of the city, "She merits this name, might is what matters here."[39] This way of naming the city without naming it has the effect of identifying Rome with might and recalling that the empire was imposed on the Greeks by armed force. In his other works, when Aristides uses the word "might" about the Romans, in talking about the emperors or some powerful person, it is to suggest the idea of intractable power.[40] No need, therefore, to elaborate on this loaded rewriting of the city's name. Aristides had said enough to make it clear that in his eyes Rome was might and nothing but might, even if this might had its good side. And there it is, the heavy truth that everybody knew, that weighs on the oration, and that there is no desire to expose.

In acting thus, the orator is once again applying the rules of rhetoric, deploying them as he pleases. Arguments based on names were indeed recommended in rhetoric, and especially in the rhetoric of the encomium.[41] So Aristides was following such advice in resorting to the etymology linking "Rome" and "might," *Rhômê* and *rhômê*, which he did not invent and for which there are some earlier attestations (although the etymology is mistaken). The word "might" suited him, since this is a perfectly laudatory word even as it conceals a subtext.

Here as elsewhere prudence was in order, and it was necessary not to go too far in plays on names. It is said that, a half century after Aristides, under the emperor Septimius Severus, who had taken the added name "Pertinax," "many men were put to death, some on true and some on trumped-up charges. Several were condemned because they had spoken in jest, others because they had not spoken at all, others again because they had cried out many things with double meaning, such as 'Behold an emperor worthy of his name—Pertinacious in very truth, in very truth Severe.'"[42]

Eighteen centuries later, in a totally different context, names still provide material for delicious subtexts. Elected to the French Academy in 1927, to the chair previously held by Anatole France, Paul Valéry had to deliver an encomium of his predecessor. Now, from a literary standpoint they were complete opposites, the one uncomplicated, or seemingly so, and a successful writer, the other given to intellectual speculation and rigorously formalist. Valéry never forgave France for refusing to publish a poem of Mallarmé in the journal *Le Parnasse contemporain* (France, it seems, had insisted, "No, people would laugh at us!"). As for political opinions, Valéry wrote in a letter concerning this session of the Academy: "In matters political,—*I could not say everything I think.*"[43]

It was in this context of constraint and mental self-censorship that Valéry spoke. It misses the point to say that he was not delivering wholehearted praise. The approach he resorted to in order to let his ill humor appear, or, to put it more positively, in order to express his devotion to the memory of his admired master, Mallarmé, was to omit his predecessor's name. Throughout a powerfully calculated text, studded moreover with killer putdowns, the orator multiplies elaborate expressions of gratitude and praise, with the sole purpose of never mentioning Anatole France by name: "My illustrious predecessor," "your great colleague," "the man whose chair we are inheriting," a buildup that finally becomes comical, once one has grasped what is going on, and ends with the showstopping, final nail in the coffin, so to speak: "He himself was not possible or scarcely conceivable save in France, whose name he took. Under this name, a difficult burden, which he must have been hoping beyond hope in daring to assume, he gained the favor of the world."[44]

Not only is the name never mentioned in this new type of *damnatio memoriae*; it turns into a reproach of the departed for having assumed it. The reproach may be a bit exaggerated, incidentally, to the extent that François-Anatole Thibault did not invent the name Anatole France out of nothing but took it over from his father, François-Noël Thibault, for whom France was a diminutive of his first name and which he used as his last name professionally as a bookseller. The pseudonym was a patronymic, or at least that is how Anatole France justified it.[45] Such is the importance of the name and the homophones it brings to mind.

This was not a new case for the academy, for in 1670, as Amin Maalouf recalls, the dramatist Philippe Quinault, in his acceptance speech, "considered it pointless to salute the memory of his predecessor" and "even omitted mentioning his name."[46] For the record, this academy immortal, who had been a disappointment to his colleagues, was called François-Henri Salomon de Virelade.

The Eloquence of Silence

In a certain sense, every subtext relies on silence, since it is all about being understood without speaking (I leave aside the case, envisaged previously, of the orator compelled to be silent because he is prohibited from speaking).[47] That is why the uses of expressive silence are extremely rich and varied. An abbé of the eighteenth century counted ten types, and his list is probably not exhaustive: prudent, guileful, ingratiating, mocking, spiritual, stupid, approving, contemptuous, ill-humored, politic.[48]

Saying nothing in a situation that not only permitted but called out for speech is in itself a significant message. Montaigne happily names this procedure "telling silence" (*taire parler*), which is "quite intelligible," and he recounts the anecdote of an ambassador from the city of Abdera who, "after having gone on at length before the ancient Spartan king Agis, asked him: 'Well, Sire, what answer do you want me to take back to my people?' 'That

I have given you the opportunity to say all you wished, for as long as you wished, without saying a word.'"[49] The king's silence showed his rejection, his laconism a switch on the legal maxim "qui tacet consentit," "silence is consent."

During the last world war in France, Vercors, in his novel *Le Silence de la mer* (*The Silence of the Sea*), provided the famous example, at book length, of flaunted indifference and systematic muteness to express refusal and resistance.

Once the orator has decided to break silence and speak, silence can still recur within his oration at the macro or micro level. Silence at the macro level weighs on the entirety of the discourse, as in the case of thorny subjects that one does not have the right to mention openly. One brings them up indirectly—for example, the past crimes of a former tyrant, which the speaker is legally bound not to discuss even though everybody knows them, because an amnesty forbids recalling the tyranny's memory.[50] Sometimes, as in the case of Aristides on Rome, forbidden items are not omitted, expected items are, which is another form of suggestion.

At the micro level, silence takes the form of specific figures, thoroughly vetted by the theorists of figured discourse.[51] "Paralipsis" is saying that one intends to "leave aside" or "pass over" something ("I will omit mentioning," "What's the good of enumerating?"); it is called "true" when one is silent about the topic and "false" when one mentions the topic all the same. "Reticence" is breaking off abruptly ("But I must pause here," "Enough said"). Such ploys serve to draw attention to a crucial item, simultaneously flagged and concealed, in the midst of other, less pertinent items.

Reading the Greek orators, with all their elaborations and deviations, one is reminded of a striking sentence in *The Blacks* by Jean Genet—mutatis mutandis, of course, and without wishing to push the so-called postcolonial approach[52] too far: "It is by stretching language that we will pull it sufficiently out of shape to wrap ourselves in it and hide, for the masters operate by tightening."[53] This is what Dio of Prusa and Aelius Aristides have done with an embarrassment of riches, including generalization, playing with masks, omissions and telling silences drowned in a flood of words, which allowed them to keep their distance from the codes of celebration. Given their refinement and cultural formation, these two authors were certainly aware of the import of their choices. But I suspect that they did not experience these as premeditated prevarications; they were incumbent on them because of who they themselves were and what they had to say. Their lengthy evasions responded to the conviction that they had a political message to deliver, and

The Subtle Subtext

the ancient notion of figured speech provided historical and rhetorical assurance for making interpretation of their works possible. In this message, it must be remembered, there is nary a word of criticism against the empire as such. Our authors accepted Rome's authority, and they could imagine no other regime in their time. The dissonances they introduce belong to the realm of individual affirmation, Hellenic identity, and cultural or ideological negotiation, a negotiation that involved no practical stakes but remained intellectual, since the Greeks were in no position to make any material demands on the Romans. Through the mouths of the orators, the subjects said what they accepted and what they wanted to last. They recalled the conditions of their fealty to the empire, the latter conceived as a system imposed on the Greeks externally.

This is the encoded counsel of the encomium. The subtext was more than an ad hoc ploy to avoid the inconvenient consequences candor would entail. Yet a ploy it certainly was, helping its users to think harder and longer. In their belonging to a subservient people who felt themselves culturally superior, the Greek orators (in the speeches we have examined, and others) experienced a tension that they eased by playing on this discrepancy, and their strategy drove them to adopt sweeping and theoretical points of view. This rich confrontation of two civilizations, Greek and Roman, gave birth to a system of double language that simultaneously brought into play the structures of discourse and the structures of power.

Greek Pretenses About Rome

6

An Ox on the Tongue

The watchman at the beginning of Aeschylus's *Agamemnon* knows the secrets of the House of Atreus, and he deplores the conduct of its queen, Clytemnestra, and the dishonor done to its absent king, Agamemnon, in his own palace. But the watchman will reveal nothing. "A big ox has walked on my tongue," he explains, using, as one of the common people might, a proverbial image. Yet in speaking so, he has already let something slip: "I speak to those who know."[1] Then he exits. This subtle opening, one of the most celebrated monologues in theatrical history, illustrates the difficulty of speaking freely about the powerful and the need, again and again, for recourse to indirection.

We are going to investigate the use of indirection in the twentieth century. In this area, everyone has personal points of reference. Mine rely on works of literature and published evidence, and they draw chiefly from the two major European totalitarian systems. Without wishing to compare historical realities with one another since each has its own specific character, I still must say that, when looking at the subtext, they present similarities as undeniable as they are instructive. It is my hope that the items here singled out have a general application and will allow readers, should they so desire, to continue their own investigation, applying them to their preferred issues.

Louis Aragon and Smuggled Poetry

During the German occupation, the poet Louis Aragon conceived a method for expressing himself and spreading his ideas under the nose of the enemy and its French collaborators. In league with the Resistance, he developed an intellectual, or, more precisely, a literary resistance. Beginning in 1940, he named his effort "contrebande," or "smuggling," at the suggestion of his friend Georges Sadoul,[2] using and explaining it as follows: "Smuggling, in literature, is the art of giving life to forbidden feelings with authorized words."[3] He goes on: "The idea here was to address everyone, so that anyone might find this poetry easily accessible, and that it would touch people's hearts, whoever these people were. That is why I thought this required a relatively straightforward poetry, but not so much so that it would attract the censor's attention. In short, a smuggled poetry."[4]

When the Second World War broke out, Aragon, born in 1897, was a celebrated poet, novelist (he won the Prix Renaudot in 1936), journalist, and leading Communist. A veteran of the last war, decorated in 1918, he was drafted again in 1939, and his bravery earned him a second Croix de Guerre in 1940. Unlike other writers who became expatriates during those dark days, Aragon and Elsa Triolet, married since 1939, decided to remain in France.

He used "contrebande" for the first time in *Le Crève-cœur* (Heartbreak).[5] This collection, published in 1941 by Jean Paulhan at the Gallimard press in occupied Paris, gathered poems that had been written, and often already published in journals or reviews, dating back to 1939. Aragon chose poetry as his means of expression because this genre seemed apparently benign and so more likely, he thought, to elude the censor than other genres considered serious and timely. The "Romance du temps qu'il fait," a learned allegory borrowing from *Hamlet*, written while he was in uniform, describes the methodology and concerted multiplicity of possible meanings:

Mais le maréchal-des-logis
À qui je montre ces versets
Se perd dans mes analogies
Veut à tout prix savoir qui c'est
Et moi je lui réponds Qui sait

Je tiens la clef de ces parades.

But the sergeant
To whom I show these verses
Gets lost in my analogies,
Wants at any cost to know who is it
And I, I answer him Who knows

I hold the key to these swordplays.

"Le Temps des mots croisés" is a poem written in 1939, when Aragon was away in the service, and which, prior to being reprinted in *Le Crève-cœur*, appeared in *La Nouvelle Revue française* and was recited in Paris by the eminent actress Madeleine Renaud at the Comédie Française and the Théâtre des Mathurins. It reveals three overlapping levels of meaning:

1. According to the usual sense of *mots croisés*, "crossword puzzle," the poem refers to the prohibition against printing crosswords in newspapers after war was declared, out of fear that they might be used for espionage purposes to convey coded messages. A former director of the then suspended Communist daily *Ce Soir*, Aragon could not help but be conscious of press restrictions.
2. In a literal way, "crossed words" means the communication between the author and his beloved wife (the joint edition of their fictional works, published in 1964, was entitled *Œuvres romanesques croisées d'Elsa Triolet et Aragon*). They recall the happy time when the war had not yet separated the couple and they could still have private exchanges. Beyond their personal history, the expression represents the exchanges of all lovers, and, even more than that, all forms of exchange and freedom of expression.
3. Through historical allusion, "crossed words" evoke the Crusades, in French "Croisades" (with the Crusaders the topic of another poem in the same collection). They symbolize the necessity for returning to roots and rediscovering historical values in undertaking the country's deliverance.

Taken as a whole, the poem gives voice to present sadness and speaks to the separation of those who are in love, their fear, their confusion. But it also contains a message of hope, for this situation cannot endure, as the poem's last line indicates: "et reviendra le temps des mots croisés" (and the time of crosswords will return). The poet underlines the role he wants to play: "Je veille c'est promis / Je veille" (I am keeping watch, I promise / I am keeping watch). Thus, behind the "lament," the "clarion call" can be heard.[6]

Each poem of *Crève-cœur* is a bearer of allusion, which is still possible to elucidate today. The events are not so remote. External information is abundant: the author and first readers have left comments, the conditions surrounding the writing and publication of the texts are often known, biographies are crammed with details, all creating a favorable environment for deciphering the subtexts. "Ils prétendent avoir mangé trop de mensonges"

(They claim to have eaten too many lies) is an obvious reply to the speech of Marshal Pétain in June 1940, "Je hais les mensonges qui vous ont fait tant de mal" (I hate the lies that have done you so much harm).[7] "Qu'est ce chant?" (What's this song?). It is "The Internationale," which some soldiers dared to hum.[8] "Est-ce Hénin-Liétard ou Noyelles-Godault / Courrières-les-Morts Montigny-en-Gohelle": these village names, which the poet boldly introduces in strict alexandrine meter amid an evocation of the Flanders campaign and the memory of labor struggles in this mining region, allude to the life of Maurice Thorez, who was born at Noyelles and as a child witnessed the disaster of Courrières (actually called les-Mines, "the Mines," not "the Dead"!): terraced row houses, coal gas, and the French Communist Party, "a Communist's credentials."[9]

Overdetermined Writing

Aragon's tendency to secrecy and disguise was of long standing in his personal as well as his literary life. An illegitimate child, he grew up under a false name and in deceitful family relationships, his father posing as his godfather or his guardian, his grandmother as his adoptive mother, his mother as his sister. He recalls this situation in a poem from 1943, addressed to his dead mother: "Ce lourd secret pèse entre nous / Et tu me vouais au mensonge / A tes genoux." (This heavy secret weighs between us / And you pledged me to deceit / At your knees).[10] Out of "mentir-vrai," or "lying truth," he made a fictional program, a combination of fiction and reality. As for coded messages, ever since 1917, if we can believe his own words, "I was preparing a language that neither censorship nor prisons would be able to prohibit, . . . I was looking for the way to get through to large numbers of people, without attracting the prohibition of those in power."[11] The second part of this sentence is of some interest, for in speaking of "getting through to large numbers of people, without attracting the prohibition of those in power," Aragon harks back unintentionally, I imagine, to the words of Quintilian concerning the arranged will, "to plead in such a way that the judges understood what had happened, but the informers could not seize on any explicit statement."[12] What a remarkable continuity between the figured speech of ancient rhetoric and the modern poet's smuggling! The two authors unite in affirming the advantage of the subtext, which is its ability, when raised to a certain level of refinement, to disarm the censors, pulling the wool over their eyes with calculated dissonances so that some understand the implied content while others do not, and even those who do understand are unable to prove

An Ox on the Tongue

conclusively that it exists. Multiple levels of comprehension and the absence of certainty are inherent in this manner of expression and give it its force.

The poetry Aragon developed during the war drew on several sources. More classical in style than the author's earlier works, it employed rhyme and alexandrine meter (without punctuation, however) and forged a bond, through surrealism and Dadaism, with Guillaume Apollinaire, Paul Verlaine, Arthur Rimbaud, or Victor Hugo. There is a certain distance, to say the least, between the unbridled literary experiences of the 1920s and the controlled wartime's contraband, between *Le Con d'Irène* (*Irene's Cunt*) and *Les Yeux d'Elsa* (*Elsa's Eyes*)! The prose manifesto *Rhyme in 1940*, published as an appendix to *Crève-cœur* at the time of the latter's second edition, stresses this choice of a more traditional poetics and points out its implications for someone wishing to mobilize the nation's cultural memory.

In this memory, Aragon fastened especially onto the Middle Ages, with their authors and tales. Another prose text explains this, *La Leçon de Ribérac ou l'Europe française*, published in 1941 and reprinted as an appendix in *Les Yeux d'Elsa*. Stationed in Ribérac, a small town in the Dordogne, in 1940, Aragon was reminded of the great local poet, Arnaud Daniel (spelling the first name with a final "d," not "t"), whom Dante mentions in the *Purgatorio*, and who practiced "closed invention" (*trobar clus*), a type of hermetic poetry with hidden meaning. This, Aragon wrote, "allowed poets to sing of their Ladies even in the presence of their Lord." The learned discussion on the troubadours prompts him to reactivate the allusive traditions of medieval poetry, at the same time as it furnished a model for the amorous and bereft poet. For "Arnaut Daniel," writes Michel Zink, "is the master of language's paradoxical and painful tension . . . , echoing that of impossible love."[13] The Middle Ages were a major period for allegory and subtext. A border also existed then between two linguistic regions in France (*langue d'oïl* and *langue d'oc*), and this prompted the allusive evocation of the frontier established by the armistice of June 1940, between Germany and the Vichy government: Ribérac was just over the line.

And then there were the women, the idealized woman. The Middle Ages also meant a culture of courtly manners. The modern dramatist Henry de Montherlant had spoken of "the culture of the silly shopgirl," and many agreed, "men taken with the ability to satisfy their misogyny, their two-bit Nietzscheism, or simply their snobbism."[14] But Aragon, in his war poems, did exactly the opposite, exalting women and merging love elegy with epic in his poems honoring Elsa and France. Later on, the poet strongly challenged interpretations that reduced Elsa to a mere symbol and submerged her identity into the country's. The beloved woman was very real, and it is by virtue of a second level of meaning, which in no way negates the first, that this feminine figure incarnates the homeland: she is no chill allegory, but a living metaphor.[15]

The collections of poetry that followed *Le Crève-cœur* continued to associate patriotism, national culture, and love, always through the smuggling method, with one change, from confusion over the defeat to a more combative, more resistant spirit. In *Elsa's Eyes*, the poem entitled "Pour un chant national" (For a national anthem) contains a new call for a coded writing:

> Il faut une langue à la terre
> Des lèvres aux murs aux pavés
> Parlez parlez vous qui savez
> Spécialistes du mystère
> Le sang refuse de se taire
>
> The earth needs a tongue
> Lips for walls for cobblestones
> Speak speak you savvy ones
> Specialists of mystery
> Blood will not be silent

This text originally appeared under the title "Pour un chant . . ." with ellipsis and no epithet, because, as Aragon later explained, "in '42 it seemed preferable not to dot the i's."[16]

Indeed, the collections of 1942 are interwoven with allusiveness. For example, in *Elsa's Eyes*, the verses from the poem "Plus belle que les larmes" (More beautiful than tears), "Il y a dans le vent qui vient d'Arles des songes / Qui pour en parler haut sont trop près de mon cœur" (In the wind that comes from Arles are dreams / Too close to my heart to speak aloud), recall the Ninth Congress of the French Communist Party, held at Arles in 1937. Similarly, "Le criminel azur d'un rêve de Crimée" (The criminal azure of a Crimean dream), from *Cantique à Elsa*, 2, refers explicitly to Elsa's eyes and implicitly to the resistance of Soviet soldiers against the German offensive in the Crimea. In *Brocéliande* (a forest in Brittany), the poem "Prière pour faire pleuvoir" (Prayer for rain) expresses the hope that the Allies will deluge the enemy with bombs; "La terre . . . ne mentira plus" (The earth will lie no more) is a fresh reply to Pétain's "La terre, elle, ne ment pas" (The earth itself does not lie). *La Nuit d'août* (August night) contains a memorial, without names,

An Ox on the Tongue

to Communist fighters shot and killed in the Resistance: "I haven't forgotten your memory, pounder of rails [that is, Jean-Pierre Timbaud, after whom a street is now named in Paris] . . . / Nor yours either, slandered one [Pierre Semard] / And I haven't forgotten your memory, philosopher with the red hair [Georges Politzer]," and so on. Allusions to names, a procedure we met in the previous chapter, are an important element of "smuggled poetry": "And you know their names without my having said them."[17]

What is most startling about these subtly evocative poems is that they are not at all difficult to read. Meant to be learned by heart and recited aloud (later they became pop hits by the singer/composers Ferré and Ferrat), they ring clearly and speak directly. One of the facets of Aragon's genius was his ability to create a poetry both learned and popular. His poems were highly successful, as successive editions with print runs in the thousands show. Nor was the public capable of understanding them limited to cultivated and alert minds, the Paulhans, the de Gaulles of this world; it was truly broad. One must also point out that Aragon was not unique in using such devices; there was an entire milieu of muzzled poets who were no less brave, as well as reader accomplices who helped to get the messages across. Pierre Seghers has painted a moving fresco of this society.[18] Nor were the adversaries deceived who, like Drieu La Rochelle, denounced (in every sense of the word) "all these muffled appeals that Aragon spreads in his literary reviews stitched with red thread."[19] A party comrade filed a report to Moscow on the poem "The Lilacs and the Roses" because it had appeared in the conservative Paris daily Le Figaro and because it mentioned the Germans as "the enemy" during the time of the Russo-German nonaggression pact.[20]

The Complexities of Coding and Decoding

The period, indeed, was not simple. One would have to be as naive as Candide to believe that the good guys were, once and for all, on one side, the bad on the other, and that the opposition between subtexts and official verities was fixed and sharply defined. On the contrary, historical circumstances and Aragon's personal situation never stopped evolving. Some spurned the Communists because they were German allies (1939–41), only to see them subsequently join the Resistance. France waged war (1939–40), was defeated and occupied. The unoccupied zone offered some freedom (1940–42) and then was itself invaded. Aragon and his wife, Elsa, went through a marriage crisis ("There is no happy love" was the title of one of his poems from 1943). The poet, who had been strongly criticized at the start of the war, became a "scout," a "leader," an organizer.[21] All this added complexity and flexibility to the smuggled poetry as events transpired. The composite character of the collections was a further complication, bringing together poems and accompanying prose texts, each with its own date and individual circumstances of initial publication.

Those circumstances varied, depending on whether texts were published in France and subject to censorship, or were published abroad, principally in Switzerland, or were clandestine. Depending on the situation, expression had to be more, or less, encoded. Beginning in 1943, with clandestine editions, the method of smuggled poetry gradually faded, giving way "to a straightforward statement of the facts."[22] As a general rule, not so surprisingly when one thinks about it, only when publication was still relatively free was it necessary to dissimulate, whereas clandestine publications required no concern for appearances. In *The Grévin Museum*, published in 1943 under the pseudonym François La Colère (Angry Frank), Hitler and Auschwitz are mentioned, even if historical references from the Bible, d'Aubigné (a nineteenth-century Swiss Protestant divine and historian of the Reformation), and Hugo persist. In *The French Diana* (1944), the role of coding is reduced.

It was time. For, while remaining generally clear and direct, the method of smuggled poetry, it must be said, led to some unevenness in comprehension and left disputes on particular points hanging. His popular success notwithstanding, Aragon posed some interpretative conundrums. In one instance he explained himself, providing a high school girl some detailed clarifications on the allusions in a stanza of *Lilacs and Roses*.[23] But what is one to make of the Latude case?

Nous reprenons après vingt ans nos habitudes
Au vestiaire de l'oubli Mille Latudes
refont les gestes d'autrefois dans leur cachot

We strike again twenty years later our normal attitudes
In oblivion's changing room a Thousand Latudes
again in their dungeon enact the deeds of yesteryear

Latude, a famous eighteenth-century prisoner, is a substitution for all the victims of arbitrary imprisonment. In this poem from 1939, entitled "Twenty Years Later," and reprinted at the beginning of *Crève-cœur*, his name symbolizes the fate of men like Aragon, called up to fight in a second world war roughly twenty years after having served in the first. But are we not also to see here an allusion to the thirty-nine Communist deputies jailed in Paris's la Santé prison for their party loyalty? Many commentators, including longtime Communists, have tended to favor this bifocal interpretation and with this poem date the start of Aragon's contraband poetry.[24] But another critique pointedly counters this interpretation and maintains that only the old warriors are meant, and, while conceding the other view "was perhaps a more or less widespread interpretation at the time," dismisses it as not "Aragon's intention."[25] Yet another, prudent approach wonders, "Did the poet, perhaps, intend the ambiguity—or the multiplicity of meanings?"[26] Even if the negative arguments do not carry conviction, the debate remains open and will remain so.

The same problem occurs in "Le Temps des mots croisés," a poem discussed earlier, where the author insists on affirming, "I am not one of theirs." Such an umbrella statement has elicited all sorts of contradictory readings.[27] "The poetic 'I' cuts itself off from the masculine universe of the war" to dedicate himself to the beloved woman entirely. In short, make love, not war! Or, rather, and it is not the same thing: "Aragon does not belong to this male world," which can lead to further questions concerning the poet's sexual orientation. And for those of political bent: "He does not howl with the wolves, when he lives among very anticommunist . . . officers." He is differentiating himself from those who led France into war, or those who suppressed the Communists, or Communists who deserted the Party. The editor of the standard Pléiade edition of Aragon, weary of the warfare, admits, "The disagreement over the referent raises the question of the intelligibility of this bit of *contrebande*."[28]

The Tribulations of Censorship

This only goes to show how difficult the censors' task was. After the war, Aragon explained how his writing "contrebande" allowed him to elude censorship.[29] For example, in the poem "Art poétique" from the collection *En français dans le texte*, a verse like "For my friends slain in May" had an "immediate" meaning and a "precise" meaning: the immediate reference seemed to be the French soldiers killed in the war in May 1940, but, to be precise, the poet was paying homage to his friends in the Resistance whom the Germans shot at Mont Valérien in May 1942 (Georges Politzer, Jacques Decour, Jacques Solomon). Thanks to the decoy, the poem, published at Neuchâtel in Switzerland, could be distributed in Free France. Similarly, "The Rose and the Reseda," an emblematic Resistance poem (reprinted in *La Diane française*), first appeared legally in Marseilles in 1943, and it was still amazing to realize twenty-five years later that the censor had let it pass.[30] The poem "Nymphée," reprinted in the collection *En étrange pays dans mon pays lui-même* (As a stranger in my own country), apparently dealt with Nymphaion, the name of the capital of King Mithridates in Racine's tragedy *Mithridate*, but was actually an evocation of Kerch, the city's modern name, where the war was raging on the Russian front. Aragon had even slipped in "a rocking chair" ("Celui qui s'assiéra dans le fauteuil-bascule . . .") to recall the Anglo-American forces.[31] This time the censors got it, and the journal *Confluences* was shut down for two months for having published the text.

Aragon cites a 1942 letter from Paul Marion, secretary of state for information, who complained about "the allusions to current political events": "These allusions, as clever as they are, though they may escape the notice of the local censors, are still noticed at Vichy. . . . These knowing winks to the alert reader tending to multiply, I find myself obliged to limit their abuse." A former member of the French Communist Party, Marion had been secretary of the party's agitprop section and a member of the propaganda bureau of the Comintern in Moscow prior to becoming a Vichy collaborator. He knew whereof he spoke.

Censorship is a more subtle activity than one might think. Censors engage with authors in a refined game of cat and mouse, as Robert Darnton shows in his comparative history.[32] In France, under the Ancien Régime, when Malesherbes was director of the Librairie, the censors were not content merely to be on the lookout for political opposition; they safeguarded morality, religion, and the reputation of nobles. This meant they needed to have a great knowledge of the world, if they were to discern subversive contents veiled in allusions and coded references. In India during the Raj, to prove that a publication was seditious, judges engaged in veritable *explications de texte*, for they had to deal with ambiguous and metaphorical writings that made establishing the meaning of words and the thrust of imagery essential. In the Democratic Republic of East Germany, censorship was meticulously organized into administrative bureaus, each with its own area of responsibility; dossiers were vetted up the bureaucratic ladder, and there was an annual schedule for the works to be published. In all these cases, as different as they are, censorship, in Darnton's opinion, is shown to be an intellectually complicated process, requiring the ability to interpret and to read between the lines, and it even includes "collaboration" and "negotiation" between the censors and the censored.

Situations of absolute brutality leave no room for nuance. On the other hand, when the oppressor, for one reason or another (desire for respectability,

An Ox on the Tongue

self-delusion, fear of international sanctions), cares to maintain a certain tolerance that is not just window dressing, subtexts are in order. Not to mention the incestuous relationship between censorship and self-censoring, which leads authors themselves to choose, consciously or not, to temper their messages.

To Write, Despite

Mention of East Germany brings us to a historical context of great importance for the subtext. I mean the Soviet bloc. Analyses are so numerous, beginning with those of witnesses and victims, that they constitute an embarrassment of riches. Ryszard Kapuściński, referring to the Poland of his student years, at the time of Stalin's death, has described it well. He was later destined to traverse the globe as an insightful reporter, and he was already keenly perceptive:

> Well . . . all our thinking, our looking and reading, was governed during those years by an obsession with allusion. Each word brought another one to mind; each had a double meaning, concealed a subtext, a hidden significance; each contained something secretly encoded, cunningly concealed. . . . The man who wrote had difficulty communicating with the man who read, not only because the censor could confiscate the text en route, but also because, even when the text finally reached him, the latter read something utterly different from what was clearly written, constantly asking himself: What did this author really want to tell me?[33]

That explains why the Polish translation of the *Histories* of Herodotus was kept under wraps for several years, for the ancient Greek historian's portraits of tyrants and the narratives of bloody reigns, extending over nine books, lent themselves to comparisons with current events. This climate of suspicion, vagueness, and oppressive uncertainty, as it obtained in Albania, also appears in the novels of Ismail Kadare.

Under such conditions, writing risks mirroring thought's enslavement, as Czesław Miłosz has emphasized about the intellectuals and writers who cooperated, more or less, with the Communist regime in Poland and the Baltic nations. Showing that transparency was out of reach and observing their ploys, their acts of cowardice as well as bravery, Miłosz highlights the Arabic notion of *Ketman*, which he borrows from a book of Arthur de Gobineau on Persia, meaning, he says, the art of dissimulation, secrecy to secure survival, to escape persecution: the art he saw at work in the politics, ethics, and literature of the People's Democracies. Among other examples, Miłosz cites a Polish poet, "D," traveling in the Soviet Union right after the war, who wrote that "everything was great in Moscow; there is only one criticism to be made: Moscow was too much like Taormina; one ate as many tangerines there as in Sicily. And he, D., did not like tangerines." Just like those bankers' acacias,[34] these Muscovite tangerines come out of nowhere and are precisely the sort of thing to arouse suspicion. Was it an over-the-top, mocking encomium? Maybe . . . "In fact," Miłosz concludes, "it was not easy, knowing D., to unravel his intentions."[35]

Discussing another country, Hungary, and another period, the 1980s, Miklós Haraszti sketches a less dramatic picture of a state-directed culture in which constraint is lighter than in the past but where the subtext has not lost its legitimacy. Artists and intellectuals write well and truly "between the lines," using diverse means, such as anachronisms, deliberate infractions of certain artistic rules, hyperbole, omission, dissonance. Only, this "space between the lines" is not meant to voice protests or win freedom of speech; it serves instead "to bring together the loyal fringes," to establish "the archive of our feelings, a welcoming environment for interests and needs still unexpressed, the laboratory of consensus."[36]

Confronting these "loyal fringes," this "laboratory of consensus," which assumes some kind of collaboration between the controllers and the controlled, one can make a connection with Aristides's *Encomium of Rome*. Similarly, one thinks of Dio's *Discourses on Kingship* while reading in Robert Darnton's book about a work admittedly more caustic than Dio's. It masks or blurs its criticism with stylistic maneuvers, like the use of several narrative voices and literary allusions, which make it possible to claim that no attack against the regime was intended, only "a lighthearted satire inspired by Diderot."[37] The East German censor, however, was not fooled and blocked the work.

Here is yet another example, this time from China:

> Question: Can political debates occur in the current Chinese Parliament?
> Answer: Criticisms are forbidden, but one can send messages, for example, by congratulating the government for something that it really did not want to do, by thanking it for its help "that continually increases and is wisely used," or by referencing only a small part of the Prime Minister's speech.[38]

An Ox on the Tongue

The deputies concerned here do not voice criticism, since that is forbidden. They use seeming approval (congratulating, thanking) to make their wishes known, or else they use silence to signal what they disapprove. Once more, the resemblances are striking between these methods and those encountered among others in Greco-Roman rhetoric. The contexts change, dogmatic pronouncements come and go, but the art of insinuation still endures.

Historical Analogy

One important approach in writing under a dictatorship is historical analogy. Vladimir Lenin, in order to denounce the Russian bourgeoisie for their oppression of Sakhalin Island, substituted Korea for Sakhalin and Japan for Russia. Berthold Brecht cites this example in his essay "Five Difficulties in Writing the Truth," a kind of anti-fascist handbook, which catalogs the different ways of "spreading the truth among the greatest number." "There are many kinds of cunning to hoodwink the suspicious State":[39] they rely, for the most part, on double meaning and the subtext.

There is a similar strategy of distancing, raised to a very high degree of power and subtlety, in François-René de Chateaubriand's nineteenth-century prose epic *The Martyrs*. Situated in the Roman Empire at the end of paganism and the establishing of Christianity as the state religion (third to fourth century), it was applied by analogy to the Napoleonic Empire, as Marc Fumaroli has shown: "To the rare readers capable of reading slowly and closely, the moral and religious allegory that utterly controls the epic *The Martyrs, or the Triumph of the Christian Religion* (a title following on *The Genius of Christianity*) revealed the principle of Neronian Terror lurking beneath the glory of the Napoleonic Empire and the underground activity of Providence in making ready sooner or later the fall of the anachronistic, military, neo-pagan dictatorship. . . . To aid his attentive and knowing reader in lifting the veils, the poet of *Martyrs* multiplied the collusive signposts."[40]

We can also cite a historical study dealing with ancient Athens that covertly eyed contemporary France, *Les Oligarques* (The oligarchs) of Jules Isaac, written clandestinely in 1942 and published in 1945 by Editions de Minuit. The author, a victim of the racial laws, lost his post and had to hide during the occupation; his wife and two of his children were deported and died. Before their recent reappearance in Russian society, oligarchs were familiar figures in ancient Greece, a social and psychological type to whom Theophrastus devoted one of his *Characters*: driven by a will to dominate, the oligarch desires power and wealth and conspires with his friends against the People,

The Subtle Subtext

whom he despises. Twice, at the end of the fifth century BC, Athenian oligarchs, taking advantage of their country's defeat, staged coups to overthrow the democracy, relying on support from Sparta, Athens's victorious enemy. Isaac saw in them certain elements of the French Right who profited from the war and the 1940 defeat and who, with German assistance, put in place a government of diminished freedoms. While claiming to be a work of serious and scholarly history, it was, in effect, a political tract. The paratext lends credence to this view, from the subtitle, *Essay in Biased History*, to the opening foreword: "It was in 404 BC that vanquished Athens had to bend its knee before Sparta. It is in 1942 AD, in a France subjugated by Hitler's Germany, that these pages are written. Two thousand, three hundred forty-six years— half of recorded history—separate the author from his subject. Rather than in space, being a sedentary sort, he has chosen to flee in time. And here is what he has found."

This foreword presents historical inquiry as an evasion, an intellectual evasion, which indeed is what it was for the old, hounded Jew, but an evasion connected to the present and putting it in perspective. Throughout the work, one picks up disguised allusions, with political analysis and denunciation conducted under cover of analogy. The attacks against the metics, resident foreigners, in ancient Athens recall the attacks against the Jews in France. Modern terms are applied to the ancient situation, like the word "collaboration," or the expression "divine surprise," which the French nationalist and anti-Semite Charles Maurras had used apropos of the situation created by the defeat of June 1940, and which reappears here to describe the Athenian defeat in the Sicilian expedition of 413 BC. One recognizes Philippe Pétain peeking out from behind Sophocles: "The venerated name of an illustrious elder looks good on the façade of certain demolition companies."[41]

Double-Talk and Cant

While I was writing this book, I received an email from the French National Railway. It went like this:

> Dear Monsieur Pernot,
>
> In order to facilitate your next trip from Paris, Gare de ***, we are activating, as of ***, an automatic boarding device.
>
> The idea is simple: once your tickets are verified when you pass through the device, you will be able to enjoy fully our on-board services and comfort.

Here is what you need to do to get yourself on the right track!

- The boarding area is open between twenty minutes and two minutes prior to the train's departure.
- Your ticket will be checked at the entry to the platform; have it in hand.
- The boarding team will welcome you and facilitate getting on board.

Given that all my senses were awakened to the subject of this book, I could not stop myself from seeing a message here that cried out for deciphering. At first glance, it was the bearer of glad tidings, since the company had decided to "facilitate" things for me, in such a way as to allow me "to enjoy fully" the new situation, and this was said with a smile, thanks to a play on words in the expression "on the right track." Nevertheless, on second thought, this message was announcing restrictions, modeled after airplane boarding, the vague word "device" designating gates in front of which the traveler had to present his ticket to be scanned automatically. Previously, one used to access the train without going through any barrier and without showing a ticket; so there was an additional formality, which set one to thinking that there was risk of a long line at a busy hour and further complication for a nontraveler accompanying someone to his assigned car. The subtextual procedure here in evidence is thus not only "attenuation" but also "inversion": the word "facilitate," used twice, qualifies an innovation liable to create, in fact, a difficulty, and its noteworthy, dare I say compulsive, repetition reveals the very point that it is meant to conceal.

I hasten to add that I have nothing against gates and I fully understand that security needs to be tightened. The objective is not at issue, but its manner of presentation is interesting. A more direct way of introducing the new arrangement might have gone like this: "We are aware of the inconvenience caused, and if we are taking this measure, it is because we deem it necessary to counter fraud and improve security; we appeal to your understanding and compliance; we are doing all we can to limit any inconvenience." Instead of preferring an informative tone, providing instructions and explanations, the railway chose to communicate in a style familiar from advertising, promoting a happy innovation and dispensing friendly advice. It does not fool anybody: we assume that most of the message's recipients were capable of deciphering it and recognizing its attempt to sweeten the pill. They probably did not even hold it against the hack writer, because they knew that he was writing within the confines of a corporate strategy (the context), and they understood that he was tasked with accentuating the positive. Is such a strategy a good or bad thing? That is for each person to decide. Admittedly, this is only an amusing and inconsequential example, but it does bring up a new aspect of the subtext.

For here is a case where a pronouncement with two ways of being read does not issue from an oppressed person seeking to be heard but rather from an entity imposing itself. The perspective changes: whereas previously subtexts arose out of positions of inferiority, now the author of the pronouncement holds the reins. There are, in essence, two sorts of "double-talk": one is the strength of the weak, the other the weakness of the strong.

In the political realm, these two aspects conjoin. The language of dissidence is existentially tied to the language of power, its dialectical opposite; it is a response to censorship and cant. Inversely, censorship is not self-sufficient either. It prepares the ground for propaganda, which aims to stifle subversive speech. Hence it follows, in a way only superficially surprising, that the language of power, stark and seemingly daunting, can itself contain aspects that stem from the subtext. If the malarkey only encounters suckers, it is not germane to our discussion. If, on the other hand, as often happens, those to whom the language of power addresses itself understand that they are dealing with a false or falsified language that is covering up ideas different from those explicitly stated, then one is in the presence of a double register of meaning. Lying differs from the subtext, to be sure, but the lying of the state is not a lie like other lies; it is a lie that fools nobody, or at least not everybody. Imposed discourse, in which the addressees place little trust, and which they decipher, is a special and superlative form of subtext, a "super-text," if you will. The subtext is a tinkling tune seeking to be heard under the bass drum. The bass drum swamps everything; there is nothing else. But it can be analyzed in its turn.

Changing the Meaning of Words

> "When *I* use a word," Humpty Dumpty said, in rather a scornful tone, "it means just what I choose it to mean—neither more nor less."
> "The question is," said Alice, "whether you can make words mean so many different things."
> "The question is," said Humpty Dumpty, "which is to be master—that's all."[42]

As Lewis Carroll observes in this dialogue, control of the meaning of words and the manipulation of their meaning are the rewards of power. In antiquity, Thucydides observed that the creation of new ways of speaking and changing the usual meaning of words accompanied revolutions; with political polarization, for example, in the effort to push out moderates, "reckless audacity came to be considered the courage of a loyal ally; prudent hesitation specious cowardice; moderation was held to be a cloak for unmanliness; ability to see all sides of a question inaptness to act on any."[43] The overthrow of linguistic power is one of the means of overthrowing the state. Another ancient historian, Tacitus, remarks that, seen from the viewpoint of the vanquished, the establishing of Roman domination involved a semantic switch. The Romans, he writes, camouflage the reality of their conquest under misleading names, employing different terms to mask their plundering: they speak of "empire" instead of "killing and pillaging," "they make a desert and call it a peace," the famous "Roman peace."[44] But one should not think that the barbarians did any better, for they, too, "bandied about specious names as excuses."[45] Such passages show that some, at least, were not duped, and discerned a hidden meaning in the official propaganda.

Here, in turn, is Aragon, different circumstances, same reality, in *The Grévin Museum*: "They may have tried to baptize the darkness light / raise ignorance to the level of virtue."

Substitute Words

A variation on the preceding is the prohibition of certain words and their replacement with others, deemed to be the solely acceptable. Thus it is that Alessandro Manzoni, in *I Promessi Sposi (The Betrothed)*, basing himself on archival documents, recounts how an epidemic of plague broke out in Milan in 1630. Although some people had recognized the symptoms, the authorities refused to acknowledge that it was the plague. The general public showed signs of disbelief, too, and self-deception. Most doctors mocked the warnings of a small number of their colleagues. After several months, however, the cases were so numerous and the evidence had become so clear that doctors were forced to recognize that they were confronting an epidemic. Yet even then, they avoided calling it "plague":

> The doctors who were opposed to the idea that this was the plague were unwilling to admit the truth of a view which they had ridiculed, but still had to find a name for this supposedly new disease, which

was now too common and too well known not to do without one. So they christened it "the malign fever," or "the pestilent fever"—a wretched evasion, in fact a mere fraudulent play on words. And yet it did great harm; for while admitting half the truth, it still concealed the fact which it was most important for everyone to believe and understand, namely that the disease was transmitted by contact.[46]

When the stubborn denials of the disease ceased, word went around that evildoers and diabolical machinations had spread it:

In the beginning, then, there had been no plague, no pestilence, none at all, not on any account. The very words had been forbidden.

Next came the talk of "pestilent fever"—the idea being admitted indirectly, in adjectival form.

Then it was "not a *real* pestilence"—that is to say, it was a pestilence, but only in a certain sense; not a true pestilence, but something for which it was difficult to find another name.

Last of all, it became a pestilence without any doubt or argument—but now a new idea was attached to it, the idea of poisoning and witchcraft, and this corrupted and confused the sense conveyed by the dreaded word which could now no longer be suppressed.

I do not think that it is necessary to be deeply versed in the history of words and ideas to see that many of them have followed a route similar to that just described.[47]

The novelist becomes historian and moralist, detaching himself from his characters and plot to comment on actual events. He denounces the mechanism of self-deception, which recompenses itself with harmful illusions and looks for scapegoats. The only remedies were rationalism, scientific analysis of the facts, courage to face reality. Yet the language of official truth triumphs instead. Without going so far as to mention Chernobyl, let me be content to cite Jean de La Fontaine, who in two verses sums up the problem: "Un mal qui répand la terreur / . . . la Peste (puisqu' il faut l'appeler par son nom)" (An evil that spreads terror / . . . the Plague [to call it, as we must, by its name]).[48]

Totalitarian Languages

Concerning "totalitarian languages,"[49] two books shed essential light while deepening reflection on the role of the subtext these languages entail. Victor

Klemperer (1881–1960), son of a rabbi, cousin of the orchestral conductor Otto Klemperer, was professor of Romance philology at the University of Dresden. Dismissed in 1935, he was placed under house arrest, where he endured daily threats, humiliations, and forced labor, escaping deportation only because his wife was not Jewish. But he did not forget he was a philologist, and for twelve years, from 1933 to 1945, he filled notebooks with his meticulous studies of the transformations that the Nazis inflicted on the German language. These studies culminated in the publication of *LTI* in 1947, that is, *Lingua tertii imperii* (*The Language of the Third Reich*). The title was the knowing acronym he sarcastically coined to parody the initials that the new regime used and abused. He clung to this work, as to a life preserver, throughout his dismissal/detention, and it embodied for him the intellectual endeavor and research that preserved his dignity and kept him going. *LTI* was "an SOS sent to myself," he wrote.[50] It is one of the ironies of history that the book had a limited press run in the German Democratic Republic, where Klemperer lived after the war, since the Communist regime evinced little enthusiasm for spreading this research dedicated to a language steeped in ideology and capable of suggesting uncomfortable parallels.[51] *LTI* became susceptible of being read on a second level, as an allusion to Communism, even though that was not the author's intention at the time of composition—yet another example of a message received without being sent, the subtext arising on its own after the fact.

Be that as it may, Klemperer's study is at once an autobiography, a denunciation of Nazism, and a treatise on totalitarian language based on numerous examples; the author imagined making it into a dictionary. The "changes in the value of words"[52] expressed itself either through existing words that assumed new senses, or through new combinations (thanks to German's predilection for forming compounds), or through neologisms. Thus: "fanatical," used to mean "heroic and virtuous"; "people" (*Volk*), omnipresent in different compounds; "historic," incessantly applied to actions of the regime, with the superlative "universally"; rejection of "the system" (yes, even then . . .[53]); "placed in safekeeping," used apropos of private libraries, definitely not "stolen"; "voluntary contribution" for a required tax. Also rampant was what Klemperer calls "alternating cold and hot shower" rhetoric, which combined incongruously in one and the same expression grandiloquence and earthiness: "wormy intellectualism," "flat-footed idiocy." Or this: "lost to their own kind" (*artvergessen*), designating Jewish house pets, animals that wound up being confiscated and killed.[54]

The other important work for our purposes is Orwell's *1984*, which targets Communism and Stalinism in a way applicable to England. In this novel the totalitarian state does not stop at physical control of the populace; it aims at mental control as well. To do this, the party in power coldly propagates falsehoods through sloganeering—"WAR IS PEACE," "FREEDOM IS SLAVERY," "IGNORANCE IS STRENGTH"—or it uses deceptive names like the Ministry of Love, which "maintained law and order" but is actually a sinister place of detention and torture. It rewrites the past, emending archives (the work of the protagonist, Winston). And, above all, it undertook a total reform of language, creating "newspeak," which is meant gradually to replace the language formerly in use. A radical reorganization and suppression of numerous words characterize newspeak, the objective to prevent not only saying but even conceiving ideas that deviate from the regime's dogma: "'In the end we shall make thoughtcrime literally impossible, because there will be no words in which to express it.'"[55] Orwell's nightmarish world offers a sort of synthesis of all the aspects of totalitarian language, compounded of official verities, adulteration of the meaning of words, and the double-talk of the state.

Who Is Fooled?

The nagging question that Klemperer and Orwell's hero pose is this: "Am I the only one not to be fooled?" Klemperer emphasizes that the LTI was largely received and adopted, including by people of his circle who were not detestable. "None of them were Nazis, but they were all poisoned," he angrily lets loose.[56] Children, in particular, were easily influenced, so that, given the length of time under discussion, many Germans of Klemperer's acquaintance were marked by an indoctrination they had undergone since their youth. And yet, for all its effectiveness, Klemperer himself did not believe the propaganda. Similarly, one comes across individuals in his pages who, without explicitly recognizing it, had no illusions about what the government was saying to them and told them to say. There was his colleague Israel, who changed his name, explaining that his family was really called Oesterhelt and that his current family name was only the mistaken result of a series of successive changes going back to the sixteenth century (Uesterhelt, Isterhal, Istrael, Isserel, Israel). There were also those who refrained from mentioning the Führer in obituary notices, and "all those who laughed at Goebbels's all-too-blatant lies."[57] Complex factors were at work, the author states, even within the LTI: "The LTI was a prison language (of jailors and prisoners), and integral to the language of prisons (as acts of self-defense) are secret words, confusing ambiguities, forgeries, and so on."[58]

If Klemperer decrypted the Nazi language with special skill, owing to his motivation, the time he spent on it, and his philological training, others, certainly, without engaging in such a profound study, sensed as well the presence of hidden contents behind the official words. These people did not have any reason to open up to him because that would have been dangerous. Naturally, it is also necessary to take into account the variations in intensity of the critical spirit that leads to some taking at face value the same message others discern as a cover-up. This is the problem *1984* poses, where the hero, Winston, wonders who can remain sane in the face of state lies. "Was he then *alone* in the possession of a memory?"[59] He gradually discovers the existence of other rebellious spirits, although none admits it. He approaches O'Brien, in whom he intuitively recognizes one of the disabused, but this very O'Brien is revealed as an agent provocateur working for the government. He becomes Winston's torturer. The half light is pervasive owing to the system of "doublethink" or "conscious deception" in favor of the party. So people believe lies, all the time knowing they are lies.[60]

To get back to reality, we may cite the witness of Albert Londres, who, already in 1920, understood the hidden dimension of the new Soviet language. Revolutionary slogans, he observed, are written "in sympathetic ink": to decipher them you must hold them up to the light. "Dictatorship of the proletariat" thus becomes "Dictatorship, in the name of the proletariat, over the proletariat, as over everybody else, by nonproletariats." "Labor force" means "forced labor,"[61] a topic that kept the author's attention: this is the same Londres who was to file horrifying stories about the French penal colony in Guyana. Another witness is Ante Ciliga, a member of the Yugoslav Communist Party who stayed in Russia during the 1920s before being arrested and deported to Siberia in 1930. He described the "country of the big lie," its mumbo jumbo, its historic fakery, but he observed that, in prison, tongues loosened up, noting sarcastically: "All social layers of Russia are represented in prison. There one can at last get to know what really happens in the country and what people really think. It is very simple; prison is the only place in Soviet Russia where people express their feelings openly and sincerely."[62]

According to Aleksandr Solzhenitsyn, in a so-called free society, informing, fear, and distrust reigned, to such a degree that everybody lied, praising the party and the government with prefabricated phrases that they used without conviction. Whether in public, in private conversation, or within the family, especially in front of children, "the permanent lie becomes the only safe form of existence," "the continuing basis of life," so that everything is covered over with its "dense, grey fog."[63] "Dense, grey fog" (in Russian, *serovatyi tuman*) unexpectedly calls to mind Verlaine's "grey song." That is how totalitarian language functions, imposing itself while leaving a secret margin for reception in a different light.

And Now, Political Correctness

In 1946, Orwell (again!) denounced a development in English, or more precisely a new language of political orthodoxy, marked by a stale style of cliché, euphemism, inflated expressions, question-begging, and nebulous generalities. In his eyes, speakers' duplicity explained these stylistic vices and betrayed a disconnect between real and alleged objectives. "But if thought corrupts language, language can also corrupt thought."[64]

Democracy, indeed, does not solve all problems. Although its material and moral superiority compared to totalitarianism is beyond dispute, it nonetheless presents features of self-surveillance and attempts at the political control of language. Every civilization constructs its own concepts meant to maintain social order, and ours today is no exception, taking the form of "political correctness." Everybody knows it: whether in the media or government, words and locutions spread in politic language that aims to soften, dress up, or mask certain realities and to promote noble-sounding objectives through the generous use of euphemisms and metaphors. For example, "affirmative action/reverse discrimination," "it's a fact that . . . ," "forces beyond our control," "inclusivity," "Black," "dialogue," "diverse," "he or she," "LGBTQ," "senior citizen," "whistleblower," "lone wolf," "open admissions," "empower," "a strong signal," "road rage," "community." The list goes on. A new lexicon, disingenuous or in any case overdetermined, abets the dodging. Behind each of these locutions another way of speaking lies hidden, older and more widespread, that remains "understood": it can be re-created mentally, and that is exactly what political correctness wants to avoid. The difference with totalitarian languages examined earlier is that political correctness means well and is reacting against a past of stern and categorical labeling. That is why it seems a little excessive to speak in France of an LQR, or *Lingua quintae reipublicae* (Language of the Fifth Republic), as some have proposed, in an attempt to connect with Klemperer's work:[65] fortunately, the situation is not the same. The subtext, this Protean phenomenon, is not finished evolving and adapting.

7

Sexorama

And where is sex in all this? Is it not the domain par excellence of the subtext? Pseudo-Aristotle notices this: "Beware of mentioning shameful acts with shameful words . . . : one must describe actions of this sort enigmatically and express the matter using words meaning something else."[1] Even the ancients, habitually portrayed as crude and bawdy, were capable of reserve. All civilized societies do the same, for reasons there is no need to dig into here, insisting upon precautions when speaking about sexual activity, bodily functions, or death. Sexual subtext satisfies a certain curiosity, moreover, and provides the added pleasure of surmise. We are all a bit like Sartre's grandmother: "She read lots of spicy novels, but it was not so much the plot that interested as the transparent veils in which it was enveloped: 'It's daring, it's well-written,' she would say with a delicate air. Gently, mortals, be discreet!"[2] So let us now lift the veil on a few scenes from the immense panorama of sex, a "sexorama," if I may use a Balzacian coinage.[3] Indeed, Balzac will be an important contributor to what follows.

The Ten Commandments of Decency

1. Thou shalt not mention organs
2. Thou shalt swear by metaphors and similes
3. Remember to proclaim psychology
4. Honor the avoidance of physiology
5. Thou shalt play on words
6. Thou shalt use italics
7. Thou shalt know when to pass
8. Thou shalt respect the reader

9. Thou shalt leave a little room for mystery
10. Thou shalt be silent about the basics.

The Art of Ellipsis

Generally speaking, the subtext in sexual matters consists of saying less to imply more. It is necessary to stop at the critical moment and to know how far is too far, as they say. For example, from top to bottom: "You are going to be mine from head to toe, and I will be Master of all: of your little bright eyes; of your little naughty nose; of your luscious lips; of your lovable ears; of your cute little chin; of your plump little breasts; of your. . . . And so, your entire Person will be mine, and I will be all set, to pet you all I want. Don't you just love this Marriage, my adorable baby doll?"[4] And now from bottom to top: "He kissed the hem of the duchess' robe, her feet, her knees; but to maintain the honor of the Faubourg St. Germain, I must not reveal the mystery of its boudoirs, where one sought everything from love, save what could prove love."[5]

Differing from a certain kind of literature with a tendency to speak at length about these things and even more than that, the crucial moment goes by in silence; all is suggested. It is an art being lost in our time, an art in which previous centuries were past masters.

At the end of Balzac's *Les Chouans* (the name of Breton counterrevolutionaries), Marie de Verneuil and the Marquis find themselves alone in the bedroom on their wedding night. They go to bed, Marie looks at the clock, and says to herself, "Six hours to live." For she knows that death awaits them on the morrow. With this the novelist ends the paragraph, and begins the next one thus: "'So I was able to sleep,' she cried out toward morning, awaking with a start." Between Marie's two remarks the night has passed, a night the novelist has refrained from relating. Nevertheless, he discreetly alludes to it a little later, when he mentions on the same page the "pleasures they had tasted."[6]

In a chapter of Stendhal's *The Red and the Black*, mischievously entitled "Cockcrow," Julien has come to find Madame de Renal in her bedchamber at two in the morning. "He did not respond to her reproaches as he threw himself at her feet, hugging her knees. As she berated him harshly, he melted into tears." Next paragraph: "Some hours later, when Julien left Madame de Renal's chamber, one might say, as they do in novels, that he had nothing left to desire." Again, the love scene becomes an ellipsis, placed in the interval between the two paragraphs, an ellipsis at once narrative, temporal, and typographical. A comment by the author fills in the lacuna, but as a deliberate cliché, which gives an amused elegance to the narrative distancing.[7]

Stendhal, again, this time in *The Charterhouse of Parma*, shows Clélia going off to Fabrizio:

> She was so lovely just then, her gown slipping off her shoulders and in such a state of extreme passion that Fabrizio could not resist an almost involuntary "movement." Which met with no resistance.
>
> In the enthusiasm of passion and generosity which followed extreme rapture, he murmured to her quite foolishly, [his words follow].[8]

Ellipsis, for greater clarity, or to draw closer attention, may be marked by dots. Thus, in Book Two of *The Red and the Black*, with, once more, a narrator's comment:

> He hurls himself into the chamber more dead than alive:
> "It's you then!" she said, throwing herself into his arms.
> . . .
> Who will describe Julien's excess of happiness? Mathilde's was almost its equal.[9]

In Leo Tolstoy, two lines of suspension points at the end of the chapter suggest the beginning of Anna Karenina's liaison with Vronsky. The ensuing chapter picks up: "That which for Vronsky had been almost a whole year the one absorbing desire of his life, that which for Anna had been a terrible but enchanting dream of bliss, that desire had been fulfilled."[10]

Here is another, somewhat more lively, example, where the marks of ellipsis are evocative: "Do you remember the first time you came to my place? You entered brusquely, with a scent of violet perfuming your skirts; we looked at each other for a long time without saying a word, then kissed madly . . . then . . . we didn't speak until the next day."[11]

In Italian literature, there are two famous ellipses. The first is in Dante's *Inferno*, "that day we read no further" ("quel giorno più non vi leggemmo avante").[12] Paolo and Francesca da Rimini have been condemned to the torments of Hell, where the poet meets them. At his request, Francesca tells how the lovers' sinful passion arose and brought them to their sad state. One day, alone, they were reading together the lay of Lancelot, and its love story had such an enormously suggestive effect on them that, when they got to the point where Lancelot kisses the mouth of his ladylove, Paolo could not resist doing the same to Francesca. Recalling this moment, Francesca speaks the verse cited earlier, whose precise interpretation has been a matter of debate. There is no doubt about the general tenor of the episode, nor, since she was a married woman, about Francesca's adultery with Paolo, who, to make matters worse, was her brother-in-law. Ever since the Middle Ages, commentators have noted the use of rhetorical "reticence" here, the poet breaking off and leaving the rest to the imagination. The debate is over whether the adultery occurs precisely at the moment following the verse in question.[13]

The second Italian example occurs in Alessandro Manzoni's novel *I Promessi Sposi* (*The Betrothed*): "the poor wretch answered him" ("la sventurata rispose").[14] Egidio had found a way of speaking to Gertrude, a young and still beautiful woman from an important family but, alas, consecrated since birth to the religious life and cloistered, willy-nilly, in a convent in Monza. Living in a house next door to the convent, on the side where the noble nun had the luxury of a private apartment, Egidio espied her from a window that gave onto a courtyard where she used to walk, and one day he was bold enough, knave that he was, to call out to her. It is here that the famous sentence occurs. We will never know a word of what they said, let alone what they did. After the sentence, the author ends the paragraph, continuing anew: "It was certainly not an unmixed happiness she felt in those first few moments, but it was a keen happiness nonetheless."

In a similar way in the cinema (in nonexplicit films), the scene changes and the camera shifts discreetly to something else. Thus, in *Gone with the Wind*, at the moment of Rhett Butler's jealous outburst against Scarlett O'Hara: "He gathers her in his arms and mounts the staircase for a night of forced passion. Dissolve to blackout. Next we rediscover Scarlett in bed, the following day, gay and 'satisfied.'"[15]

The ellipsis is therefore a preference for proper tone, which leaves to the reader the task of filling in the blanks and imagining as he or she pleases what was left unsaid. It is such a common practice that it no longer has the aspect of happy discovery or prudish choice; it is a writing convention, a code in force at a given time between authors and readers or viewers. We can gauge its power by comparing it with texts that break the codes.

Half-Rapes

The chapter in Jules Renard's *L'Écornifleur* (*The Sponger*) entitled "The Half-Rape" is not easy reading.[16] The protagonist forcibly possesses Marguerite, his hosts' daughter, without enthusiasm and full of self-reproach for taking advantage of the young girl's naiveté. "What is this carnal appetite that has suddenly taken hold of me and passes before it's sated?" he asks himself. Without descending to obscene detail, the description is evocative all the same:

> "Are you in pain, then?"
> Her paleness scares me. Oh! The resistance of that delicate flesh! I am ashamed of my inexperience, like an intern at his first operation on a living body, with tools that don't cut.
> "I can't take any more!" Marguerite cries. "Do you want to kill me?"

Such a scene conveys to the reader, along with its brutality, the sense of self-loathing that the protagonist experiences. The author was fully aware of what he was writing and knew what effect his narrative produced. It infringed not only the laws of hospitality but also the rules of literature. "My fault humiliates me like a stylistic flaw," the hero, a would-be poet, ruminates. Behind or beside Renard's legendary ferocity, as his *Journal* makes clear, was a chaste and sensitive Renard, and this double dimension is perceptible in this excerpt from the novel.

The same literary tour de force occurs in Philippe Hériat's novel, a saga about the Boussardel family, *Les Boussardel*. An entire chapter recounts the wedding night spent in a compartment on board the Paris-Marseilles night train, the eagerness of an inexperienced Victorin with Amélie, a convent girl as willing as she is ignorant, the repeated, and not fully successful, attempts between each station stop.[17] The novelist writes from Amélie's perspective: "Men are another species . . . This unknown will be horrible . . . Don't be stupid and don't cry . . . You have to believe he's within his rights." Despite her good intentions, the young girl resists without meaning to. Even at the last try: "Once more, the reflex of a body in revolt had placed its barrier between them, but without preventing Victorin the superficial contentment he seemed to be getting used to."

Can one still speak of the subtext? In fact, just as there is half-rape, so there is also half subtext. Even if they do not reveal all the physical details, the authors suggest a great deal. The need to create a dramatic atmosphere topples the barriers of allusion.

Giving "a 'Less Pure' Sense to the Words of the Tribe"

Metaphors are another method; Sterne's nose,[18] Proust's orchids (Odette's *catleyas*)[19] are famous. Later on in Proust's novel, to stick with flowers, the meeting of the Baron de Charlus and Jupien is likened to a bumblebee's flight toward an orchid.[20] So it is not at all surprising that the linguist Agnès Pierron was able to compile a dictionary of French sexual vocabulary six hundred pages long.[21] It has twenty-five hundred entries, more than five thousand words and expressions, divided under seventeen headings according to the area they borrow from, starting with "artisanal" and "arts" and ending with "vesture" and "voyage." This is not a question of jargon but of normal words like "offal," "butchering," "meat packer," and so forth that take on a special meaning whether in a writer or in common parlance. In view of this richness (not exactly Mallarmé's "purer sense"!), it is quite apparent that we are no longer dealing with a case of occasional veiled expressions but with a parallel language, and that is why it needs a dictionary.

In English, we can cite the volume of the lexicographer Eric Partridge, *Shakespeare's Bawdy*,[22] a glossary of more than two hundred pages that impressively lists the sexual and scatological double-entendres in the playwright's works, from "Abhorson," the name of a secondary character in *Measure for Measure*, meaning "whore's son," down to "weakness and debility [the means of]" in *As You Like It*, referring to onanism.[23] These double meanings naturally offered players, able to accentuate their actions as they saw fit, rich possibilities for fun. Thus, the Nurse announces in suggestive metaphors the terribly romantic device of the ladder that allows Romeo to reach Juliet for a night of love:

Hie you to church; I must another way,
To fetch a ladder, by the which your love
Must climb a bird's nest soon when it is dark;
I am the drudge, and toil in your delight;
But you shall bear the burthen soon at night.[24]

The Impossibilities of Love

Now to the difficult cases. When somewhat detailed, or startling, information has to be provided on the sexual act, if one wants to observe the proprieties, silence and imagery no longer suffice; more elaborate strategies are called for. This is a challenge, especially for writers, one we are going to examine through what Stendhal calls "the greatest of the *impossibilities* of love."[25] First, it involves talking about what does not happen, and the negative is less inspiring than the positive. Then, the writer has to deal with unsettling surprise, or even an embarrassing disgrace: no priapic triumphs here. So the subtext needs to be used with particular subtlety.

Recall the plot of Stendhal's *Armance*. Subtitled "Scenes from a Parisian Salon in 1827," the novel recounts the stormy relationship of Octave and Armance. The young girl's modesty and scrupulosity hold her back; being poor, she does not want to give the impression of marrying for money. As for Octave, he reveals himself to be a difficult person who is hiding a secret. Misunderstandings add to these obstacles, as do the machinations of secondary characters who thwart the couple. Despite everything, the two heroes become progressively aware of their mutual love and confess it to one another. Armance unexpectedly inherits a fortune that makes her well off; yet Octave's hesitancy persists. He is ready to reveal his secret to his fiancée, when their enemies provoke a mutual misunderstanding, and Octave thinks he is no longer loved. Still, he marries Armance, only to commit suicide thereafter. She will retire to a convent.

One of the narrative's chief interests is the psychological portrait of a brilliant graduate from a prestigious school who is at the same time a melancholy and misanthropic young man, "a totally mysterious being." "Octave desired nothing, nothing seemed to cause him either pain or pleasure." Fierce, desperate, he might be a romantic hero in the throes of the sickness of the age, were it not for thoughts dropped here and there that suggest the existence of a specific torment: "Perhaps some singular factor, deeply imprinted on this young heart, that found itself in contradiction with the events of actual life such as he beheld them developing about him, led him to portray himself in guises too dark, both his future life and his relations with his fellow man."[26]

Octave's particular preoccupation is marriage. He envisaged for a time consecrating his life to God, and he rejects the idea of marrying. He is a "person whom some bizarre prejudice against marriage makes unhappy." At a performance of one of Scribe's comedies, where there is some stage business with the key to the bridal chamber, he runs out of the theater. Love terrifies him. When the famous Madame de Claix pays him "a very pointed compliment," he hurries away blushing. Once he has met Armance, he dreams of her: "I could love her passionately . . . I COULD LOVE HER! Me, wretched me!"—and he almost gets himself run over by a carriage. The idea dawns on the reader that this woman is not to be Octave's, and that this is crucial, as the accident he barely escaped shows. He reproaches himself for having fallen in love: "My heart . . . has done something that I forbade myself under pain of death." And yet Octave is responsive to the physical charms of the opposite sex, "stirred by Armance's beautiful arm" and nuzzling her cheek with his lips.

The Subtle Subtext

There is a "but," a "frightful but," a "fatal secret" that Octave cannot bring himself to reveal. At the end, at the moment of his suicide, he pours everything out in a letter, but we will never get to read it, for the novelist refrains from reproducing its contents.

These are the facts that have provoked the remark, "Never has a book been more in need of a preface. It is incomprehensible without an explanation."[27] The author himself provided this explanation in manuscript notes that he included in a copy that subsequently came into the possession of Donato Bucci: "The protagonist is troubled and angry because he realizes he is impotent, something about which he assured himself when he went to Madame Auguste's with his friends, and then by himself." He is "Octave the impotent."[28] Stendhal's plan was to make this situation understood without saying anything explicitly, out of respect for convention, perhaps to avoid turning his hero into a comic figure, and the better to pique, no doubt, the interest of his readers, male and female, by appealing to their intelligence and imagination. The subject, moreover, was in the air, for a novel, *Olivier, or the Secret*, dealt with the same theme and caused quite a stir in literary circles. It also appears that Stendhal, without being in the least impotent, was acquainted with the disappointments that had impressed him and that may have contributed to his interest in the matter. But with a sure hand the novel transcends its immediate context and aims for literary and psychological depth.

The author was therefore led to use deliberate ploys, in order to create a double level of meaning. Stendhal's breadth of mind obviously alerted him to the resources of concealment and revelation equally inherent in language. In *Armance* he cites, through the mouth of Madame d'Aumale, a "major principle" that he was fond of: "Speech was given to man to hide his thought."[29] This cynical and witty generalization shows the author's sharp awareness of the artful subtext.

In the Bucci manuscript, certain notes do, in fact, reveal a conscious effort in this direction, an effort Stendhal, editing himself, judged still incomplete. For example, at the very beginning, in the margin of the sentence quoted earlier ("Perhaps some singular factor"), the Bucci manuscript sets forth a less vague correction: "A singular and incurable woe induced him to exaggerate certain types of happiness that he was unable ever to enjoy and to picture to himself in overly dark guises the situations he had to confront in life. [...] Since he could only dream of a certain happiness that he took to be enormous, his imagination could no longer find in life any pleasure or anything at all that seemed to make living worth the effort."

Compared to the original version, the gloss introduces the words "happiness," "enjoy," "pleasure," and "unable ever," which guide understanding, and it twice uses the word "certain," a marker of the subtext. But this is still insufficient, and Stendhal concludes: "I am unable to find a way of saying this honestly in the work: in the preface instead."[30] This key passage is a lesson in the subtext, given by the author himself, offering in a note a clearer rewriting of what he indicated obliquely in the novel itself.

Likewise, in the margin of the other excerpt cited previously, "I COULD LOVE HER! Me, wretched me," the Bucci manuscript has the comment: "Try to suggest *impotence*, insert here: *and how could I be loved by her?*"[31]

In light of these clarifications, some details take on added significance, like the visit to Abelard's tomb, or the promise made to Armance by Octave's mother, a statement heavy with tragic irony: "You will have the sweetness of being loved as few women are today."

Stendhal is just as clear in his correspondence as in the Bucci notes, and he goes even further. To Sutton Sharpe, he writes: "The hero Octave is *impotens*."[32] In a letter to Prosper Mérimée, entirely devoted to *Armance*, he asserts right off: "There are many more impotent men than you think," and he names this malady "Babilanism." He goes on bluntly to explain a detail in the novel that might appear confusing. During the week the newlyweds spent in Marseilles between their marriage and Octave's leaving for Greece, Armance was "happy" and experienced "the height of felicity," was "drunk with happiness and *swooning* [italics Stendhal's] in Octave's arms the night before his departure." The letter to Mérimée explains. "A skillful hand, a probing tongue gave Armance vivid climaxes. I am sure that many young girls do not know exactly what physical marriage entails. . . . In 2826, if civilization lasts . . . , I will relate how Olivier [the character's name was not yet Octave at the time of this letter] bought a Portuguese dildo of elastic rubber, carefully attached it to his waist, and with said dildo, etc."[33]

In view of these documents, whose authenticity is not in doubt, the reaction of some critics, including the most authoritative, has been puzzling. Instead of rejoicing at having paratexts at their disposal to enlighten and ground interpretation, they reject them, or else they become enraged as though deprived of the possibility to speculate as they like. One of them harrumphs: "Octave's character, Armance's, the extreme reserve Stendhal always displayed toward his readership, prevents us from thinking that *the happiness of this young wife* could derive in any way from the auxiliary means Stendhal cynically described in the Mérimée letter. The image of Armance, 'exhausted from happiness and *swooning* in the arms' of her husband must

The Subtle Subtext

not shake our opinion that the two spouses rigorously maintained separate bedrooms."[34]

Another critic would prefer the Mérimée letter not to exist and does not hesitate to write (seriously?), "One might almost regret that it has been preserved for us,"[35] while a third strives to belittle it: "It shows an intention of the author, but it in no way guarantees the meaning of a text."[36] Still others have thought that Octave's secret was homosexuality,[37] although there is no evidence in the novel of masculine attraction. Critics do not like having the meaning of a text dictated to them, even when the author himself does the dictating, so much so that Stendhal's novel is misunderstood (or, should I say, is differently understood?), despite its internal indications and despite the express statements of the novelist. These debates are instructive for problems of interpretation and enlarge upon previous remarks about the multiple difficulties inherent in the subtext: difficulty in knowing whether it is intentional, difficulty in understanding it, and, once understood, difficulty in being sure and in sharing one's certitude. In the present case, the risk of falling into arbitrariness is great, if one seeks not only to remove the author but also to contradict him. It is more judicious, it seems to me, to take into account all the items of the dossier and to accept the explanation that follows accordingly.

Balzac, who knew Stendhal well, recommended *Armance* to Domenico Fiore in 1841.[38] Did he have the novel in mind in 1836 when he wrote *La Vieille Fille* (*The Old Maid*)? Be that as it may, a parallel exists between the two works, for without resembling each other they show important affinities on this specific issue.

In his short novel, Balzac presents what amounts to a type of enigma in the character called du Bousquier. We learn that he had been a "speculator," a wheeler-dealer leading a luxurious and dissolute life during the Directoire, only to find himself suddenly ruined because of Napoleon Bonaparte's victory at Marengo, when he expected to enrich himself in anticipation of a French defeat. "This alternative, of millions to be gained and actual ruin, deprived the army supplier of all his faculties, he lost his mind for several days, having so abused his life with excess that this sudden upheaval found him enfeebled."[39]

At the time of the narrative, when the plot is centered in the city of Alençon, du Bousquier is in his forties, with "sharply etched facial features" and the "chest of the Farnese Hercules." But, as Balzac makes clear (he was an adept in physiognomy and a reader of its eighteenth-century Swiss proponent, Lavater), the man has "a flattened nose" and "he showed evidence of some clinical indicators contrasting with his general appearance," notably a "whispery" (*étouffée*) voice, "the voice of a worn-out speculator." One senses from the outset that external appearances can be deceptive.

Keeping the reader in mind, Balzac strews the novel with indicators like this: "Still in bed, du Bousquier mulled over his financial plans, for he was nothing if not ambitious, like all men who have squeezed the orange of pleasure too hard." With the rumor circulating that du Bousquier had a child with the beautiful Suzanne, an anonymous letter reveals that he "was never destined to amount to much in such adventures." Balzac even uses the word "impotent," although in a context that does not make the thrust of the adjective explicit: "Abrupt, energetic, his manner sweeping and brusque, curt and rough of speech, dark-complexioned, dark-haired, and dark-eyed, frightening to behold, in reality impotent as an insurrection, well did he represent the Republic."[40]

Du Bousquier, the liberal, is contrasted, both in personality and in intellectual bent, with a rival, the chevalier de Valois, his complete opposite, an elegant and witty monarchist, seemingly weak but "endowed with a prodigious nose," who will prove to be a great seducer. They are two types, representing two worlds, the old and the new, which collide in a changing society. In this sense, *The Old Maid* is a political fable.

The object of the two men's rivalry is the hand of the rich Mademoiselle Cormon, who after many plot twists chooses du Bousquier. "Finally the impotent Republic carried the day over the valiant aristocracy, and at the height of the Restoration." Alas, the novelist makes clear, it does the wife no good. "Madame du Bousquier would never be anything but Mademoiselle Cormon." Once married, du Bousquier becomes a leader in society but turns out to be a tyrant at home, and that is that. Word went round in the region: "Du Bousquier is quite powerful! . . . But unfortunately for his wife, this word is a horrible contradiction." "The most horrible of despotisms," the chevalier de Valois will say, "is that of the impotent riff-raff."

The Old Maid is therefore a story of a "fake marriage," of a marriage "essentially nonexistent." One might think the husband suffered from sterility, but that is not an adequate explanation, considering the word "impotent," used several times in the novel, and the word "Mademoiselle," which continues to be applied to Rose Cormon after her wedding. The subtext lets the reader understand that du Bousquier has lost his virility as a result of the physical and emotional shock he endured earlier when he lost his fortune. But we are still not done with the enigmas; for Balzac observes that "during the first two years of her marriage, Madame du Bousquier looked . . . quite satisfied" and that "sexual urges no longer troubled her, whereas previously "it was really true that sexual urges seriously troubled Mademoiselle Cormon in the opinion of the folk of Alençon," owing "to the trials of her endlessly and overly prolonged virginity." Balzac mentions her "occasional depressions" over not being pregnant. These contradictory bits of information have prompted commentaries that are not free of a certain confusion and seem all the more embarrassed since their authors, observing the rules of decency and good taste, do not permit themselves, just like the novelist, to use crude words and to call a spade a spade; it is possible, moreover, that the novelist's plan evolved during the course of writing.[41] So what, then, happened to Mademoiselle Cormon? To all appearances, the old maid in her inexperience thought she had consummated her marriage when in fact she had not. Her sensualist of a husband had more than one trick up his sleeve and knew how to satisfy her with means perhaps reminiscent of those mentioned earlier concerning Armance. Madame la Vicomtesse de Troisville and the old Marquise de Castéran will have to take her aside and open her eyes. "Madame du Bousquier was then disabused of the thousand disappointments of her marriage, and since she had remained 'zipped up,' she amused her confidantes with her delectable naiveté." Naturally, her misfortune made the rounds of the city. At first du Bousquier looked "odious and ridiculous," "but the ridicule eventually weakened." "At fifty-seven, the soft-spoken Republican seemed to many to have a right to retire from activity."

So here we have, once again, the example of a work built on allusions, one that puts to use, as the editor P.-G. Castex has highlighted, "a subtle rhetoric, which does not always proceed without obscurity."[42] Balzac had to bend to the linguistic norms of his time, what he elsewhere called "the prudish phraseology of the period,"[43] which did not allow expressing in frank terms certain physiological realities. But the allusive method, despite its being imposed, was not without its advantages. It titillated readers: when the novel was serialized in *La Presse*, "letters of indignation denouncing the novel's immorality poured in to the paper's editor," but they did nothing to stop the considerable increase in print runs.[44] From a literary point of view, the narrative's obscurity corresponded to the lived reality of the work's characters, for these did not know anything clearly either, with the exception, of course, of the interested party and some of his sexual partners.

If *Armance* and *The Old Maid* are not the best known of their authors' works, they still have an interest for the history of ideas about sexuality. Our two novelists chose to treat the topic of impotence seriously, to make it a factor weighing upon the entire narrative. They treat it within the context of marriage, considering the wives in a way that today might be thought a bit simplistic or condescending but displaying a largeness of mind that was not a given in their time. The very titles of the works reveal as much, since they feature women. Male torments are not forgotten, at least with Octave, but the reader is spared an overly detailed look inside men's pants to keep the heroine in the foreground by portraying her as the victim in the situation. The process of the subtext may have permitted expressing the feminine point of view, or at least it participates in this expression.

Balzac distinguished works where he allowed himself to be racy (the *Contes drolatiques, Droll Stories*) from *The Human Comedy* where he meant to depict married life. *The Old Maid* is in this latter vein. It also connects to the issue of *The Physiology of Marriage*, the concern for the rearing of girls with a view to their wifely estate, reiterated in the last pages of the novel with a humor that does not gainsay its seriousness: "If Mademoiselle Cormon had been educated, if a professor of anthropology had lived in the *département* of Orne, if finally she had read Ariosto, would the frightful misfortunes of her conjugal life have ever occurred?"[45]

This preoccupation jibes with what Stendhal expressed in the letter cited earlier, when he wrote, "Many young girls do not know exactly what physical marriage entails." Our two authors converge, and that explains why, in a sketch tacked onto *The Human Comedy*, Balzac introduces a character recognizable as Stendhal, who, in a salon, tells an anecdote illustrating and decrying the ignorance in which women are kept before marriage.[46]

The "Cunsciousness" of the President

Change of scene: even if not afflicted with impossibility, loves can have dire outcomes. Here is such a case.

On February 16, 1899, France was amazed to learn of the sudden death of the president of the Republic, Félix Faure.[47] Elected in 1895, he distinguished himself while in office with the care he took to maintain the dignity of his role, having the greatest regard for protocol and pomp, and earning himself the nickname "Sun President," recalling the sobriquet of Louis XIV, the Sun King. Fifty-eight, a dedicated hunter, he carried himself well. Only his intimates and doctors had noted signs of cardiac fatigue in this heavy smoker with the flushed complexion.

The official reports paint an edifying picture of the president's last day. That Thursday, feeling tired, he had canceled his daily horseback ride and devoted himself entirely to affairs of state. At the end of the afternoon, and now feeling unwell, he summoned his chief of staff, who immediately called for a doctor. The patient was conscious, but his condition worsened. Everyone was gathered around him, his associates, other doctors, priests, his wife and two daughters, until he began to lose consciousness. He breathed his last at ten o'clock in the evening.

Just one detail was kept in the dark: in the course of the fatal afternoon, the president had received a visit from Madame Steinheil, and it was while in her company that he experienced the onset of his illness. Marguerite Steinheil, called Meg, only in her thirties, was a *demi-mondaine* whom he had met two years earlier; she became his mistress. She was to find herself later, in 1908, at the center of a notorious court case in which she was acquitted of the charge of murdering her husband.[48] In the present moment, she left the president in an embarrassing situation. It was later said that he was discovered half-naked, his fingers still entwined in the lady's hair, which had to be cut to disentangle him. But this point is debated.

Despite the silence of the authorities, bits of information seeped out and rumors grew. Public opinion sensed that something was being kept secret, as this remark in *La Lanterne* for February 18 shows (the epitome of insinuation): "May we be permitted to observe what everyone was already observing yesterday evening and insistently commenting upon, namely, that this grief is shrouded in unusual, and poorly explained, mystery, just the sort of thing to cause I cannot say how much upset to public opinion, which was hardly expecting this disturbing news and will be as amazed as we are at confronting this web of silence, which may be perhaps nothing more than clumsiness but is in any case dangerous, because it leaves room for so many suspicions. . . ."

There was even a rumor that the president had been assassinated, which explains the article in the newspaper *L'Aurore* for February 19 headlined "Who Killed Him?" The *Journal du peuple* clearly answered on February 22: "We can confirm that he was not poisoned, but that he died by making the ultimate sacrifice to Venus, testing the limits of the *Code Napoléon* and the code of official ethics, of which he was the chief representative."[49]

The circumstances surrounding the decease, and all the conflicting versions in circulation, gave rise to speculation and wisecracks that were not always in good taste. Famous is the witticism of the leading politician Georges Clemenceau (we cite only the best of the best): "He wanted to be Caesar, he died Pompey"—not only a political put-down but a wicked pun on the Roman general's name and "*pompé*," vulgarly "blown." A fierce critic of Faure's, because the latter turned down the appeal of the Dreyfus case, Clemenceau provided the departed with a cruel epitaph in *L'Aurore* for February 17: "Félix

Faure has just died. No one in France is the less for it. Still, an attractive post is up for grabs. Claimants will not be wanting." Another epitaph is attributed to him: "Félix Faure has returned to nothingness; he must feel right at home." Others nicknamed Madame Steinheil "la pompe funèbre," again a wicked pun, literally "funeral obsequies," "Morticia," say, but really "The Fatal Blow." This apocryphal dialogue made the rounds: "The priest summoned for the last rites: 'Is the president still possessing his consciousness (*connaissance*)?' Guardsman of the Presidential Palace: 'No, Father, she has left by the back door.'"

Nevertheless, it was inconceivable in newspaper articles to mention the visit of Madame Steinheil explicitly, so they went about it indirectly.

On the day after the death, Léozon le Duc, in *Gil Blas* for February 17, devoted to Faure a portrait that was nuanced ("One could not reproach him for being detrimental any more than one could admire his accomplishments") but also enlivened by a suggestive sentence or two: "M. Félix Faure has gone in the pink of good health, actually because of his excess of good health. His death without suffering mirrored his happy life."

Or again, in the "Logbook" of *La Presse* for February 21:

Félix Faure has died! It seems impossible to me. What, this man dead, who only yesterday was alive and kicking, smiling and indefatigable! ... *Friday evening.* An intelligent woman of the world, after dinner, in intimate lamplight, tells me the gossip about the death of Félix Faure: "He departed in the daytime. ... Do you catch my meaning? You know, at his age one has to be prudent. The work stress in the life of a powerful man does not sit well with the workouts of Don Juan, upon my word, Pouf! ..." Here, a gentle gesture sends across the room the dark butterflies summoned by the Pouf. ...

This delightful exchange employs several characteristic features of the subtext: ambiguous words (alive and kicking, indefatigable), a question inviting collusion (Do you catch my meaning?), and generalization (work stress in the life, etc.). In short, people surmised, people hinted. It is in this context that one has to place the editorial from *Le Figaro* of February 17:

Monsieur Félix Faure died yesterday evening at 10 o'clock, carried off in two and one-half hours by an attack of apoplexy. Seeing him fighting fatigue and wearing out his assistants, one could never have imagined that this man in his 50s, vigorous and erect, was so close to death. Death was kind to him, since, without imposing upon him the long-suffering of sickness and the despair of cruelly felt separations, it still left him time to bid farewell to his own, to put his mind at rest, to prepare his soul for the great journey, and to beg like a good Christian the forgiveness of those against whom he had trespassed.

It is not without regret, however, that he had to quit this world below, where the risks of politics and the jolts of our national life had given him an office unhoped for, unexpected, if not unmerited. He savored its delights and intoxications with a boundless satisfaction whose honesty disarmed envy, and he fulfilled the duties of his office with devotion, tact, and firmness in the face of every test.

He tasted as well the various pleasures that multiplied and enhanced its attractions. . . .

I do not think that a word of hatred or truly deserved criticism will fall upon this coffin opened too soon.

After this homage, ordained as much by sincerity as courtesy, we may be permitted to think a little of the country and to ask what will be the consequences for it of this untimely death.

What is interesting about this eulogy is that there is no obvious subtext, if one can put it that way. First of all, it seems that this elegant prose aims to depict, all in all sympathetically, a parvenu who took up the highest office with energy and relish. One has to read more closely, taking the context into consideration, to understand that the author, the Dreyfusard Jules Cornély (1845–1907), founding member of the Union of French Journalists, carefully weighed his words and did not use by chance those evoking health and pleasure, in order to summon up with "courtesy," in a thoroughly equivocal manner, what he did not say expressly.

The way in which journalists reported the death of Faure illustrates the statement of a character of Paul Morand, the *bon vivant* wit, brilliant writer, and Vichy diplomat, in a narrative entitled, fittingly, *Shut Up*: "The press doesn't always say what it's thinking, it doesn't always think what it's saying, but it always thinks what it is not saying. IMPLIED, there's the big secret."[50]

8

What About Being Frank?

Perhaps amid this onslaught of subtlety ancient and modern, readers will have asked themselves at some point whether it would not be simpler just to talk frankly and say outright what one has to say in the first place, avoiding any other level of meaning. It seems to go without saying. The study of the subtext would therefore not be complete if it did not take into account its opposite, frankness, which is a path, let it be said immediately, that is as full of pitfalls as it is of promise.

Death to the Subtext!

The subtext certainly does arouse hostility. The great Catholic poet Charles Péguy, for example, gets carried away against those who write "between the lines." "The strictly classic high style," "the strictly French high style" consisted, he thought, in writing and reading "within the lines" and required banishing all forms of connivance. The epithet "discontemporary" (*mécontemporain*) that Alain Finkielkraut has applied to him[1] fits him here like a glove:

> It is even one of the cardinal superstitions, the cardinal vices, of the modern world, this idea, this illusion, this error, that one who writes between the lines is allegedly superior in some way to one who writes within them, that he possesses a kind of silent and latent superiority that makes the aware, the hip, smile; I do not know what superior understanding and secret sharing makes them, ever so discreetly, wink their eyes, these witty ones, once they are clued in; this is also, this is eminently, a French vice, intolerable, worldly, one of the most disagreeable of all the innumerable French vices, a hateful vice of veritable frivolity.[2]

Another scourge is the critic René Pommier, who made it his business to overturn all sorts of exceedingly far-fetched and, he thought, utterly fantastic interpretations, especially in literary criticism, summing up his polemics with the funny outburst "Decoding Deschmoding!"[3] In the eyes of its detractors, there is something really convoluted and off-putting about the subtext. It betrays a hermetic, elitist bent, as if basic truths could not be openly revealed. It harks back to a social state of closeted constraint. It evokes secrecy, dissimulation, taboo. Ultimately, it is immoral, an engine of deception and manipulation. People in Antiquity used to cite two lines of Homer that seemed to contain in essence all the possible criticisms against speaking, so to say, "with forked tongue": "For as I detest the doorways of Death, I detest that man, who / hides one thing in the depths of his heart, and speaks forth another."[4] What is more, the subtext spotlights a disturbing reality, the malleability of language. It shows that there are several ways of saying the same thing effectively: just as one can mold a piece of wax as he pleases, a message can take several forms, like an admonition that can be expressed just as well as an accusation or some suggested advice or a question.[5]

In the ancient schools of declamation, abuse of double-meaning discourse was criticized. No sooner was a topic assigned than certain orators undertook to treat it in unnecessarily figured fashion, desiring to shine by showing off their refinement and virtuosity. The "rush to figures,"[6] when it would have been better to speak simply, became a banal tick. This was the failing of the expert, Junius Otho. While he was orating, his listeners had the impression that his line of argument was sound, but they wound up asking themselves in amazement why he had not said it all more directly. When someone makes a mystery out of something that could be openly expressed, he "is whispering *The Congressional Record* in your ear."[7] Another, one Moschus, who had a penchant for verbal fussiness, became the target of an associate's mockery, who greeted him by resorting to the same tactic. Running into him one morning in Marseilles, instead of just saying, "Hello, Moschus," he humorously jibed, "I could have said: Hello, Moschus."[8] His parodic use of a figured flourish instead of a plain, everyday expression sought to reveal the absurdity of the stunt.

But there is an even more radical criticism, the subtext's futility. An objection as famous as it was stinging circulated in rhetorical circles: "What good is a figure if it is understood? What good is it if it is not understood?"[9] Given that the method of figured discourse consists in insinuating without saying, this criticism poses a dilemma: either listeners understand what has been left implicit, in which case there is little use in enveloping it with figured speech, or they do not comprehend, and the figured speech also serves no purpose. This apparently devastating objection deserves a response. Should the subtext be dismissed as superfluous, or even impossible? Yes and no; it depends on the objective of the discourse. When informing or instructing in a disinterested and factual manner, the alternative "either say it or do not say it" can be justified; the objection applies, and doing without the subtext is conceivable. It is when the issue is communicating and persuading that the discourse has grounds for borrowing from indirection. Thanks to implicit suggestion, a speaker is able to act upon listeners without their awareness, or he can make them understand things tacitly, through collusion, without the need to say anything expressly, or he can even induce them to discover on their own what they have not been told. This is why the subtext exists.

In short, criticisms and rejections do not rule out, happily, what has been said in the previous chapters concerning the utility and ubiquity of the subtext. But these reactions do reflect the thoroughly legitimate concern for seeking something else, another way. They betray a yearning for frankness, sincerity: "Free speech," as the contemporary rallying cry would have it.

Talking Turkey, for Better, for Worse

Of course, there exist any number of situations that call for direct expression, without mental reservation or subtext, like confession, testifying, satire, or cheers ("So-and-so for president!"). In these cases one may say, with Molière, that "speech has been given to man to set forth his thinking":[10] the exact opposite of Stendhal's aphorism cited earlier,[11] which is really a reversal of the common opinion. But the Molière passage is comic, and Doctor Pancrace, who is asserting the need for explaining what is on one's mind, is just then cutting off his interlocutor and preventing him from speaking. Once more, things are not as pat as they seem, and we find interesting complications.

Take the case of friendship. In theory, it is the friend's role to speak frankly, should there be some unpleasant truth to discuss. Yet moralists have observed that, even in the context of such a relationship, it is sometimes better to sweeten one's remarks and present them obliquely. Frankness is like a medicine: carelessly administered, it risks doing harm. "Causing unnecessary pain is the nastiest way to disavow flattery."[12] We must not be too quick to label sweeteners "insincere," lest, without them, our speech becomes "rude" and "ineffective."[13]

Likewise, moral theologians in the seventeenth century counseled preachers not to criticize too sharply and to use instead a more watered-down approach, not so much because they feared reprisals, thinking that directness was dangerous, but rather because it risked being pointless. For it is only too true that the powerful do not examine their consciences gladly, and they do not heed faultfinding unaccompanied by flattery.[14]

"Tell it all," "The whole truth and nothing but the truth," and "State the obvious" are commands whose implementation is not always easy or desirable, something doctors know quite well when delivering a diagnosis to a patient. History and literature are full of characters who would have done better to hold their tongues and not said what they were thinking, going all the way back to Thersites, the deformed and brazen loudmouth of the *Iliad*,[15] up to the nasty Toto in the satirist Georges Courteline's *Coco*, who cannot keep from mentioning the nose of General Suif, even though his parents have previously preached to him that he should not make the slightest allusion to the valiant soldier's disfigurement.[16] The unveiling of intimate thoughts is best left for "interludes," as in Eugene O'Neill's *Strange Interlude*. The quest for transparency cost Rousseau dear.[17] Often, direct expression shocks and surprises, as happened one day to Laurence Sterne when he had the honor of traveling with Madame de Rambouillet. As she was stopping the carriage, he asked her "if she wanted anything—*Rien que pisser*, said Madame de Rambouillet"[18] to her flabbergasted and slightly discombobulated traveling companion (the French is in Sterne's text: "only to piss").

To sum up, if one "talks turkey," to use a folksy turn of phrase, calling things by their name, one risks losing the advantages of the subtext, security and civility. "One forsakes ambiguity at his peril," so goes a rather cynical maxim attributed to Cardinal de Retz.[19] And philosopher Emil Cioran, nobody's fool, as always:[20] "Useless to construct this model of frankness: *life is only tolerable to the degree of mystification one puts in it*. Such a model would be the sudden ruin of society, the 'sweetness' of life in common residing in the impossibility of giving free rein to the infinity of our hidden thoughts. It is because we are, all of us, imposters that we put up with one another. Someone who would not accept lying would see the earth crumble beneath his feet: we are *biologically* bound to the false."

In these circumstances, the rejection of the subtext, on the contrary, becomes an expressive choice, or at least a weapon. Theodor Adorno went so far as to write that speaking directly, tossing in someone else's face what one has to say, smacks of fascism.[21]

Certain linguists, moreover, have maintained that it is impossible to speak directly and that every utterance carries an implied content in addition to its explicit meaning.[22] A simple remark like "It's cold today" never boils down, they say, to mere mention of the temperature but always contains a message, which, depending on the situation, can be: "Shut the door," "Turn on the furnace," "Let's move to another room," even "You are not being very nice to me."

And so we come full circle. The same objections addressed to the subtext apply to direct expression: dangerous or disagreeable character, uselessness, impossibility. To understand this connection, it is necessary to deepen the study of frankness, with the aid of established theories.

Boldness

A Latin rhetorical treatise, the *Rhetoric to Herennius*, devotes three pages to a figure of thought called "license" or "boldness" (*licentia*), the berating of those one is supposed to respect or fear.[23] A tribune of the people will reproach citizens who have given their votes to the enemies of the *plebs*. An attorney will fault judges for deferring their decision instead of condemning the accused forthwith. The speaker breaks the rules or fails to observe the requisite deference in order to assert his right and to rectify a mistake. But how to go about it? Will he expose the bald truth? By no means. On the contrary, the Latin rhetorician counsels mitigation. For example, one may temper an acrimonious statement with compliments ("I appeal to your courage, your wisdom") or with protestations of affection ("Talking to you as a friend").

More subtly, our author continues, one can happily feign boldness by using a tone all the more heated the less controversial the actual content. One may criticize listeners as they themselves wish to be criticized: "You are too good, too merciful, too trusting." Or a speaker will make a big confession, pretending to fear the listener's reaction, an inconsequential and even flattering avowal: "I am not sure how you are going to take this, but I will say it anyway: you have deprived me of a friend, for I have chosen to renounce this man's friendship, since he was your enemy."

Against all expectation, what looked like boldness at the start is transformed in attenuation and flattery. That explains why this discussion is a part of figure theory. In principle, Quintilian remarks, boldness should not be a stylistic procedure, since it consists in expressing oneself overtly, but vaunted freedom is, precisely, often nothing more than an appearance behind which adulation lurks.[24] Thus it is that sincerity becomes a rhetorical figure! This confirms our initial statement: direct expression is a complicated matter, as difficult to analyze as it is to use.

The Subtle Subtext

Michel Foucault Confronts Frankness

We owe to Michel Foucault a modern attempt to conceptualize frankness and plumb its implications. He devoted his last research efforts to this theme, research made available to readers some twenty years after his death, thanks to the publication in three volumes of courses he gave at the Collège de France from 1981 to 1984, entitled *The Hermeneutics of the Subject, The Government of Self and Others*, and *The Courage of Truth*.[25] Foucault chose to highlight the Ancient Greek noun *parrhêsia* (the stress falls on the "i"),[26] a word rich in meaning, which encompasses etymologically the act of "saying everything," whence "freedom of speech" and "frankness." This is the word the rhetoricians use to designate in Greek the figure of "boldness" that we have just been discussing,[27] and to identify the opposite of figured speech.[28] It was used, however, much more broadly, occurring often outside of rhetoric, in different authors and different contexts. By keeping the Greek term instead of being content with a French translation like *"franc-parler"* ("frankness"), Foucault in effect enshrines it, emphasizing its polyvalence and establishing it as a philosophical concept. All in all, Foucault's various writings and discussions about parrhêsia amount to a good thousand pages or so. They are a standard reference work, and for that reason they merit our tarrying here awhile, looking at them from our own perspective.

Foucault came upon parrhêsia at the end of a series of investigations that he had rehearsed several times or, rather, that he had recomposed after the fact in the introductions of his books and courses. Without going back all the way to the earliest publications, we can take as our point of departure the inaugural lecture, given in 1970, *The Order of Discourse*, in which he untangles the concepts of speech and truth. Foucault observed that every society produces various discourses and that these are set forth as true: for example, medical discourse, psychiatric discourse, sociological discourse, penal discourse, which define officially who is sick, who is crazy, who is asocial, who is delinquent. These discourses betray a "will for truth" based on "institutional support."[29] The study of these discourses, which vary in every period, is portrayed as a history of the "will to know,"[30] a "history of the truth."[31]

Then the notion of the subject intervenes, representing a "displacement"[32] of the question, to the extent that Foucault was no longer examining discourses of truth for themselves but the "subjectivity" they express: "On the other hand, it seemed to me that it would be equally interesting to analyze the conditions and forms of the type of act by which the subject *manifests* himself when speaking the truth, by which I mean thinks of himself and is recognized by others as speaking the truth."[33]

Foucault is interested, therefore, in "the discourse of truth which the subject is likely and able to speak about himself"—for example, "avowal, confession, examination of conscience."[34] He notes that a precept of ancient Delphic wisdom has defined the effort one makes in knowing and saying the truth about oneself and in obtaining awareness of one's own limits: Know Thyself (*gnôthi seauton*). But he judged that this precept, as famous as it is, does not settle the question, and that the "know thyself" is part of a larger problematic, "care of oneself, application to oneself" (*epimeleia heautou*).[35] Self-concern then leads him to frankness. "I saw a figure emerge who was constantly present as the indispensable partner, at any rate the almost necessary helper in this obligation to tell the truth about oneself." This figure is "the other person who listens and enjoins one to speak, and who speaks himself." His qualification is "a practice, a certain way of speaking, which is called, precisely, *parrhêsia* (free-spokenness)."[36] Care of oneself requires exposing oneself to the judgment of the other; one who speaks the truth wants to receive it in return. For that a counselor or director is needed, who speaks frankly, in the name of his personal subjectivity, and who holds sway. This is the source of the word "government" in the titles of the final courses: the government of self harks back to the care of self, the government of others to parrhêsia.

The Varieties of Frankness

In its most ancient and most current meaning, parrhêsia (plus its derivatives) belongs to the political domain and designates the freedom of speech granted to all citizens in democracies, Athens in particular, at least theoretically. It is the right of "the citizen in the public space," as Luigi Spina puts it,[37] a right that plays a critical role in the history of Greek institutions. All express themselves freely, and then the majority opinion prevails. There exists, additionally, a second type of political parrhêsia: the act of speaking by which the weak individual, in the face of power, decries the injustice that victimized him or her. Such individuals assert their right in public and challenge the mighty in the name of their own personal authority and their own courage.[38]

To these political forms, Foucault opposes what he characterized as a "new problematic of *parrhêsia*,"[39] envisaging it as an ethical attitude and a technical procedure aiming to guide the individual conscience. This was the aspect that really interested him and about which he thought he had the most to contribute to the existing discussion on the topic.[40]

Telling the truth is the issue, but what does that mean?[41] To prove it? No, because the counselor does not accomplish a scientific demonstration; he gives advice. To persuade? No, because that would be a rhetorical matter (I will get back to this point). To teach? No, because the counselor does not act like a pedagogue, his sole aim is not to endow a subject with abilities, with previously unpossessed knowledge; rather, he seeks to change the manner of being of this entity he addresses. To debate? No, because the counselor does not want to confront his interlocutor in a competitive, antagonistic manner. His intention is not to have a point of view prevail. Following upon these negative responses, frankness, as Foucault defines it, appears as an individual and specific choice that is defined by the speaker's role. He is neither braggart nor jokester: parrhêsia exists when the speaker courts a risk in telling the truth and has a personal stake in this effort. He does not merely tell the truth, he says what he actually believes to be true and is determined to proclaim because he has concluded a sort of pact with himself, a pact requiring him to be free and courageous and to exercise "the profession of truth,"[42] the "free questioning of men's conduct by a truth-telling which accepts the risk of danger to itself."[43]

Compared to the political and institutional frankness previously discussed, this new form of frankness has a far larger frame of reference. It is no longer connected only with democracy and can have a place in autocratic regimes, when the counselor addresses a king or tyrant to act upon his character and shape his being. It proceeds from an ethical choice and ends up identifying itself with philosophical discourse. Indeed, philosophic individuals, three preeminently, embody frankness by their courage to tell the truth to kindred spirits. Socrates, according to Plato's *Apology*, busied himself in encountering his fellow citizens and pestering them with questions in order to get them to recognize that they were mistaken about the meaning of life, values, their own selves; and they made him pay for it, condemning him to death. Plato, in turn, defined an ideal of "veridiction"[44] in politics. The third and final representative of parrhêsia is the Cynic philosopher, Diogenes in particular, who seeks wisdom by means of physical and provocative conduct. The cynic breaks with society's accepted rules and values; he desires to be self-sufficient, a global citizen, and in harmony with nature. That is why frankness is one of his characteristics. The words and the entire way of Cynic living are "a manifestation of the truth," "the scandal of the truth."[45]

What About Being Frank?

Weighing in the Balance

To assess briefly, then, "this great history of *parrhêsia* and truth-telling."[46] The work of Foucault is the leading study, both quantitatively and qualitatively, that exists on a difficult concept, what he calls a "spidery kind of notion" (*notion-araignée*),[47] and his contribution consists in bringing out the least recognized aspect of the topic. For the majority of commentators, the most stimulating question, with incessantly amplified contemporary resonance, is political freedom of speech. For Foucault this was secondary; he preferred to insist on the truth discourse of the counselor and the director of conscience in an ethical and personal relationship. He still remained within a basically pagan context and did not have time to consider the evolution of the problem in Christianity.[48]

Rather than a historical description, he elaborated a model built on ancient texts that were transferable to later periods. The parrhêsiast, he who risks exposing the unvarnished truth, is a figure with many guises, like princely counselor, government minister, political critic.[49] Cynicism for Foucault was an especially fruitful and significant stance, not limited to the ancient philosophy but with many recognizable avatars in the West, be they ascetics, revolutionaries, devotees of the artistic life, and including militants, nihilists, and leftist politics.[50]

The topic also had real-world ramifications; for at the time, at the beginning of Mitterrand's first term as president, a debate arose in France over the responsibilities of intellectuals, whom some pilloried for being silent and for not lending a hand to the left in power.[51] Foucault's research on parrhêsia could be seen as a contribution to this debate—an essentially negative one, since Foucault, who was not a big militant and preferred to support causes on an individual basis, demonstrated that the idea of an intellectual engaged with those in power is nebulous. He felt that there was a need to go as far back as classical antiquity truly to understand the issue, thereupon to discern a very high bar of truth and courage, something, in short, beyond the reach of the current culture. During those years, Foucault intervened against the government or in some way annoyed it, opposing the policies of General Wojciech Jaruzelski in Poland, or not hesitating to hit back in the affair of the so-called Irishmen of Vincennes, whom the government falsely accused of terrorism: "When socialists speak of the silence of intellectuals, they are speaking of their own silence and their own regret that they have nothing to offer in the way of political thought or reason."[52]

Personally, Foucault remained faithful to the program begun a dozen years earlier. In his focusing on parrhêsia, one recognizes the fundamental intuition that truth, power, and "subjectivity" are not immutable and universal standards but exist shaped by contingent and changing discourses. The slogan of frankness is not "I speak the truth"; it is, rather, I speak *my* truth, in the name of my ethos, in certain circumstances, before a certain type of interlocutor, in view of a certain objective. This did not prevent, however, a difference in method compared to his earlier efforts; for, in the case of parrhêsia, the philosopher displayed a kind of empathy toward his subject. As Susan Jarratt has rightly observed, one no longer recognizes the subversive spirit, whether Nietzschean or iconoclastic, that Foucault had demonstrated on other occasions.[53] His is a classical approach, based on canonical texts of Greco-Roman literature and on great figures from ancient history. Not insisting on critical distance, unwilling to bring to light differing witnesses or unexploited sources, Foucault tends to espouse the viewpoint of his authors. With Plutarch, he praises Plato and denigrates Dionysius of Syracuse; with Thucydides, he praises Perikles.[54] In this way, Foucault offers a sort of manifesto in favor of an ideal of parrhêsia assimilated to the philosophic discourse of Socrates and Diogenes.

This word "discourse" brings up the problem of the connection to rhetoric. Foucault highlighted the ties between parrhêsia and rhetoric but sought to erect a barrier between the two, because rhetoric, as he conceived it, was by definition a traditional and opportunistic art of persuasion, using false and manipulative arguments, while parrhêsia, on the contrary, was a candid and truth-telling stance.[55] He nursed an undeniable grudge against rhetoric, in line with a still widespread feeling in French philosophy of his time, inducing him to isolate parrhêsia at all costs, since it was something he held dear and idolized. This isolating, this barrier has been justly criticized.[56] In sum, Foucault made rhetoric perhaps too ugly and frankness too handsome. Better to accept parrhêsia in its totality, not only as a stance taken toward life but also as a discourse befitting this stance; whether one calls this "rhetoric" or not is secondary. As for the political-legal aspect, the existence of a discourse of parrhêsia is obvious; when the citizen wants to speak truthfully, that is, frankly, and to set forth his viewpoint during democratic deliberations, he can only do so by addressing the assembly of the people and using oratory. As for ethical parrhêsia, it too supposes a discourse, because the philosopher questions the powerful, reprimands them, admonishes them. This speech is characterized by a content (the moral message), by the position of the speaker (the philosopher, with the authority his courage and way of life confer on him), by the status of the recipient (the wealthy individual, the sovereign), by the objective of the speech (having an effect on someone else), and by procedures (such as irony, criticism, or invective). Foucault's work thus permits us to identify several types of discourse, which obey rules as well as specific and convergent ends, all with the goal of telling the truth. These are the discourses of frankness.

Two Sides of the Same Coin

Foucault was not interested in the subtext and so has no cause to observe what for us is essential—namely, that frankness is the opposite of the subtext, or, if one prefers, subtext is the opposite of frankness. A deep kinship unites these two notions and they are like the obverse and the reverse, two sides of the same coin. It is telling that Foucault relied on Dio Chrysostom's *Fourth Discourse on Kingship* to illustrate the candor of Diogenes, his life literally laid bare to the gaze of all, and his quality as true king; but Foucault did not notice the ploys and double meanings characterizing Dio's work. In Foucault's account, Dio's discourse emerges as a reference work on parrhêsia; in the present undertaking, it has provided an illustration of the subtext.[57]

Subtext and frankness are forms of speech, and truth is what they have in common, hence the paradoxical complementarity that unites them. In the first case, one transmits in veiled manner truths not easy to say or understand. In the second, one reclaims or arrogates to him- or herself the right of being frank, rhyming verity and liberty, like a character in Racine: "Je répondrai, Madame, avec la liberté / D'un soldat qui sait mal farder la vérité" (I will answer, Madam, with a soldier's liberty / one poorly equipped to travesty verity).[58] We are dealing, then, with two parallel ways. As a right and duty to say what one is thinking and to speak openly and truly, parrhêsia in all its forms presents itself as an alternative solution to counterbalance the subtext. But parallel lines tend to meet; that is where the paradox lies. Indeed, frankness is often less direct and spontaneous than one might assume. It results from maturely considered choice and consists in a subtle and conditioned approach, using ploys and laden with ulterior motives. To sum up, speaking simply is not so simple. It is an option that harbors as many complications as the subtext.

9

Catalog of Further Examples and Practices

This final chapter is a running, random list of concepts, methods, and fields, some of them not widely known, meant to enrich the depiction of the subtext. The catalog makes no claim to in-depth study.

The Hidden Clue

One may call the "hidden clue" the insertion of an offhand reflection into a narrative, which casts the entire presentation in a new light. The Greek rhetoricians analyzed this tactic, illustrating it with a speaker who, after elaborating on an opinion with which the listener readily agrees, introduces finally, as incidental, a more important addition that is his most critical, or most risky, point, and his true gist.[1] Leo Strauss, in turn, imagined the case of a historian living in a totalitarian country, who might lay out carefully, even tediously, accepted ideas before presenting the opposite opinion in three or four jarring sentences to give his readers a fleeting glimpse of "forbidden fruit."[2]

An example from Antiquity is the encomium of Athens (the *Panathenaicus*) written by Aelius Aristides in the second century AD. The orator surveys the city's history, from mythological times to Philip of Macedon's decisive victory over the Greeks at the battle of Chaeronea (338 BC), and after more than one hundred pages he appears to remember that, at the time he was writing, Athens belonged to the Roman Empire. He then slips in two sentences to recall this new situation.[3] Following his usual practice, he expresses no criticism; on the contrary, he asserts that Athens prospers under Roman domination because it is freed of the political and military responsibilities it previously had to shoulder, while still enjoying its prestige and preeminence. Essentially, Athens is relieved of burdensome duties and left only with advantages. So is everything for the best? If we examine the text more closely, we notice two nuances. Athens today is "almost" (*mikrou dein*) as prosperous today as in the past, and one would "not easily" (*mê rhadiôs*) desire its return to its former status. Allowing these words their full weight betrays some reservation and casts doubt upon the vaunted approval. Occupying ten lines in total, the remarks raise the question, the essential question, of Athens's situation in the Roman Empire (and, through Athens, the situation of all the Greeks), and they imply that this evaluation of the situation is not straightforward. The issue was a sensitive one, which Aristides, therefore, did not want to pass over in silence. Yet neither did he want to confront it directly, judging it more effective to include telling words surreptitiously within his text. It was up to listeners and readers to discover them and personally to draw the meaningful conclusions.

Moving on from politics to literary creation, we highlight two admirably hidden clues in twentieth-century novels.[4]

In Proust's *The Guermantes Way*, the following remark occurs: "before the invisible vocation of which this book is the history declared itself."[5] This is a highly important statement, since it reveals ahead of time the novel's true subject—how the narrator became a writer—which will be revealed in *Time Regained*. "This is the first time in *In Search of Lost Time* that one finds a prolepsis or anticipation concerning the work that will be fulfilled, a work we, the readers, are in the process of reading."[6] But this phrase within a sentence that encapsulates everything receives absolutely no emphasis and remains as something hidden within the monumentality of the whole enterprise.

In Alain Robbe-Grillet's *La Jalousie* (*Jealousy*) we find: "It is no doubt the same poem that continues on. If the themes sometimes fade, it is to come back, a little later, strengthened, almost identical. Yet these repetitions, these tiny variations, these interruptions, these fallings backward can give rise to modifications, even if barely discernible, leading in the long run quite far from the point of origin."[7] If these observations deal, in the first instance, with a native song heard on a plantation, they also apply to the novel itself, for its structure is actually composed of scenes, nearly identical, that are repeated and rewritten with variations. One is in the presence here, as critics have remarked, of a metaliterary commentary that explains and justifies the chosen style of narration, all the while remaining doubly discreet both because of its position deep inside the novel and because of its allusive character, resting, as it does, on a "mise en abyme."[8]

How to Respond to the Subtext

The subtext is like an unseen dart that sticks in the wound after one is hit and that is difficult to extract, precisely because it is invisible.[9] The harder one tries, the greater the risk of worsening the situation. In other words, it is dangerous to refute what has only been hinted at; it would be much easier to react to something said openly. So what, then, are the best ways of responding to the subtext? According to Quintilian, there are principally two: one may rise up and openly state the insinuation to refute it, or else one may assume a look of incomprehension and continue as if nothing had occurred.[10] A third way may be added, defined by the Greeks as "antifiguration" (*antiskhêmatismenos*), which is trying to outsmart by answering a subtext with another subtext.[11]

At the opening night of Alexandre Dumas père's *Mademoiselle de Belle-Isle*, Balzac ran into the author on the stairway of the Théâtre Français. "When I am all dried up, I will try playwriting," Balzac said to him, revealing a certain amount of sour grapes over the playwright's success. The latter took care not to acknowledge the insult directly but without missing a beat riposted, "Start right away, my dear."[12]

Here is another, more recent example: a witty exchange in 2016 between Nicolas Sarkozy, former president of the French Republic, and François Hollande, the incumbent, as reported in a satirical weekly.[13] After the two had held foreign policy discussions, Sarkozy asked Hollande, "So, what about this primary business?," alluding to the announcement of a coming primary election on the left to choose a presidential nominee in 2017. The spiteful question underlined the difficulty in which Hollande found himself, having not yet decided whether he would be a candidate. Just as maliciously, Hollande replied, "So, what about this primary business?" For Sarkozy was indeed a candidate in the primary on the right and center, his still uncertain victory making his life difficult, too. In this subdued exchange, innuendo answered innuendo, and all the more effectively in that repeating the same words made sense, two identical statements having an opposite meaning and serving as a weapon for each camp. One knows what followed: both men are now former presidents.

The Fairy Tales of Charles Perrault

Everybody is familiar with *Little Red Riding Hood* or *Puss in Boots*. If the tales in all their simplicity delight so many readers, it is because of the narrative structures and psychological archetypes they employ. Basing himself on these observations, Marc Fumaroli brought to light a further dimension: the "second meaning" supporting royal policy.[14] Charles Perrault (1628–1703) was an important figure on the literary and political scene during the reign of Louis XIV as an advocate for the cause of the Moderns in the Quarrel of the Ancients and the Moderns; he was also supervisor of the king's buildings and Colbert's right-hand man. Thus, his *Tales* are full of allusions to the events of his time. For example, the theme of the "toilette" (found in *Cinderella* with the stepsisters' quest for elegance and the magnificent dress Cinderella received from her fairy godmother) reflects the development of haute couture, jewelry, and hairdressing in Louis XIV's court. The ogres, those ravenous monsters who inhabit the forest and castles (in *Little Thumb* or *Bluebeard*) evoke the feudal aristocracy whom the king was trying to get rid of. Perrault's *Tales* emerge as an allegory of economic and social change and celebrate the progress made under the Sun King. But this message is not explicitly stated; it leaves itself to be discovered, making it all the more persuasive. Following the words of Fumaroli: "The *Tales*' allegorical structure has probably not been adequately discerned, a structure that allows them to double back on themselves in a literal meaning of pure narrative delight and in a second meaning quietly polemic and apologetic. . . . The collection of the *Tales*, in its own day and for some time to come, aims to raise in muted fashion . . . the cause of the Moderns. . . . It is this impressive ensemble of 'progress' that the second collection of Perrault's *Tales* celebrates under various veils."

Dionysius at Corinth

When King Philip of Macedon was threatening the Spartans, they replied to him, "Dionysius at Corinth," alluding to the fact that Dionysius the Younger, tyrant of Syracuse, had taken refuge at Corinth after being overthrown in 344 BC. The three words were a scathing reply that implied an entire line of reasoning: Dionysius, who was more powerful than you, was reduced to the condition of a mere individual, exiled in a foreign city; you, Philip, could suffer the same fate. This expression became proverbial and is cited as an example of meaningful conciseness and laconic speech, befitting Spartans.[15] Short and cryptic, the statement draws its force from the recipient's having to surmise the meaning and supply the missing elements.

Diction and Phrasing

In a written text, the merest comma may count.[16] In oral delivery, there are the ways of enunciating the sentence—tone, pauses, flow, all the things linguists call "prosodic acts"[17]—to reinforce meaning. Thus, in Sophocles's *Oedipus Tyrannos*, the Chorus Leader says to the Messenger who is looking for Oedipus: "Here is his palace, stranger, and there you will find him. / Here is she whom he has for wife and mother of his children."[18]

This response is equivocal. Recited in one breath to the end, the second verse means that Jocasta is the wife of Oedipus and the mother of his children (his two sons, Eteocles and Polynices, and his two daughters, Antigone and Ismene). But if one observes a pause after "mother," the verse secretly reveals that Jocasta is simultaneously both Oedipus's wife and his mother (and the mother of his children as well), exposing the terrible incest of which no one in the play is yet aware. Ancient and medieval commentators on this reply speak of "ambiguity"[19] and "figured speech."[20] Indeed, expressions with multiple meaning, enabled by the play of pauses, sprouted all over in figured declamations. For example, in a classroom exercise where the assignment concerns a father carrying on an incestuous relationship with his daughter, the latter, being unable to bring herself to accuse the guilty man directly, hints at the truth in the following exchange: "Father: Who raped you? Daughter: You, father, don't you know?"[21] The effect rests on the tone used in the response "You, father" and on how the pause is observed after these words. There is a similar situation in another declamation, where the father is the lover, this time, of his daughter-in-law, and his son surprises him hiding his face as he comes out of the woman's bedchamber. In the courtroom, turning to his father, the son recounts the scene as follows: "Having grabbed the lover, I cried out, father, it is you whom I was looking all over for."[22] If one separates the words "father, it is you," as representing the son's cry, they make clear the identity of the hooded adulterer; if, instead, one marks a pause after "cried out" and the phrase "it is you whom I have been looking all over for" is delivered as a separate proposition, appearances are maintained.

The following elegant turn is attributed to the great nineteenth-century actor Frédérick Lemaître, called "the lion of the boulevard." Needing to apologize for having viewed the audience as a "bunch of idiots," he reportedly came forward and said: "Gentlemen, I claimed that you were a bunch of idiots, it is true, I offer my apologies, I am mistaken."[23] Now *there* is a cunningly ambiguous statement! At first glance, "it is true" and "I am mistaken" bear on "I claimed that you were a bunch of idiots," and the guilty party clearly begs forgiveness. But, if "it is true" bears upon "a bunch of idiots," and "I am mistaken" on "I offer my apologies," the contrition morphs into impertinence. This anecdote shows the rich potential of diction and phrasing.

Telling the Truth

"Two Jews meet in a railway car at the station in Galicia, Poland. 'Where are you going?' asks one. 'To Cracow,' answers the other. 'What a liar you are,' the first retorts. 'If you say you are going to Cracow, you want me to think that you are going to Lemberg. But I happen to know that you really are going to Cracow. So why are you lying?'"[24] This funny story, reported and analyzed by Freud, challenges the very act of telling the truth. It reminds us, in its "skeptical" fashion, to use Freud's word, that what matters is not only the content of words but the way the recipient receives them, and that saying the truth can be a means of suggesting the false. In the case at hand, the traveler off to Cracow perhaps did not expressly intend to confuse things, and the responsibility for the misunderstanding rests with his interlocutor, who is overly suspicious. But one may also imagine, in other situations, deliberate manipulation in telling the truth as a way to fool the other because one knows full well that he will not be believed. The card player who "says he passes may be concealing a good hand (first-degree cleverness), or maybe he is lying to us by telling us the truth so as to make us doubt it (cleverness squared)."[25]

Lip Service

Paying lip service means not committing oneself to what one says, sensing and recognizing a distance between the content of one's words and one's true intent. Often the recipient understands what is going on, and the distancing is mutual. This reserve can be gentle, in the case of subdued love, for instance, as the chanteuse Barbara used to sing: "Speak to me half-heartedly / I will listen with half my heart." But lip service becomes acidic when it is reluctant praise and the recipient is unreceptive. For reasons difficult to pinpoint, having to do, perhaps, quite simply with our own personal vanity, praise is a touchy subject. Sometimes the praise directed our way flatters us or arouses our suspicions; praise awarded others, or that others award themselves, irks us; and praise we are forced to give pains us. Being closely bound up with the emotions of the human comedy, praise accordingly lends itself to multiple meanings and subtexts. Lauders, rightly or wrongly, give the impression of saying too much, or of not saying enough, or of slipping in devious innuendos. Nietzsche, who was exceptionally perspicacious, almost morbidly so, about these problems, frequently sketched out cases of forced praise from both angles, where doubt and subtext equally contend. These little episodes speak for themselves:

PRAISE. You see someone who wants to praise you. You bite your lips; your heart shrivels. O, that this cup might pass from you! But it does not pass; it comes near! Let us drink in, then, the sweet impertinence of the payer of compliments, let us transcend the disgust and deep disdain the essence of his praise inspires within us, let us put on a happy face dimpled with gratitude! He wanted to be nice to us! And now that that's over, we know how exalted he feels, he has vanquished us—and himself too, the cur!—since it was not easy for him to wring these praises from himself.[26]

Here we have a written page which is covered with praise, and you call it flat, but when you realize that revenge is concealed in this praise, you will find it almost too subtle, and you will experience a great deal of pleasure in its numerous delicate and bold strokes and figures. It is not the man himself, but his revenge, which is so subtle, rich, and ingenious: he himself is scarcely aware of it.[27]

We demonstrate a subtle and also noble self-control—assuming that we want to praise at all—by praising only where we do *not* agree (otherwise, after all, we would only be praising ourselves, which is contrary to good taste). To be sure, such self-control offers a nice impetus and occasion for being constantly *misunderstood*. If we want to grant ourselves this truly luxurious moral and aesthetic taste, we cannot live among intellectual fools, but rather among people who can still be amused by the subtleties of misunderstandings and misconceptions (or else we will have to pay dearly for it!). "He praises me: *therefore* he thinks I am right"—this sort of idiotic conclusion is always ruining life for us hermits, for it sends the idiots our way, as neighbors or friends.[28]

ATTITUDE TOWARDS PRAISE. When good friends praise a talented nature, he will often exhibit pleasure at it, though he does so out of politeness and benevolence: in truth he is indifferent to it. His real being is quite languid in its presence and it cannot drag him a single step out of the sunshine or shadow in which he lies; but men want to give pleasure when they praise and one would grieve them if one did not rejoice at their praise.[29]

The Time Factor

Time plays a big role in the subtext. An utterance meaningful through reference to a specific moment changes meaning if connected to another time. That is why worldly ladies set aside a day: "The Marquise: . . . when one says, I am at home Tuesdays, it is clear that this is as good as saying: The rest of the time, leave me in peace."[30] The sentence "I am at home Tuesdays" carries simultaneously the positive content "Come on Tuesday" and an implied negative, "Don't come on the other days." The most frequent instance concerning time is saying "later" instead of saying "no," a type of shrouded refusal of the utmost usefulness in everyday life, as everybody knows, and which has proved itself in international relations as well. Ancient history was familiar with situations of this sort, when a deliberative assembly had to decide on declaring war or not. The passions of the citizenry were inflamed, and they would be ready to vote for any warlike measure whatsoever. In this case, the orator seeking to dissuade them avoids taking them head-on. He does not say he is opposed to the war, but he counsels them against declaring it immediately, and he urges them in the meantime to prepare for it, thereby leaving a door open for future developments.[31]

This is what Dominique de Villepin, the French foreign minister, did at the UN Security Council in New York on February 14, 2003. He intended to make known French opposition to military intervention in Iraq, contrary to the wishes of the US government. He did so by insisting on the time factor: "The use of force is not justified today," he said. "Premature recourse to the military option would incur heavy consequences." "In the present state of our intelligence, . . . nothing entitles us to confirm such ties [between Al-Qaida and the Baghdad regime]." "We do not exclude the possibility that one day we may have to resort to force." "At no time, within this Security Council, will acting out of hastiness, ignorance, suspicion, or fear have a place."[32] This speech, which all opponents of the war hailed as very forceful, was no less so for its skillfulness: firm in its conviction, polished in form, and prudent, because it was not predetermining the future. There was no vote, and the United States undertook its intervention without a UN mandate.

Procrastination is a weapon women resort to in societies where they are pressured and where they have to make use of "rhetorical byways."[33] One of the first examples is Penelope in Greek mythology. As she was being courted by men of the area, who were eager for her hand and her property, her husband Odysseus being reported missing, she conceived a stratagem, saying she would choose among the suitors after she had finished weaving a shroud for him.[34] What happened next is well known: after three years, an acceptable delay for a "spousal mourning period,"[35] her task was still incomplete, and the suitors learned, thanks to a maid's indiscretion, that Penelope got up every night to undo what she had woven the previous day. The drama intensifies, the situation becomes difficult, but luckily for Penelope, Odysseus returns. Saved by the bell . . .

In the *Aethiopica* of Heliodorus (an ancient and influential Greek novel Racine knew by heart), brigands carry off the young and beautiful heroine, Chariclea. Their leader, Thyamis, ever the gentleman, wants to marry her. She is quite careful not to reject this offer, which, given her situation, is still a godsend; she only asks permission to go off first to a city where there is a temple of Apollo, in order to lay down her emblems of office as a priestess. Thyamis has to accept this delay, even if he does not like it.[36] Attack by a rival band will free Chariclea from keeping her promise. The same subterfuge occurs in another novel, by Xenophon of Ephesus, where, this time, it is the chief of police who falls in love with the fair Anthia. In order to gain time, she pretends to give her consent and asks for a delay of thirty days.[37] What happens next is more complicated. The appointed day arrives, Anthia drinks poison, but it is only a sleeping potion; she awakens in her tomb. Happily, tomb robbers rescue her.

The cases of "yes" meaning "no" are innumerable, provided there is an accompanying "not right now." Reciprocally, there are, let me add parenthetically, cases where "no" means "yes," as in this exchange between Balzac's ardent Montriveau and the coquettish Duchess of Langeais:

> "So you never loved me," he said with a rage that leapt like lightning from his eyes.
> "No, my dear."
> This no was really yes.
> "What a big fool I am," he replied.[38]

Human psychology and social constraints are such that acquiescence, like refusal, cannot always be frank. One recalls the advice of the Evangelist: "But let your communication be Yea, yea: Nay, nay: for whatsoever is more than these cometh of evil."[39] Alas, easier said than done!

Alongside "later" meaning "no," we highlight "when" meaning "never." Jorge Luis Borges recounts that *"When then, dear?* was the typical form of address in a fight when one dodged the blow of the hot poker or the adversary's knife." Thus, it was an ironic expression, a provocative but indirect way of saying, "You'll never succeed, you wimp." "When will I ever get around to that blonde?" is similarly to be understood as a praise of brunettes.[40]

The future tense, rich by definition with every possibility, is a bearer of subtexts depending on the context. Catherine Kerbrat-Orecchioni cites, for example, a sentence like, "You will go to Timbuktu," which, according to the circumstances, can be "a court sentence, a promise, a prophecy, a recommendation, praise, or blame."[41]

In the Roman Empire, provincial governors changed annually. Upon their entry into office, they usually visited the cities under their jurisdiction, where they were welcomed with grandiose ceremonies and eloquent speeches. But behind all the hoopla, the situation was delicate, full of expectations and misgivings on both sides. In these circumstances, the sophists, among other means, used anticipatory praise to bring out the viewpoint of the governed, praise in the future tense. "I am certain that our new governor will render justice equitably and that he will defend the poor against the rich," the orator essentially asserted; "I predict that he will courageously promote our province's case at the Imperial court; it is obvious that he will govern for the good of his subjects," and so on.[42] At first glance, these pronouncements look like flattery. But if one thinks about it, one sees that, like the expression "You will go to Timbuktu," these statements carry implied meanings. Assuming as a certainty that the recipient will display a given virtue is tantamount to wishing that he does display it and respectfully to map out for him a course of conduct; it is, in short, a halfway approach between outright begging and negotiation.

Figures of Speech

The subtext depends on the figures, those ways of speaking that depart from the normal and spontaneous in an effort to suggest something more. Since we have already encountered several of them in the course of this work, it seems useful, for the convenience of the reader, to provide a brief recapitulation of the most relevant procedures. To ensure consistency, I deemed definitions from a single source preferable, since classifications vary widely from one author to another. I have chosen Pierre Fontanier (1768–1844), whose reliable handbooks were published between 1818 and 1830, before Gérard Genette, in an effort of rehabilitation, gathered them into one volume fifty years ago.[43] The name "figures of speech," which gives the volume its title, includes figures in the strict sense (bearing upon thoughts or multiple words) and tropes (bearing essentially upon an isolated word). It does not include, however, the special form found in theorizing about the subtext called "figured speech" in ancient rhetoric, which Fontanier did not consider.[44]

Here with Fontanier's definitions are some of the figures of speech at play in the subtext. One will notice in the definitions the omnipresence of double meaning, the unspoken, veiling, and feigning.

Allegory and Allegorizing: "Allegory . . . is a statement with double meaning, a literal and an imaginary sense in combination, through which one thought is presented beneath the image of another, suitable for rendering the first more palpable and striking than if it had been stated directly and without any type of veil." "Allegorizing, an imitation of Allegory, is a prolonged and continuous Metaphor."[45] According to Fontanier's subtle distinction, allegory occurs when two levels of meaning coexist, and allegorizing when the only thing that matters is the figurative meaning. We have stressed the power of allegory from the very outset of this book.[46]

Allusion: "Allusion is making felt the connection of something said with something unsaid, the very connection prompting the idea."[47] Allusion can be historical, mythological, ethical, or verbal. We saw earlier, for example, historical allusions in the form of analogy.[48]

Antiphrasis: In antiphrasis, one uses a word or manner of expression in a sense contrary to what is or what seems natural to it."[49] A thank-you in the form of "Oh, you shouldn't have" may be considered as a kind of antiphrasis.

Apostrophe: "Apostrophe . . . is that sudden switching in a speech by which one turns from one recipient to address another, real or supernatural, absent or present."[50] Not every apostrophe involves a subtext—far from it. But in certain cases this figure allows one to speak indirectly, as its name indicates (in ancient Greek, *apostrophê* means "the act of turning oneself away"), for example, in order to accuse someone while pretending to address someone else. To blame the troops, one turns to the general and deplores with him the cowardice of his men;[51] to reprimand students, one speaks in front of them to their teacher, regretting the poor example their unruliness presents.[52]

Euphemism: "Well-meaning speech . . . that is, speaking in a courteous and pleasing way."[53] Stretching distinctions further, there is metaphoric euphemism ("a life in the lap of luxury"), double negative euphemism ("the republic, the last, and not the least malfunctioning, type of authoritarian governments"), and euphemism by allusion, innuendo, metaplasm (word reshaping), invented words, ellipsis, and so on.[54] Political correctness and the language of "sexorama" teem with euphemisms.

Hyperbole: "Hyperbole augments or diminishes things by exaggeration, and presents them as quite superior or inferior to what they are, with a view not to deceive but to lead to the truth itself, and to establish by saying something unbelievable what must really be believed."[55] Statements like, "I am, Sir, your humble servant"[56] or "The Roman Empire is a democracy"[57] are blatant hyperboles.

License: "License, also called Parrhêsia, is that freedom of expression used sometimes toward important persons, or with which one says more about something than is permitted or seemly."[58] We have seen earlier how this figure (also called "boldness") should, in theory, be the opposite of the subtext but actually reintroduces false appearances.[59]

Litotes: "Litotes, also called Understatement . . . , instead of positively affirming something, categorically denies its opposite, or understates the thing in question somewhat, with the actual aim of lending more energy and weight to the affirmation it disguises."[60] The classic example in French literature is from the *Cid*, in the scene where Chimène, caught in the demands of honor with her beloved Rodrigue, dismisses him, saying, "Go, I do not hate you" when she means "Go in the certainty of my love."[61]

Preterition: "Preterition . . . is a feigned unwillingness to say what one nevertheless is saying quite clearly, and often even forcefully so."[62] This is a figure of silence.[63]

Prosopopoeia: "Prosopopoeia . . . is bringing on the scene in some way those who are absent, the dead, supernatural beings, or even inanimate entities; making them act, speak, respond, as one sees fit." Akin to prosopopoeia, insofar as they introduce external characters, are Ethopoeia, "description that focuses on the habits, the character, the vices, the virtues, the talents, the weaknesses, in sum the good or bad moral qualities of a real or fictitious individual," and Fictitious Dialogue, which is reporting directly, and exactly as coming from the mouth, imaginary statements one attributes to his characters."[64] The play of masks in Dio Chrysostom makes use of these three figures all at once.[65]

Reticence: "Reticence is breaking off and stopping suddenly in the midst of a sentence, making understood through the little one has said . . . what one pretends to be suppressing, and often even more than that."[66] It is another figure of silence, which Dante, for example, uses with Paolo and Francesca.[67]

Tropes: Tropes are subdivided into "Tropes of association, known as metonymies," "Tropes of connection, ordinarily called synecdoches," and "Tropes of comparison, that is, . . . metaphors."[68] It is not always easy to

The Subtle Subtext

determine with what category one is dealing. We have encountered earlier, for example, Empson's reflections on the ambiguity of metaphor, the name as a synecdoche (the part for the whole), Elsa as a metaphor for France, or even imagistic language in sexual matters.[69]

Gastronomastics

The linguist Eva Lavric scrutinized restaurant menus and came to the conclusion that "the more numerous the ingredients listed and the more detailed the preparation described, the more expensive the dish became"[70]— an iron-clad rule that has certainly not escaped the notice of any patron of a Michelin-starred establishment. Examples make the mouth water, like "Lobe of duck liver from So-and-So's farm, cooked *au torchon*, seasoned in coffee and cacao butter flavored with spiced port," or "Shank of milk-fed Dordogne veal, slow-braised until it melts off the bone, bone stuffed with veal sweetbreads, classic Lyons dumplings of ground veal with mushrooms, in veal pan sauce." This rhetoric of the *nouvelle cuisine*, which Lavric characterizes as "gastronomastics," spells out in minute detail on the menu, which is tantamount to saying, what is ordinarily passed over in silence. To all appearances nothing more than information, in reality this luxury of detail, this "overinforming," carries an implicit message that aims to convey the exceptional quality of the products used as well as the care and innovation employed in the conception and realization of the recipes. Lavric adds that there is one strategy of subliminal valorization, and one only, which does not work in French but is unfailingly effective in other European languages. It consists, as one might have guessed, in introducing a little French into the names of dishes ("*Schweinsmedaillon*," "*patatas soufflé*," "New York strip steak, *sauce béarnaise*").

The Infrapolitics of Subordinate Groups

Parting with the principle that political science is chiefly interested in the organization and ideas of those who exercise power, James Scott, in his *Domination and the Arts of Resistance: Hidden Transcripts*, turns in the opposite direction to show that the dominated also have political ideas and voice.[71] His transhistorical study encompasses the black slaves of the United States as well as the untouchables in India, the serfs and peasants of the Ancien Régime in France, and different categories of European workers as he seeks to tease out a unity behind the described phenomenon that transcends temporal differences.

This phenomenon he calls the "hidden transcript," as opposed to the "public transcript." It is no coincidence that the author refers to Leo Strauss, while still maintaining some distance.[72] Both look for the ways of subtle resistance, but Strauss focuses on the intellectual elite, whereas Scott deals with the ideas of "subordinated groups," what they say and think without the power to speak it publicly, in contrast to the flattering image that dominant groups give of themselves. These ideas constitute an "infrapolitics."[73] This is the voice of the lowly, in short, the discourse they carry on among themselves, or confronting other classes when they let loose. Openly they flatter, parade their submissiveness, swallow their anger. Playing dumb is another of their favorite tactics. But the tone is not the same when they gather in a tavern or carry on conversations in dialect.

An intermediate form of communication is expressing the hidden message while disguising it through various means. Among those Scott enumerates, one notes equivocation, anonymity, rumor, gossip, linguistic tricks like metaphors and euphemisms, or even folktales:[74] all of them types of subtexts. The critical issue is ascertaining if these forms of indirect expression serve as a safety valve or if, on the contrary, they fuel pride and resistance.[75]

Artificial Intelligence

Can artificial intelligence produce subtexts? That is not really important, for we are fully capable all by ourselves. The more interesting question is: can artificial intelligence discern subtexts? A dictator's dream . . . As it happens, this is an area where internet providers are busy; apparently a research team at Yahoo, in particular, is seeking to develop some relevant investigative tools.[76] The networks are used to tracking down forbidden images and terms considered hateful or indecent, in order to block the messages containing them. The difficulty arises when an improper message is only suggestive and fails to employ the forbidden word. This means developing an algorithm that would take account of the contexts and produce vector diagrams of words' meanings, in terms of probable similarity and statistical variance compared to other words. Among the three sorts of AI distinguished by Luc Ferry—Weak AI, which calculates; Super AI, which contextualizes; and Strong AI, which does not exist yet and would be capable of emotions and independent judgment[77]—our problem concerns the second. This method of Super AI would permit detecting automatically, among the billions of messages, those that break rules previously set and would recognize, for example, that a sentence is hurtful, even when none of the words it uses is listed as such. The algorithm, however, has not yet advanced this far. Human intelligence still has good days ahead, but artificial intelligence is not to be underestimated.

Irony

Irony is an immense subject, frequently studied.[78] Traditionally it is defined through use of the contrary, as in Fontanier: "Irony is saying in a bantering way, whether joking or serious, the opposite of what one thinks or what one wants to have thought."[79] Most often it entails flattery, awarding praise, for example, in order to convey something bad—namely, criticism or blame.

When defined through the "contrary," irony overlaps with the type of figured speech that relies on the same concept,[80] an overlapping that troubled ancient rhetoricians. Quintilian chose to separate the two, thinking that the contrary belonged to irony, and only irony, whereas figured speech cannot resort to it. A contradictory statement is admissible, he felt, in the case of irony, because it is a figure of speech, while it would be absurd for an entire oration to be contradictory and for an orator consistently to sustain the view opposed to his case.[81] But Quintilian is alone in this opinion. Other theorists accept a type of figured speech based on the contrary, without raising the problem of irony. They are content to mention irony occasionally, as a method of figured speech, without spelling out the connection between the two concepts.[82] A continuation of the debate begun by Quintilian led Empson to oppose his teacher, I. A. Richards, by including contradiction among his types of ambiguity, referring to dream logic and the Freudian notion of "condensation," while Richards did not accept that a poem could have an unresolved conflict that left an enduring contradiction.[83]

Taking a broader perspective, there is an undeniable resemblance between irony and the subtext. They are both double-meaning discourses that signal their effects with internal and external markers. Nevertheless, they are not to be confused. Subtext without irony is possible; numerous works, speeches, and statements with hidden meaning are not ironic (e.g., *Armance* or Aristides's *Panegyric of Rome*), even when they rely on the contrary (e.g., "You shouldn't have," or Agamemnon's speech in the second book of the *Iliad*, discussed in chapter 2). Conversely, irony goes beyond the subtext, even far beyond. Indeed, it includes Socratic irony, which raises the question of the "form of philosophy," in the full sense of this expression, as Denis Thouard, in another context, uses it.[84] It also includes, among other things, irony like Voltaire's, tragic irony, and even irony as a stance toward life, a sentiment that can be noble and profound and is bound up with liberty, modernity, individualism, and disenchantment, to say nothing of self-irony. There can be, perhaps, a little of all that in the subtext as well, but these two still remain distinct issues of inquiry.

"I'm Not Saying That, But…"

"Denegation" in psychoanalysis is the forceful rejection of an idea or urge, revealing that one is considering or experiencing it.[85] This psychological mechanism, the negation that amounts to affirmation, is found in literature and in everyday life. From the speaker's point of view, it comes down to saying that one does not want to say something, yet leaving it understood that one is saying it well and truly. "Far be it from me the idea of. . . ." Here, in contrast to the patient in analysis, the tactic is conscious. In the famous scene in the *Misanthrope*, Alceste protests he is not criticizing Oronte's sonnet, repeating: "That's not what I'm saying."[86] The more he uses this formulaic denial, the more it takes on the opposite sense, and Oronte's reactions show he has caught on: "That is all well and good, sir, and I think I take your meaning," he finally tosses out at Alceste.

For listeners, who find themselves somewhat in the situation of the analyst, it comes down to hearing someone's denial of an act or idea and then drawing the inference that what is being denied must be true, either totally or partially. The use of strengthened negation creates an ambiguity or functions as a signal betraying ambiguity; by repeatedly saying "No, that's not it," I suggest to the reader the possibility, "This *is* it," "I wish it were so."[87] It is no different with conspiracy theories: every effort to deny the existence of a plot appears, in the eyes of the convinced, like so much additional proof of its actual existence, and refutation produces the opposite of the effect it seeks. It must not be forgotten that argumentativeness is one of the mechanisms of communication, whence this admission by a suspicious political opponent: "The Secretary of Defense . . . said on television: 'There are no uniformed combat troops on the ground in Cambodia.' I immediately thought that then there must be uniformed troops in the air space, or else troops on the ground not in uniform, etc."[88]

Unspoken English

"Left unsaid" or "unspoken" is a very common expression in English applied, even though a cliché, to varied situations. It covers what is not said openly

The Subtle Subtext

out of discretion or out of a fear of giving offense but also what one regrets not having said to someone who has now left or is dead. Adding "better," as in "better left unsaid," it designates what it is preferable not to speak of: all truths are not good to say. Naturally, others, for the most part, figure out this "unspoken." That is why "left unsaid" is connected to the subtext.

A simple internet search reveals recurrent titles using the expression. There are song titles: "Left Unsaid" (Maura Gabriella), "Better Left Unsaid" (Ariana Grande), "Things Left Unsaid" (Pink Floyd), "Some Things Are Better Left Unsaid" (Daryl Hall and John Oates). Among books, we have *Things Left Unsaid* (Stephanie Hemphill), *Few Things Left Unsaid* (Sudeep Nagarkar), and *Everything I Left Unsaid* (Molly O'Keefe). From the world of film documentaries, we find *Nothing Left Unsaid* (Liz Garbus), and in print articles, "What the Presidential Candidates Left Unsaid in the Debate" on health-care costs[89] and "What Comey Left Unsaid" (on FBI Director Comey's testimony before Congress).[90] If the quality of these efforts is quite uneven, their quantity is telling. "Left unsaid" is an evocative expression, which takes on shifting nuances, whether they be romantic, mysterious, or something else. It is associated with secrecy or regret and fascinates for this very reason.

Dog Whistle Politics

Dogs, as is well known, have a very developed sense of hearing and are able to pick up high frequencies inaudible to humans. A dog whistle emits these, which the animal receives but humans present do not. By analogy, during the past few decades, the expression "dog whistle politics" has spread in the English-speaking world to mark the practice of engaging in a seemingly neutral and general discussion that actually contains hidden messages specifically aimed at certain categories of listeners. Theorists of anti-racism are particularly fond of this expression when they criticize conservative political discussions that they fault for harping on certain themes and values meant to be understood between the lines, they say, by a limited part of the electorate to whom messages are being sent on the sly.[91] The notion of "dog whistle" itself carries a withering implication, since it lumps together the recipients of the messages with dogs.

Leading Questions

It is hot outside; you go into a drugstore and order a Coke. There are two choices. If the clerk asks you, "Large or small?" you might be tempted to answer, "A small will do," and the business is out a nickel (in America, in the 1930s). If, however, the clerk simply asks, "A large?" there is a 70 percent probability, according to some studies, that you will answer, "Yes."[92] The difference results from how the question is phrased.

The handbook by Elmer Wheeler (1903–1968), for the use of vendors, medical salesmen, Avon ladies, product reps, and door-to-door salesmen, studies in detail the most effective formulas for connecting with customers and getting them to buy. He unabashedly gets right to the point, in the name of efficiency, and, among other things, awards decisive importance to the manner of questioning. That is Rule 4: *"Don't Ask If—Ask Which!"* "Does this vacuum cleaner interest you?" and "Do you want me to give you a demonstration?" are poor questions, leading nowhere, because they offer the customer a chance to say no. "Which do you prefer?" or "When do you want delivery?" are more effective approaches.[93] In a tony establishment, "What's it gonna be?" is too ordinary; much better to ask, "What may I serve you, Sir? A Martini, a Manhattan?" "Will you be having some eggs?" is less persuasive than "Do you want one egg or two?" "Fill it?" has long been recognized as more of an inducement than "How much do you want?" (at least until gas tanks get bigger and consumer habits change).[94] Going through these analyses and recommendations, one is amazed to see how each type of question conceals a hidden power and prompts a certain type of response. All of this is also true, naturally, outside a commercial context:

- "Is a global natural treasure going to disappear?" contains at least three or four implied arguments in support of the thesis.[95]
- "Don't you find it unacceptable to tax internet search engines?" already suggests the answer.
- "Why don't you call me a little later?" is nothing more than an unspoken prayer.[96]

Teaching Tricks

Emperor Marcus Aurelius recalls in his *Meditations* how his teacher, Alexander "the Grammarian," had a particularly elegant way of correcting a student who committed a barbarism or a solecism. Instead of reprimanding him, he not only introduced the correct form but did so discreetly, as if in passing, in the guise of a reply, as a supporting remark, or a discussion on the topic itself.[97] It was certainly not easy being the instructor of a young prince, and one understands that Alexander chose prudence, which may not have required much effort, tactfulness seeming to have been a part of his makeup.[98] In any case, the model he offered, considerateness combined with ability, left a grateful student in his debt.

In our own day, the indirect method of classroom correction is seen as a teacher's responsibility and belongs to a larger collection of "teaching tricks." One must "act like a strategist to mobilize his students," a standard guide counsels, which implies using "well-intentioned tricks" to overcome the barrier of inattentiveness or resistance, employing all sorts of means, such as play, give-and-take, reverse psychology, rituals, and many others. In this arsenal, the subtext has its role, if we may believe the testimony of one instructor. In order to get her students to turn off their cell phones during class, she gave up on direct prohibition, "as common as it is ineffective," and preferred to issue an alert: "I remind everybody not to forget to reactivate your phones during the next break. I am counting on you."[99]

Figured Sarcasm

An ancient scholar, writing in Latin, Macrobius (fifth century AD) loved witticisms and devoted an in-depth study to the different types of jesting, identifying the category oblique or "figured" sarcasm (*morsus figuratus*).[100] Unlike straightforward insult, it dissimulates, sometimes with a whiff of urbanity, suggesting more than is said explicitly. It is a redoubtable weapon, all the more dangerous for its slyness, just as a hook can stick in the flesh more firmly than a straight blade. Its finesse tickles listeners, so much so that it wins over scoffers.

For example, it is a direct insult to hurl at some nouveau riche, "Do you forget that you used to peddle fish and chips?," but it is figured sarcasm to say, "I remember when you used to wipe your nose on your sleeve." For a reader today, the tonal difference between these two is scarcely noticeable, one must admit, but it was clearly significant. Ironic praise inevitably falls under this rubric, as when one says to a coward, "You're a veritable Hercules"; the sarcasm wounds underneath the praise. We can also cite the following exchange, which pitted Cicero against Laberius. When the latter was looking for a seat in the rows of the theater reserved for knights and senators, Cicero, who was already seated, said to him, "I'd make room for you if the seating weren't so cramped," a reply that killed two birds with one stone, pushing back Laberius and criticizing at the same time the policy of the latter's patron, Julius Caesar, who had packed the Senate with a considerable number of new senators. But Laberius, a celebrated author of comic mimes, had a ready rejoinder, replying, "Odd that you're cramped, given that you usually occupy two seats," an allusion to Cicero's political flip-flopping.[101]

The Iceberg Theory

Ernest Hemingway conceived and employed a type of writing that kept to the essentials, not saying everything and leaving something for the reader to infer. He theorized about this method, writing in *Death in the Afternoon*: "If a writer of prose knows enough about what he is writing about he may omit things that he knows and the reader, if the writer is writing truly enough, will have a feeling of those things as strongly as though the writer had stated them. The dignity of movement of an ice-berg is due to only one-eighth of it being above water."[102]

Because of the concluding comparison, this reflection is sometimes called "the iceberg theory." Hemingway started his career as a reporter, and American journalism of the period put a premium on rapidity and factualness. It was a training ground for an author in search of a minimalist style, a minimalism pushed to paradox, if the unspoken must represent seven-eighths of the total to assure a proper reception for the remaining eighth.

One also speaks of the "theory of omission" on the basis of the following passage, which appears in *A Moveable Feast* (a collection of reminiscences published posthumously in 1964) and refers to the short story *Out of Season*, first published in 1923: "It was a very simple story called 'Out of Season' and I omitted the real end of it, which was that the old man hanged himself. This was omitted on my new theory that you could omit anything if you knew that you omitted and the omitted part would strengthen the story and make people feel something more than they understood."[103]

For a "very simple story," *Out of Season* is a complex text, which, on the one hand, relates to the author's own biography (for the omitted suicide at the end actually took place) and contains, on the other hand, a double level of meaning. The "season" in question, which is over, is both the trout-fishing season and the season of love for the two protagonists.[104] The omission recalls and gives a glimpse of some profound problems.

"Kill Me!"

Once again, here is an utterance that does not mean what it seems to. One who says, "Kill me!" does not want to be killed. Still, nothing is ever assured in the world of the subtext. When Don Diègue hurls at the Count, who has just slapped him: "Finish it and take my life after such an affront,"[105] he does think, perhaps, what he is saying. When Phèdre implores Hippolyte, "Here is my heart. Here is where your hand must strike,"[106] the situation is less clear; for she then immediately imagines stabbing herself and winds up fleeing without doing anything. But finally, leaving aside the rare moments of heroic and tragic rage, the most frequent case, by far, is this false "Kill me!"

To go from the sublime to daily life, in a confrontation, it amounts to a sort of challenge or one-upmanship, whereby one fakes provocation in order actually to dissuade. Crying "Kill me!," that is, "If that's so, kill me!," "Don't just hit me, kill me!," "Kill me while you're at it," is to say something different from what you really desire in order to restrain the adversary.[107]

Figured declamations in which the orator pleads against himself and feigns a request for death follow the same principle. We have seen examples earlier in the case of self-denunciation, where the speaker takes the initiative.[108] Another type serves as a defensive tactic when one is being charged like Demosthenes. Accused of official corruption and threatened with exile, the imagined orator of the declamation demands a more severe sentence and asks for the death penalty. To all appearances, he is overcome with remorse and is delivering himself up to any punishment, out of despair, but also perhaps to win a little clemency. His self-condemnation notwithstanding, he recalls his glorious deeds, develops arguments on his own behalf, and points out the inconsistencies in the accusation, secretly hoping for acquittal. Technically, the rhetorical procedure he uses is "maximization" (in Greek *ek tou meizonos*, "argument proceeding from the greater"), the request for a greater penalty than the one mandated.[109]

The Latin grammarian Servius (fourth century AD) highlighted two passages in Vergil's *Aeneid* of the same sort. In one, Aeneas, seeing his ships on fire, prays to Jupiter, asking him either to preserve the fleet from destruction or else, "if I so deserve," to destroy it completely. In this prayer, phrased as a dilemma ("Save us" or "Kill us"), the second option is a pretense, the commentator explains. Aeneas is offering himself up to death only to make his salvation all the more certain, and that is what will happen with the arrival of a providential rainstorm to extinguish the fire.[110] In the second passage, it is Juno who addresses Jupiter to defend the cause of her protégé, Turnus, king of the Rutulians, who is in a difficult combat situation. If you still loved me as you once did, she says to her divine spouse, you would spare Turnus to please me. "But no, let him perish!" Once again words do not accurately convey thought, as Juno only speaks to provoke Jupiter and to arouse some

Catalog of Further Examples and Practices

reaction in him. She says "Kill him!" in order to save Turnus. Success crowns this figurative ploy, for Jupiter gives in, making clear that it is only a reprieve: death awaits Turnus, no matter what.[111]

Jupiter was certainly one very entreated god. In Ovid, it is Earth who turns to him. Victim of Phaethon's reckless behavior, who lost control of the Sun's chariot, she is about to be incinerated and begs the king of the gods to use his lightning bolt to put an end to her sufferings.[112] But what follows upon her speech shows that she has no wish to die. Jupiter, getting the message, strikes down Phaethon.

In *The Robbers* by Friedrich von Schiller, a monk comes to offer the robbers their lives, provided they surrender their leader to justice. The latter, Karl Moor, encourages the men to accept the offer and piles up arguments to convince them, to the monk's great astonishment. "See, I have no defense," the captain cries. "Who is going to be the first to abandon his captain in distress?" This paradoxical speech wins him the result he hoped for. Far from succumbing to temptation, his men show him their loyalty. First one, then a second of his lieutenants, then all the robbers stand beside him and cry, "Save the captain!"[113]

There is a variant of this in Heliodorus's novel. King Hydaspes makes a long speech, offering the people his daughter's life in accordance with a local custom that demands human sacrifices. All the time he expects his listeners will protest and not allow her to be immolated.[114]

The paradoxical injunction "Kill me!" offers a significant example of the subtext's continuity, from everyday, real-life situations to rhetorical efforts in both ancient and modern literature.

A Final Word

As we conclude, and I look back over my shoulder, I realize that I had no idea, when I undertook this investigation of the subtext, how far it would take me. Wearied of studying straightforward argumentation, which I had chiefly focused on till then, I imagined that a descent into "the subterranean depths of language"[1] would be a brief excursion. But there, where I was only expecting a basement, I discovered the "underworld." In oral and written exchanges, in politics and literature, in our witty remarks, in our bedroom intimacies, everywhere subtexts! There they are, hidden away, lying in wait for us. What can I say? They nag us! They are not only a fact; they raise epistemological issues. All theories attempting to explicate methods of communication, the aims of discourse, and the conditions of interpretation confront the problem of the multiplicity of meaning: in philosophy, in rhetoric, in linguistics, and in literary criticism, in religion, too, in psychoanalysis, and in the social sciences. The first step, therefore, was to acknowledge the breadth of the territory to be explored and then to analyze how the subtext functions and to understand what impulses it obeys.

In my exploration, I found no guide. Superior minds were not wanting; they instructed and inspired me, and I tried, as much as I could, to profit from their teaching. But as for a single, all-encompassing mentor, not a one. That is why the present study employs multiple and multidisciplinary approaches, seeking to establish the coherence of a broad topic, which is both an object of reflection and a collection of ways of acting in society.

The broad character of the subtext reveals itself in improbable encounters and unexpected similarities over the centuries—for example, between La Fontaine and Leonardo Sciascia, Isocrates and Pascal, the rhetorician Tiberius and Molière, Aragon and Quintilian, between the Roman Empire and Hungary or China, between Solzhenitsyn and Verlaine, Hermogenes and

William Empson.[2] An ancient Greek, a Roman, an Englishman, and a Frenchman have the same insight.[3] One gets the feeling one is dealing with constants, as much in the usage of the subtext as in theories about it, about its intrinsic and its momentary possibilities. While it may be too bold to extrapolate to human nature, the subtext is in any case a common thread running through European history and culture.

As for that coherence, it rests on the unity of a central definition. The initial assertion, with which I began, and the most obvious, is the observation that the subtext supposes two levels of meaning, one apparent, one implicit. That now needs an added refinement: the subtext is not static but dynamic. It aims at a target through roundabout means. The best image, in this regard, is the game of billiards, where a "carom" is hitting two other balls in a row, the red ball and the opponent's white ball, with one's own cue ball, by ricocheting from one to the other or using the table's side cushions. That is how the subtext works. To borrow again from a master of the subject some words he wrote on another topic, Aragon goes right to the heart of the problem. Speaking about the Russian poet and playwright, Vladimir Mayakovsky, who had a fraught relationship with the early Soviet regime, he says:

> Le monde est pour lui du billard et rouge en tête la parole
> Roule à travers le tapis vert et fait à tout coup carambole.

> The world for him is a billiard game and red head-on speech
> Rolls over the green baize and at every hit caroms.[4]

The difference with billiards is that, with the subtext, the trajectory is not necessarily the fruit of premeditation and may result from conventions, a psychological state, or chance. Such are the courteous or becoming turns of phrase that one uses almost unconsciously, the vague expressions that betray indecision, the evasions that we automatically blurt out when broaching a subject, or the statements that become charged afterward with unintended allusion.

For "caroming" speech, whether calculated or spontaneous, one can identify five chief functions, which I list here in conclusion, such as I think they can be discerned. These are interpretative keys, the reasons that explain why this is a necessary and useful art. The diplomatic function consists in avoiding explicit pronouncements and letting ambiguity buy us time without having to decide something or without having to change a position and contradict ourselves. The poetic and philosophic function suggests without saying, through the use of allusion, shadings of chiaroscuro, and allegory, thus to evoke another dimension, a parallel universe of ideas and feelings. The humorous function produces witticisms out of cleverness or malice; an expression like "pregnant with meaning" notwithstanding, the subtext can also be fine and light. The hypocoristic function, the use of diminutives and endearments, has an immense range of application; it is employed in all situations where there is occasion for being polite, affable, or deferential, for not shocking, for imperceptibly persuading, for insinuating, for covering up the crudeness of a reference, for sweetening or disguising an accusation, for introducing some advice or criticism, for confronting the addressee about values (or what one thinks are such) and guiding him to a conclusion without compulsion. The polemical function, finally, makes a weapon of the subtext, for defense and offense, serving under the cover of pretense to convey cutting messages that one does not want, or is unable, to express outright.

The question inevitably arises whether all this is moral or immoral, a question, like all naive questions, that does not admit of a simple and definitive answer. We repeat that the subtext is not lying; it is not hiding what ought to be said but speaking obliquely, which is quite different. We have no leave, therefore, to consider the subtextual approach as inherently evil; how one uses the subtext will determine whether it is blameworthy or not. Furthermore, no one has ever thought of using the subtext always and everywhere. When Balzac attributes half of language to it, when Hemingway allocates seven-eighths, these are high-side estimates, verging on the outrageous.[5] It is also true that billiards is not for everyone. In this case, one is free to try straight shooting: transparency, frankness, parrhêsia—even though all of these are less direct than one might think.

And what about usage? The art of the subtext enables both using the subtext oneself and deciphering it when used by someone else. This book will have achieved its objective if it helps in both veiling and unveiling, in better speaking and in better hearing. Once you have finished it, dear readers, it will be your turn.

Translator's Note on Citations

Professor Pernot naturally cites literary works and scholarship either in their original French or in French translations from another language. Normally, for the convenience of the English-speaking reader, I would have provided these in published English translations, where available, or in their original English, when that was the case.

But these are not normal times. The current COVID-19 pandemic has shut research and public libraries, making the tracking down of such references more difficult, not to say impossible. Professor Pernot and I have been thrown back upon the resources of our personal libraries; internet searches have proved helpful, but not in every case.

Accordingly, for scholarly works, I have continued to cite the references to French editions, alerting the reader to the existence of English-language versions, whether original or translated, but which I could not examine personally. I have, however, provided published English language translations in lieu of the French citations when I could verify the actual English text and its pagination. I have followed the same practice with literary works. The reader should be aware that there are usually multiple English translations available for the French literary classics Professor Pernot mentions or quotes. Those I use for cited quotations are those to which I happened to have access.

Otherwise, I have translated myself all quoted passages within the text, whether from scholarly or literary sources, even though this sometimes involves the parlous practice of giving an English translation of a third language through a French filter.

Professor Pernot has also made a few minor adjustments to his original text and notes either to update or clarify, especially for the Anglophone reader. With the same reader in mind, I have added, with Professor Pernot's approval, a few explanatory words or phrases in the text and notes. The latter are marked within square brackets with the initials WEH or "Translator's Note."

Once again I am grateful for the kind assistance of Gerald Heverly, the Classics librarian at New York University, who could patiently consult the Loeb Classical Library online for me and who had some limited access to the Bobst Library's physical collection to assist me in providing or verifying several references.

Notes

Preface

1. M. Jullian, *De Gaulle: Pensées, répliques et anecdotes* (Paris, 1994), 139. This sentence is cited with slight variation on the website Académie française (academie-francaise.fr/les-immortels/alphonse-juin), where the past verb tenses in French are different.

2. An upsurge of collections and acts of conferences, with evocative titles, attests to a growing interest in recent years for oblique writing and the unspoken. So, in chronological order, see: *La parole masquée*, ed. M.-H. Prat and P. Servet (Geneva, 2005); *Les Écritures secrètes*, ed. M. Briand, C. Camelin, and L. Louvel (Rennes, 2009); *Paralangues: Études sur la parole oblique*, ed. P. Hummel (Paris, 2010); *Allégorie et symbole: voies de dissidence? De l'Antiquité à la Renaissance*, ed. A. Rolet (Rennes, 2012); *Ne pas dire: Pour une étude du non-dit dans la littérature et la culture européennes*, ed. P. Schnyder and F. Toudoire-Surlapierre (Paris, 2013); "Le non-dit," *Cahiers internationaux du symbolisme* 134, 135, 136, ed. C. Gravet and H. Kohler (Mons, 2013); J. Sorba, C. Cusimano, and S. Brocquet, eds., "Sens multiple(s) et polysémie," *Études romanes de Brno* 35 (2014); *The Art of Veiled Speech: Self-Censorship from Aristophanes to Hobbes*, ed. H. Baltussen and P. J. Davis (Philadelphia, 2015); *Revealing and Concealing in Antiquity: Textual and Archeological Approaches to Secrecy*, ed. E. Mortensen and S. G. Saxkjaer (Aarhus, 2015); *La Parola "elusa": Tratti di oscurità nella trasmissione del messaggio*, ed. I. Angelini, A. Ducati, and S. Scartozzi (Trent, 2016); *Latenza: Preterizioni, reticenze e silenzi del testo*, ed. A. Barbieri and E. Gregori (Padua, 2016); *Le Dit et le Non-Dit. Langage(s) et traduction*, ed. S. Berbinski (Frankfurt, 2016); *Tours et détours de la parole dans la littérature antique*, ed. C. Hunzinger, G. Mérot, and G. Vassiliadès (Bordeaux, 2017); and *Autour des formes implicites*, ed. S. Anquetil, J. Elie-Deschamps, and C. Lefebvre-Scodeller (Rennes, 2017).

3. Leo Strauss, *Persecution and the Art of Writing* (repr., Chicago, 1988), 23.

4. In the preamble to *Honorine*.

5. Chapters 2 and 5 of this book rely on studies I have published previously, especially: *Éloges grecs de Rome* (Paris, 1997), 15–56; "Les faux-semblants de la rhétorique grecque," in *République des lettres, République des arts: Mélanges offerts à Marc Fumaroli, de l'Académie française*, ed. C. Mouchel and C. Nativel (Geneva, 2008), 427–50; and *Alexandre le Grand, les risques du pouvoir: Textes philosophiques et rhétoriques* (Paris, 2013), 31–56. The analyses offered in these publications have been refashioned and put in a new perspective for the present work. I must warmly thank Marc Philonenko, member of the French Institute, for his valuable and kind critique.

Chapter 1

1. G. della Casa, *Galateo, or The Rules of Polite Behavior*, chapters 14–17 and 22.

2. I thank Lynette Hunter and Jameela Lares for this example.

3. P. Bourdieu, *Distinction: A Social Critique of the Judgment of Taste*, trans. Richard Nice (Cambridge, MA, 1984).

4. S. Bern, *Piques et Répliques de l'histoire* (Paris, 2017), 142.

5. *L'Île des pingouins*, in Anatole France, *Œuvres*, ed. M.-C. Bancquart (Paris, 1994), 4:25.

6. Ibid., 85.

7. G. Orwell, *Animal Farm* (New York, 1959), chapter 10, 123.

8. Letter to D. Macdonald, December 5, 1946, in *The Complete Works of George Orwell*, ed. P. Davidson (London, 1998), 12:507–8.

9. B. Sansal, *2084: La fin du monde* (Paris, 2015), 11. Available in English translation by A. Anderson as *2084: The End of the World* (New York, 2017).

10. Molière, *The Miser*, act 1, scene 3; *Tartuffe*, act 2, scene 2; *Dom Juan*, act 1, scene 2.

11. Molière, *Tartuffe*, act 4, scene 5.

12. L. Spina, "Una suocera invadente," *I quaderni del ramo d'oro online* 6 (2013–2014): 123–29.

13. Molière, *The Imaginary Invalid*, act 2, scene 5.

14. Molière, *Les précieuses ridicules* (*The Follies of the Prissy Misses*), scene 9.

15. Racine, *Iphigénie*, act 2, scene 2.

16. Sophocles, *Ajax* 646ff.

17. M. Thompson, *Enough Said: What's Gone Wrong with the Language of Politics?* (New York, 2016), 27–31.

18. T. Herzl, *Le Palais-Bourbon: Tableaux de la vie parlementaire française*, trans. P. Kessler (Paris, 1995), 167.

19. A. Orioli, *Gli oracoli della moneta: L'arte della parola nel linguaggio dei banchieri centrali* (Bologna, 2016).

20. *Le Figaro Magazine*, March 15, 2013, 27.

21. *L'Express.fr*, July 7, 2016.

22. Cf. the pages of René Huyghe on "La suggestion indirecte" in his *Dialogue avec le visible* (Paris, 1955), 263–88.

23. La Fontaine, *Fables* 6.1: The Shepherd and the Lion.

24. Horace, *Satires* 1.1. 69–70.

25. Rabelais, *Gargantua*, book 2.

26. Nietzsche, *Thus Spake Zarathustra*, part 3, chapter 46 ("The Vision and the Enigma"), Modern Library trans. (New York, 1954), 171–78.

27. *Les Hain-teny*, a collection of texts whose first version dates to 1910–13, republished in J. Paulhan, *Œuvres complètes*, ed. B. Baillaud (Paris, 2009), 2:131–66.

28. Ibid., 167–94.

29. Baudelaire, "*Correspondances*," poem 4 in *Les fleurs du mal*.

30. P. Hadot, *Le Voile d'Isis: Essai sur l'histoire de l'idée de nature* (Paris, 2004).

31. Plato, *Republic* 7.

32. Proverbs 25:2 (AV).

33. Herodotus, *Histories* 1.53, 91.

34. Fragment 93, *Die Fragmente der Vorsokratiker* (ed. Diels-Kranz).

35. The traditional definition, going back to Quintilian, *On the Education of the Orator* 8.6.44.

36. *Aeneid* 6.280–81.

37. F. Jourdan, *Le Papyrus de Derveni* (Paris, 2003). An English translation by R. Janko is available in *Classical Philology* 96 (2001): 1–32, which can be consulted online as well.

38. Philo, *The Political Life, or On Joseph* 2.32, 35.

39. 2 Corinthians 3:14; Galatians 4:24.

40. Pascal, *Pensées*, 260, in *Oeuvres complètes*, ed. L. Lafuma (Paris, 1963), 533. G. Couton's *Ecritures codées: Essais sur l'allégorie au XVIIe siècle* (Paris, 1990) remains important.

41. R. Brotherton, *Suspicious Minds: Why We Believe Conspiracy Theories* (New York, 2015).

42. *Dernières Nouvelles d'Alsace*, January 29, 2018, 2.

Chapter 2

1. Quintilian, *The Orator's Education* 9.2.65–99, available in the Loeb Classical Library, trans. D. A. Russell (Cambridge, MA, 2001); Pseudo-Hermogenes, *On Invention* 4.13, in the *Corpus rhetoricum*, vol. 3.1, ed. M. Patillon (Paris, 2012); *On the Method of Forceful Speaking*, 22, in the *Corpus rhetoricum*, vol. 5, ed. M. Patillon (Paris, 2014). These last two treatises are available in English, *Invention and Method: Two Rhetorical Treatises*, trans. G. Kennedy (Society of Biblical Culture, Atlanta, 2005). [WEH: "Invention" in rhetoric is akin to legal "discovery," not innovation or finding new devices.]

2. Demetrius, *On Style* 287–98; available in English trans. by D. C. Innes in the Loeb Classical Library, Aristotle, vol. 23: *Poetics* (Cambridge, MA, 1995).

3. Pseudo-Dionysius of Halicarnassus, *On Figured Speeches*, 1 and 2 (equivalent to his *Rhetoric*, 8 and 9), in *Dionysii Halicarnasei opuscula*, vol. 2.1, ed. H. Usener and L. Radermacher (Leipzig, 1904).

4. Fortunatianus, *The Art of Rhetoric*, 1, in *Rhetores Latini minores*, ed. R. Halm (Leipzig, 1863), 84–86; Martianus Capella, *The Wedding of Mercury and Philology* 5.470–72, in *Martianus Capella, De nuptiis Mercurii et Philologiae*, ed. J. Willis (Leipzig, 1983), 165–66.

5. Like the four books of Junius Otho the Elder (first century AD), which, while probably not dealing only with figured speech, still allotted it considerable space [Seneca the Elder, *Controversiae* 1.3.11; 2.1.33; available in the Loeb Classical Library, trans. M. Winterbottom (Cambridge, MA, 1974)]; or like the treatise of Aspasius of Byblos (second century AD), cited in Suidas, the Byzantine dictionary, A 4203, *Suidae Lexicon*, vol. 1, ed. A. Adler (Leipzig, 1928).

6. Isocrates, *Oration 12* (the *Panathenaicus*), 200ff.; available in the Loeb Classical Library, Isocrates, vol. 2, trans. G. Norlin (Cambridge, MA, 1929).

7. Or inversely, in Rufinianus (following Quintilian here), as a kind of introduction to these: Julius Rufinianus (fourth to fifth century AD), *On the Figures of Thought*, in *Rhetores Latini minores*, ed. R. Halm (Leipzig, 1863), 59–60.

8. Pseudo-Hermogenes, *Forceful Speaking* 22.1; Pseudo-Dionysius, *Figured Speeches* 2.5; Apsines (third century AD), *On Figured Problems* 26, in *Apsinès, art rhétorique: Problèmes à faux-semblant*, ed. M. Patillon (Paris, 2001).

9. Seneca the Elder, *Controversiae* 2.1.33.

10. Demetrius, *On Style* 294 (Loeb trans. adapted).

11. Homer, *Iliad* 15.201–2 (Lattimore translation), a passage analyzed by Pseudo-Dionysius, *Figured Speeches* 2.3.

12. Homer, *Iliad* 9.434ff. (Lattimore translation); Pseudo-Dionysius, *Figured Speeches* 1.11.

13. Homer, *Iliad* 2.72–75 (Lattimore translation); Pseudo-Dionysius, *Figured Speeches* 1.15 and 2.5.

14. Apollonius of Rhodes, *Argonautica* 1.872; 2.638–39.

15. J. C. Iglesias-Zoido, "Un ejemplo de *logos eskhêmatismenos* a finales del XVI," in *Homenaje al Profesor Juan Antonio López Férez*, ed. L. M. Pino Campos and G. Santana Henriquez (Madrid, 2013), 405–12.

16. A. Ascani provides a recent example of this approach, *De sermone figurato quaestio rhetorica: Per un' ipotesi di pragmatica linguistica antica*, PhD thesis, Vrije Universitcit Amsterdam, 2006 (available online at https://dare.ubvu.vu.nl), ii–vi and 123.

17. Figured topics are found among the Latin declamations transmitted under the names of Quintilian and Calpurnius Flaccus (second century AD), the Greek declamations of Libanius (fourth century AD), and the analyses and citations of Seneca the Elder, Philostratus (third century AD), and Sopater (fourth century AD).

18. Pseudo-Hermogenes, *On Invention* 4.13.4.

19. Libanius, *Declamation 39*, in *Libanii opera*, vol. 7, ed. R. Foerster (Leipzig, 1913).

20. Pseudo-Hermogenes, *On Invention* 4.13.14.

21. Respectively: Quintilian 9.2.69; Syrianus, Sopater, and Marcellinus, in the scholia to Hermogenes, found in *Rhetores Graeci*, ed. C. Walz (Stuttgart, 1833), 4:122; Pseudo-Hermogenes, *On Invention* 4.13.15.

22. Hermogenes, *The Stylistic Categories of Speech* 2.8.10–12, in *Corpus rhetoricum*, vol. 4, ed. M. Patillon (Paris, 2012): this work, unlike the two others cited previously, is genuinely by Hermogenes.

23. Quintilian 9.2.85.

24. Libanius, *Declamation 35* in Foerster's edition, vol. 7.

25. Libanius, *Declamations 28, 30*, and 26 in Foerster's edition, vol. 6 (Leipzig, 1911). Declamations 26 and 28 are available in English, *Libanius: Imaginary Speeches*, trans. D. A. Russell (London, 1996).

26. But not all: F. M. Ahl saw the political implications of figured speech in "The Art of Safe Criticism in Greece and Rome," *American Journal of Philology* 105 (1984): 174–208; P. Chiron, "Quelques observations sur la théorie du discours figuré dans la *Technê* de Pseudo-Denys d'Halicarnasse," in *Papers on Rhetoric*, ed. L. Calboli Montefusco (Bologna, 2000), 3:75–94.

27. Demetrius, *On Style* 289 (Loeb trans., adapted).

28. Quintilian 9.2.68, 74 (Loeb trans.).

29. Libanius, *Letters* 369.4, in the Loeb Classical Library, Libanius, *Autobiography and Selected Letters*, ed. A. F. Norman (Cambridge, MA, 1992), 1:446–47.

30. Menander Rhetor (third century AD), 2 (*On Epideictic Orations*), 388 and 390, in *Menander Rhetor*, ed. D. A. Russell and N. G. Wilson (Oxford, 1981).

31. Pseudo-Dionysius of Halicarnassus, *Figured Speeches* 2.1.5, 15.

32. Julius Victor (fourth century AD), in *Julius Victor, l'art rhétorique, suivi de Pseudo-Augustin, sur la rhétorique*, ed. P. Fleury and J. Aubin (Paris, 2016), 121.

33. Martianus Capella, *The Wedding of Mercury and Philology* 5.472.

Chapter 3

1. N. Sarraute, *L'Ère du soupçon* (first pub. 1950), in *Œuvres complètes*, ed. J.-Y. Tadié (Paris, 1996), 1579. Available in English as *The Age of Suspicion* (New York, 1963, paperback ed. 1990) and also online.

2. P. Ricœur, "La psychanalyse et le mouvement de la culture contemporaine" (first pub. 1965) in P. Ricœur, *Le Conflit des interprétations: Essais d'herméneutique*, new ed. (Paris, 2013), 210–11; available in English as *The Conflict of Interpretations: Essays in Hermeneutics*, ed. Don Ihde (Evanston, IL, 1974), 121ff.

3. P. Ricœur, "Le problème du double sens comme problème herméneutique et comme problème sémantique" (first pub. 1966), reprinted in, ibid., 102 (Ihde, 62ff.).

4. P. Ricœur, "Herméneutique philosophique et herméneutique biblique" (first pub. 1975) in P. Ricœur, *Du texte à l'action: Essais d'herméneutique* (Paris, 1986), 2:132; available in English as *From Text to Action: Essays in Hermeneutics, II*, trans. K. Blamey and J. B. Thompson (Evanston, IL, 1991), 89ff; H.-G. Gadamer, "The Hermeneutics of Suspicion," in *Hermeneutics: Questions and Prospects*, ed. G. Shapiro and A. Sica (Amherst, MA, 1984), 54–65.

5. For this and the two following paragraphs, cf. C. Kerbrat-Orecchioni, *La connotation* (Lyons, 1977); *L'Implicite*, 2nd ed. (Paris, 1998). She recognizes that the difference between "connotation" and "implication" (*l'implicite*) has not been made clear, *La connotation*, 164.

6. Kerbrat-Orecchioni, *La connotation*, 17, 197.

7. Kerbrat-Orecchioni, *L'Implicite*, 342.

8. Kerbrat-Orecchioni cites Quintilian once, in *L'Implicite*, 277.

9. R. Martin gives the first illustration in "Flou, approximation, non-dit," *Cahiers de lexicologie* 50, no. 1 (1987): 173; the second is from O. Ducrot, in the works cited in note 11.

10. G. Roudière, *Traquer le non-dit: Une sémantique au quotidien* (Issy-les-Moulineaux, 2002).

11. Oswald Ducrot, in turn, reserves the word "subtext" (*sous-entendu*) strictly to mean deliberate implication, calling "presuppositions" (*présupposés*) those contents that are not deliberate, in his *Dire et ne pas dire: Principes de sémantique linguistique* (Paris, 1972) and in his *Le Dire et le dit* (Paris, 1984).

12. Boileau, *Art poétique* 1.153–54.

13. D. Mornet, *Histoire de la clarté française: Ses origines—Son évolution—Sa valeur* (Paris, 1929).

14. Verlaine, *Art poétique*, 5–8. A freer English translation of the whole poem is available in *One Hundred and One Poems by Paul Verlaine: A Bilingual Edition*, trans. Norman R. Shapiro (Chicago, 1999). *L'Art poétique* ad hoc, 5–6, in *Œuvres poétiques complètes*, ed. Y.-G. Dantec (Paris, 1940), 206, 684.

15. Mallarmé, "Magie" (Magic), in *Œuvres complètes*, ed. B. Marchal (Paris, 2003), 2:309.

16. J.-P. Sartre, *Orphée noir*, preface to L. Sedar Senghor, *Anthologie de la nouvelle poésie nègre et malgache de langue française* (Paris, 2011), xix–xx; A. Glucksmann, *Le Discours de la guerre* (Paris, 1974), 273.

17. Mallarmé, "*Toute l'âme résumée . . . ,*" in *Œuvres complètes*, ed. B. Marchal (Paris, 1998), 1:60. An English trans. ("The entire soul evoked") is available in Mallarmé, *Collected Poems: A Bilingual Edition*, trans. Henry Weinfield (Berkeley, 1994), 77.

18. Edmond de Goncourt, *Journal*, February 23, 1893, in Edmond and Jules de Goncourt, *Journal*, ed. R. Ricatte (Paris, 1989), 3:800.

19. R. Barthes, "Critique et autocritique," in *Œuvres complètes*, ed. É. Marty (Paris, 2002), 3:640.

20. *S/Z* (Paris, 1970), 11. Available in English, trans. Richard Miller (New York, 1974).

21. Ibid., 206.

22. R. Barthes, "Texte (théorie du)," in *Œuvres complètes*, ed. É. Marty (Paris, 2002), 4:451.

23. G. Pasquali, "Arte allusiva," in *Pagine stravaganti di un filologo*, ed. C. F. Russo (Florence, 1994), 2:275–82.

24. G. Genette, *Palimpsestes: La littérature au second degré* (Paris, 1982).

25. L. Fraisse, "L'autoréflexivité en pratique," *Poétique* 166 (2011): 155–70.

26. A. Gide, *Journal*, ed. É. Marty (Paris, 1996), 1:171 (September, 1893).

27. J. Haffenden, *William Empson*, vol. 1 (Oxford, 2005), chapter 9.

28. W. Empson, *Seven Types of Ambiguity*, 2nd ed. reprint (New York, 1966), 48.

29. Ibid., 68.

30. Ibid., 1.

31. R. Caillois, *Cohérences aventureuses* (Paris, 1976), 19.

32. Ibid., 93–105.

33. Ibid., 187–88.

Chapter 4

1. Marcel Proust, *In Search of Lost Time: Swann's Way*, trans. C. K. Scott Moncrieff and T. Kilmartin, rev. by D. J. Enright, Modern Library paperback (New York, 2004), part 1, chapter 1, 29.

2. Ibid., 46.

3. E. Zola, *L'Assommoir*, chapter 11, in *Les Rougon-Macquart*, ed. A. Lanoux and H. Mitterand (Paris, 1961), 2:719.

4. Molière, *La Critique de l'École des femmes*, scene 5.

5. *Les Femmes savantes*, act 3, scene 2, with the note of G. Couton on *La Comtesse d'Escarbagnas*, act 1, scene 7, in Molière, *Œuvres complètes* (Paris, 1971), 2:1461–62. Cf. Pascal *Pensées*, No. 553 (Brunschvicg), "The Mystery of Jesus." [WEH: Fans of the American musical will recall the disgusted relish with which Hermione Gingold trills off the name of the salacious French author in the film version of *The Music Man*.]

6. *Much Ado About Nothing*, act 2, scene 3.

7. Ibid.

8. Cardinal de Retz, *Mémoires, Seconde partie*, in *Œuvres*, ed. M.-T. Hipp and M. Pernot (Paris, 1984), 567.

9. Leo Tolstoy, *War and Peace*, book 4, part 4, chapter 10, trans. Rosemary Edmonds, Penguin ed. (Harmondsworth, 1957), 1303.

10. *L'Avant-Scène Cinéma* 234, October 15, 1979, 12.

11. G. G. Clérambault, *L'Érotomanie* (Le Plessis-Robinson, 1993).

12. Paris, 2016.

13. Cicero, *Pro Sestio* (*In Defense of Sestius*), 118, 120; available in the Loeb Classical Library, Cicero, vol. 12, trans. R. Gardner (Cambridge, MA, 1958).

14. Suetonius, *Lives of the Twelve Caesars*, "Julius Caesar," 84.2, trans. Robert Graves, Penguin paperback (Baltimore, 1957).

15. J.-P. Migne, *Patrologiae cursus completus, Series Latina*, vol. 23 (Paris, 1883), cols. 1471–72.

16. St. Jerome, *Letters* 81.1.

17. Demetrius, *On Style* 291; available in the Loeb Classical Library, trans. D. C. Innes, included in the vol. of Aristotle, *Poetics* (Cambridge, MA, 1995).

18. John of Sicily, *Commentary on Hermogenes*, in *Rhetores Graeci*, ed. C. Walz (Stuttgart, 1834), 6:198, 439–40.

19. *Les Fleurs du mal*, poem 100.

20. The speech can be found at https://www.ina.fr/politique/allocutions-et-discours/video/CAC96001699/declaration-de-jacques-chirac.fr.html.

21. Isocrates, *Oration 4* (the *Panegyricus*), 130. Available in the Loeb Classical Library, Isocrates, vol. 1, trans. G. Norlin (Cambridge, MA, 1928).

22. Pascal, *L'Art de persuader*, in *Œuvres complètes*, ed. L. Lafuma (Paris, 1963), 357–58.

23. See chapter 1, p. 4, this volume.

24. S. Brocquet, "L'Histoire de *Rāghava et des Pāṇḍava* de Kavirāja: Un exemple de poésie sanskrite à double sens," *Comptes rendus de l'Académie des inscriptions et des belles-lettres* (2016): 1093.

25. Letter to Mme. de Grignan, November 29, 1679, in *Madame de Sévigné, Correspondance*, ed. R. Duchêne (Paris, 1974), 2:748.

26. Guy de Maupassant, "La moustache," in *Contes et Nouvelles*, ed. L. Forestier (Paris, 1974), 1:919.

27. *Le Père Goriot*, ed. R. Fortassier, in Honoré de Balzac, *La Comédie humaine*, ed. P.-G. Castex (Paris, 1976), 3:235, 238.

28. Letter to Louis Bouilhet, September 4, 1850, in Flaubert, *Correspondance*, ed. J. Bruneau (Paris, 1973), 1:678–79. The letters of Flaubert are available in several English translations, most notably by Francis Steegmuller (Cambridge, MA, 1979–1982).

29. C. Perelman, L. Olbrechts-Tyteca, *Traité de l'argumentation: La nouvelle rhétorique*, 3rd ed. (Brussels, 1976), 25.

30. Gospel according to St. Matthew, 11:15; 13:9, 43 (AV).

31. H. R. Jauss, *Pour une esthétique de la réception*, trans. C. Maillard (Paris, 1978), 49, 259; available in English as *Toward an Aesthetic of Reception*, trans. Timothy Bahti (Minneapolis, MN, 1982).

32. Alan Cameron, "The Last Days of the Academy of Athens," *Proceedings of the Cambridge Philological Society* 195 (1969): 7–29; H. D. Saffrey, *Recherches sur le néoplatonisme après Plotin* (Paris, 1990), 210–11; P. Hoffmann, "Un grief antichrétien chez Proclus: L'ignorance en théologie," in *Les Chrétiens et l'hellénisme: Identités religieuses et culture grecque dans l'Antiquité tardive*, ed. A. Perrot (Paris, 2012), 161–97.

33. Quintilian, *The Orator's Education* 9.2.71; available in the Loeb Classical Library, trans. D. A. Russell (Cambridge, MA, 2001).

34. J. Paulhan, *Traité des figures ou la Rhétorique décryptée*, in *Œuvres complètes*, ed. B. Baillaud (Paris, 2009), 2:282.

35. Leo Strauss, "Persecution and the Art of Writing," in *Social Research* 8 (1941): 488–504.

36. Theophrastus, cited by Demetrius, *On Style* 222; Quintilian 9.2.65, 71–72; J. Paulhan, *Entretien sur les faits divers*, in *Œuvres*, 2:124; W. Empson, *Seven Types of Ambiguity* (New York, 1966), 23.

37. *Essays* 3.13.

38. Demetrius, *On Style* 288, citing Plato, *Phaedo* 59 C.

39. Plato, *Phaedo* 59 B.

40. *Tardieu, Œuvres*, ed. J.-Y. Debreuille, with A. Turolla-Tardieu and D. Hautois (Paris, 2005), 392. [Translator's Note: This translation (WEH) adapts Tardieu's "funny" French to English; a literal translation would be both impossible and pointless. Performances of the scene in French can be found on YouTube.]

41. Ibid., 373.

42. Translator's Note: The Anglophone reader may wish to compare, apropos of this discussion, Lewis Carroll's nonsense poem "Jabberwocky," which occurs early in *Through the Looking Glass*. It plays with English and certain of its poetic and linguistic conventions in a way similar to Tardieu's funny French. Cf. the old but still pertinent, as well as concise, discussion in John Ciardi's *How Does a Poem Mean?* (Boston, 1959), 683–85.

Chapter 5

1. R. MacMullen, *Enemies of the Roman Order: Treason, Unrest, and Alienation in the Empire* (Cambridge, MA, 1966).

2. See chapter 2, p. 15, this volume.

3. Philostratus, *Lives of the Sophists* 1.21.5 (519); 1.25.10 (542–43); 2.4.2 (569); 2.17 (597); 2.25.1 (609); available in the Loeb Classical Library, Philostratus, vol. 4, trans. W. C. Wright (Cambridge, MA, 1921).

4. Dio Chrysostom, *Discourse 43 (Political Oration in his Homeland)*, 6; available in the Loeb Classical Library, Dio Chrysostom, *Discourses*, vol. 4, trans. H. L. Crosby (Cambridge, MA, 1946): "If a certain person should say to me something I do not deserve, whether in plain terms or in figured speech to win renown as an orator . . ." (Loeb, adapted).

5. Dio, *Discourse 18 (On Training for Eloquence)*, 16, in the Loeb Classical Library, Dio, vol. 2, ed. J. W. Cohoon (Cambridge, MA, 1939). See chapter 2, pp. 17–18, this volume.

6. Aelius Aristides, *Oration 4 (To Capito)*, 33, in *P. Aelii Aristidis opera quae extant omnia*, vol. 1.3, ed. C. A. Behr and F. W. Lenz (Leiden, 1978). Available in English trans. in C. A. Behr, *P. Aelius Aristides: The Complete Works*, 2 vols. (Leiden, 1981–1986). Cf. Demetrius, *On Style* 287–88, available in the Loeb Classical Library vol. of Aristotle's *Poetics*, trans. D. C. Innes (Cambridge, MA, 1995); Pseudo-Dionysius of Halicarnassus, *On Figured Speeches* 1.2.

7. Aelius Aristides, *Oration 33 (To Those Who Criticized Him for not Declaiming)*, 25, in *Aelii Aristidis Smyrnaei quae supersunt omnia*, vol. 2, ed. B. Keil (Berlin, 1898): "You criticize while applauding." This oration is

available in English trans. in Behr, *Complete Works*.

8. Dio Cassius, *Roman History* 59.20.6; 67.12.5; available in the Loeb Classical Library, trans. E. Cary and H. Foster (Cambridge, MA, 1924–25).

9. Theon, *Preparatory Exercises* 106.8, in *Aelius Théon, Progymnasmata*, ed. M. Patillon (Paris, 1997), 62. This treatise is available in English in *Progymnasmata: Greek Textbooks of Prose Composition and Rhetoric*, trans. George Kennedy (Atlanta, 2003).

10. Suetonius, *Lives of the Twelve Caesars*, "Domitian," 10.1: *"propter quasdam in historia figuras."* In this passage, as in the following citation from Suetonius, the word *"figuras"* does not mean "stylistic figures" but, more probably, "figured speech" in its technical sense. The use of the simple Greek term *"skhêma"* in this sense appears in Quintilian, *The Orator's Education* 9.2.65 (cf. also Petronius, *Satyricon*, 44); the Latin term *"figura"* has this special usage, too, in both the singular and the plural (Quintilian 9.2.69, 72, etc.).

11. Suetonius, *Lives*, "Vespasian," 13.1: *"Amicorum libertatem, causidicorum figuras ac philosophorum contumaciam lenissime tulit."*

12. Philostratus, *Lives of the Sophists* 2.1.11 (561).

13. These discourses, numbered 1 through 4 in the catalog of Dio's works, have been edited and translated into English by J. W. Cohoon in the Loeb Classical Library Dio Chrysostom (Cambridge, MA, 1932), 1:1–233. Discourses 2 and 4 can be found in an annotated French translation by L. Pernot, *Alexandre le Grand: Les risques du pouvoir: Textes philosophiques et rhétoriques* (Paris, 2013), 29–107.

14. Pliny the Younger, *Panegyric of Trajan* 3.5; available in the Loeb Classical Library, Pliny the Younger, vol. 2, trans. B. Radice (Cambridge, MA, 1969).

15. Dio, *First Discourse on Kingship* 9.8, 49.

16. Ibid., 15 and 36 (Loeb trans.).

17. Dio, *Third Discourse on Kingship*, 25 (Loeb trans.).

18. *The Greek Anthology* 9.562; Martial, *Epigrams* 14.73.

19. Tiberius (third to fourth century AD), *On the Figures in Demosthenes* 21, in *Tiberii de figuris Demosthenicis libellus*, ed. G. Ballaira (Rome, 1968).

20. Molière, *La Critique de l'École des femmes*, scene 6.

21. See chapter 3, p. 34, this volume.

22. For these notions, cf. J. Assmann, *Cultural Memory and Early Civilization*, English trans. from the original German (Cambridge, UK, 2011); T. Pavel, *L'Art de l'éloignement: Essai sur l'imagination classique* (Paris, 1996).

23. Aristotle, *Rhetoric* 3.17, 1418b26; available in the Loeb Classical Library, trans. J. H. Freese, rev. by G. Striker (Cambridge, MA, 2020).

24. Pseudo-Hermogenes, *On Invention* 4.13.10.

25. Demetrius, *On Style* 292 (Loeb trans.). Also, Pseudo-Dionysius of Halicarnassus, *On Figured Speeches* 2.7, 8.

26. Tiberius, *Demosthenes* 11–12.

27. Dio, *Second Discourse on Kingship* 1.

28. Ibid., 17.

29. Dio provides this detail in *Discourse* 57.11, which can be found in vol. 4 of the Loeb Library Dio.

30. Pliny the Younger, *Letters* 10.82; available in Radice's Loeb, with the *Panegyric*.

31. Aelius Aristides, *Oration 47 (First Sacred Oration)*, 23, 38; *Oration 51 (Fifth Sacred Oration)*, 45; both orations found in *Aelii Aristidis Smyrnaei quae supersunt omnia*, vol. 2, ed. B. Keil (Berlin, 1898).

32. Aelius Aristides, *Oration 50 (Fourth Sacred Oration)*, 101–2.

33. Ibid., 31 and 36.

34. *Encomium of Rome*, the usual title; literally the Greek title means *"In Honor of Rome."* This oration is number 26 in the corpus of Aristides. The standard edition remains Keil's, 2:91–124. Behr, *Complete Works*, has an English trans., and there is another by S. Levin, *To Rome, by Aelius Aristides* (Glencoe, IL, 1950). James H. Oliver, "The Ruling Power: A Study of the Roman Empire in the Second Century after Christ through the Roman Oration of Aelius Aristides," in *Transactions of the American Philological Society* 43 (1953): 871–982, offers an English translation along with a Greek text, substantive introduction, and extensive notes. L. Pernot has done an annotated translation in French, *Éloges grecs de Rome* (Paris, 1997), 13–120.

35. Menander Rhetor 1.358 (*The Types of the Epideictic Oration*); 2.371 and 372 (*On*

Epideictic Orations); Pseudo-Dionysius of Halicarnassus, *Rhetoric* 2.6, in *Dionysii Halicarnasei opuscula*, vol. 2.1, ed. H. Usener and L. Radermacher (Leipzig, 1904).

36. Aelius Aristides, *Oration 1 (Panathenaic Oration)*, 332; available in the Loeb Classical Library, Aelius Aristides, vol. 1, ed. M. Trapp (Cambridge, MA, 2017).

37. K. Burke, *The Philosophy of Literary Form* (rev., New York, 1957), 24.

38. Aelius Aristides, *Oration 3 (For the Four)*, 127 and 250, in *P. Aelii Aristidis opera quae extant omnia*, vol. 1.2 and 1.3, ed. C. A. Behr and F. W. Lenz (Leiden, 1978).

39. Aelius Aristides, *Oration 26 (Encomium of Rome)*, 8.

40. Aelius Aristides, *Oration 27 (Panegyric of Cyzicus)*, 34; *Oration 50 (Fourth Sacred Oration)*, 77.

41. Theon, *Preparatory Exercises* 111.3–11; Menander Rhetor 2.357.9–11 (*On Epideictic Orations*); Emporius in *Rhetores latini minores*, ed. R. Halm (Leipzig, 1863), 568, 7–17.

42. *Historia Augusta*, "Life of Septimius Severus," 14.13 [Loeb trans. by D. Magie (Cambridge, MA, 1921)].

43. M. Jarrety, *Paul Valéry* (Paris, 2008), 678.

44. The French text of the speech is available in *Discours de reception à l'Académie française* (Paris, 1927), 44; Paul Valéry, *Œuvres*, ed. J. Hytier (Paris, 1957), 1:729.

45. G. Girard, *La Jeunesse d'Anatole France, 1844–1878* (Paris, 1925), 30–34.

46. A. Maalouf, *Un fauteuil sur la Seine: Quatre siècles d'histoire de France* (Paris, 2016), 44.

47. See chapter 2, pp. 17–18, this volume.

48. Joseph Antoine Toussaint Dinouart, *L'Art de se taire, principalement en matière de religion*, ed. J.-J. Courtine and C. Haroche (Paris, 1996), 40–43.

49. Montaigne, *Essays* 2.12.

50. Quintilian, *On the Orator's Education* 9.2.67, 97.

51. Quintilian 9.2.71; Apsines, *On Figured Problems*, 27; Gregory of Corinth, *Notes on Hermogenes*, in *Rhetores Graeci*, ed. C. Walz (Stuttgart, 1834), 7:1170–71.

52. M. Hose, "Von der Bedeutung der griechischen Literatur für Rom: Eine Betrachtungen aus der Sicht de post-kolonialistischen Literaturtheorie," in

Antike Literatur: Mensch, Sprache, Welt, ed. P. Neukam (Munich, 2000), 38–58.

53. Jean Genet, *The Blacks*, in *Théâtre complet*, ed. M. Corbin and A. Dichy (Paris, 2002), 488.

Chapter 6

1. Aeschylus, *Agamemnon* 36–39. The saying lives on, not only in the pages of Aeschylus. We note that none other than the British prime minister, Boris Johnson, used it recently in a witty sally against the silent leader of the Labor opposition in the House of Commons, as reported in the *New York Times*, June 18, 2020, A11.

2. G. Sadoul, *Aragon* (Paris, 1967), 28.

3. Aragon, *La Lumière de Stendhal* (Paris, 1954), 114.

4. Interview with Fernand Seguin (1969), cited in P. Juquin, *Aragon: Un destin français* (Paris, 2013), 2:152.

5. The poems dating from the Second World War are collected in vol. 1 of his *Œuvres poétiques complètes*, ed. O. Barbarant (Paris, 2007). [Translator's Note: Aragon's poetic corpus still awaits English translation. A few poems are available, especially from the *Elsa's Eyes* collection; cf. *Poetry* 67 (1945), available online at poetryfoundation. org. Other translations are scattered here and there. Those in this chapter are my own, mere stabs that do not pretend to do justice to Aragon's chiseled metrics and polished diction. Some poems have been "translated" into classical music, like "C" by Francis Poulenc].

6. Sadoul, *Aragon*, 26.

7. In *Le Crève-cœur*, the poem "Ombres."

8. *J'attends sa letter au crepuscule*: Juquin, *Aragon*, 2:35.

9. *Enfer-les-Mines*: Juquin, *Aragon*, 2:152–53.

10. *Le Mot*, in *En étrange pays dans mon pays lui-même*.

11. *Écrit au seuil*, in *Œuvres poétiques complètes*, 2:1404.

12. See chapter 2, p. 24, this volume.

13. M. Zink, *Les Troubadours: Une histoire poétique* (Paris, 2013), 291–92.

14. *La Leçon de Ribérac*, in *Œuvres*, 1:813. Aragon refers here to the expression "culture of the silly shopgirl" from a 1941 article by Montherlant in the *Nouvelle Revue française*.

Notes to Pages 65–74

15. O. Barbarant, in *Œuvres*, 1:1466–67.

16. Ibid., 1474.

17. *"Elsa au miroir,"* a 1943 poem reprinted in the collection *La Diane française*.

18. P. Seghers, *La Résistance et ses poètes: France 1940–1945*, 2nd ed. (Paris, 1974).

19. Cited in *Aragon, Œuvres*, 1:1476.

20. Juquin, *Aragon*, 2:76–77.

21. P. Forest, *Aragon* (Paris, 2015), 476, 480, 511.

22. *Œuvres*, 1:1564.

23. Ibid., 737–39.

24. Sadoul, *Aragon*, 25–26; Seghers, *Résistance*, 43–44; P. Daix, *Aragon, une vie à changer* (Paris, 1975), 303; Barbarant, *Œuvres*, 1:1438.

25. W. Babilas, *Études sur Louis Aragon* (Münster, 2002), 1:424–30.

26. Juquin, *Aragon*, 2:28.

27. The following three interpretations are, in order, those of Barbarant, *Œuvres*, 1:1439; of Babilas, *Études*, 2:478–84; and of Juquin, *Aragon*, 2:36.

28. Barbarant, *Œuvres*, 1:1439.

29. "De l'exactitude historique en poésie" (On historical exactitude in poetry), Aragon's introduction to *En étrange pays dans mon pays lui-même*.

30. Sadoul, *Aragon*, 38.

31. Aragon himself, commenting on this line, explained this touch in "On Historical Exactitude in Poetry" (cited above, note 29), in *Oeuvres*, 1:859: "the rocking chair is an American invention, unknown to the Greeks and inhabitants of Pontus."

32. Robert Darnton, *Censors at Work: How States Shaped Literature* (New York, 2014).

33. R. Kapuściński, *Travels with Herodotus*, English trans. K. Glowczewska (New York, 2007), 6 (adapted).

34. See chapter 4, p. 48, this volume.

35. C. Miłosz, *The Captive Mind*, English trans. (London, 1953), chapter 7.

36. M. Haraszti, *The Velvet Prison: Artists Under State Socialism*, English trans. (New York, 1987), 142ff.

37. Darnton, *Censors*, 209–10, 215–16.

38. J.-L. Domenach, "La machine parlementaire chinoise," in the leftist Parisian newspaper *Libération*, March 6, 2015, 7.

39. The essay can be found in English translation online and in the volume *Brecht on Art and Politics*, ed. S. Giles and T.

Kuhn (London, 2003), part 3, item 39; the quotation occurs on page 145.

40. M. Fumaroli, *Chateaubriand: Poésie et Terreur* (Paris, 2003), 426, 428.

41. J. Isaac, *Les Oligarques: Essai d'histoire partiale*, ed. P. Ory (Paris, 1989), 54, 143, 58.

42. Lewis Carroll, *Through the Looking Glass*, chapter 6.

43. Thucydides 3.82, revolution on Corcyra (Crawley translation).

44. Tacitus, *Agricola* 30; *Histories* 4.14.

45. Tacitus, *Histories* 4.73.

46. A. Manzoni, *The Betrothed*, chapter 31, trans. B. Penman, Penguin ed. (London, 1972), 574.

47. Ibid., 582–83.

48. *Fables* 7.1: "Animals Sick from the Plague."

49. J.-P. Faye, *Introduction aux langages totalitaires: Théorie et transformations du récit*, new ed. (Paris, 2003).

50. V. Klemperer, *The Language of the Third Reich: LTI—Lingua Tertii Imperii*, trans. M. Brady (London, 2006), 8.

51. S. Combe, preface to the French trans. of Klemperer, *LTI, la langue du IIIe Reich: Carnets d'un philologue* (Paris, 2013), 13, 22.

52. Klemperer, *Language*, 14, 103–4.

53. Ibid., 91–92.

54. Ibid., 94, 238.

55. George Orwell, *1984* (London, 1949), part 1.5, 54. The quoted slogans are *passim*.

56. Klemperer, *Language*, 90.

57. Ibid., 69, 113–14, 207.

58. Ibid., 76.

59. Orwell, *1984*, part 1.5, 61.

60. Ibid., part 3.4, 278.

61. A. Londres, *Dans la Russie des Soviets, 1920* (Paris, 1992), 49–51.

62. A. Ciliga, *The Russian Enigma* (Ink Links, 1979), 137; English trans. available online.

63. A. Solzhenitsyn, *Gulag Archipelago*, trans. T. P. Whitney (New York, 1973), vol. 2, part 4, section 3, 647–49.

64. Orwell, "Politics and the English Language," essay reprinted as a stand-alone pamphlet (New York, 2013), 16.

65. E. Hazan, *LQR: La Propagande du quotidien* (Paris, 2006).

Chapter 7

1. *Rhetoric to Alexander* 35.18.

2. *Les Mots* (*The Words*), trans. B. Frechtman (New York, 1981), 12.

3. Balzac, *Le Père Goriot*, ed. R. Fortassier, in *La Comédie humaine*, ed. P.-G. Castex (Paris, 1976), 3:223. The explanation for this lexical formation is given earlier in the novel: "The recent invention of the Diorama, which raised optical illusion to a higher degree than Panoramas, had introduced into certain painting ateliers the pleasantry of speaking in 'rama,' the sort of kick that a young painter had injected into the Vauquer pension which he frequented" (91). Cf. M. Drevon, J. Guichardet, "Fameux sexorama," *L'Année balzacienne* (1972): 257–74.

4. Molière, *Le Mariage forcé* (*The Forced Marriage*), scene 2, in *Œuvres complètes*, ed. G. Forestier (Paris, 2010), 1:943–44.

5. Balzac, *La Duchesse de Langeais*, chapter 2, ed. R. Fortassier, in *La Comédie humaine*, ed. P.-G. Castex (Paris, 1977), 5:978.

6. Balzac, *Les Chouans*, part 3, chapter 31, ed. L. Frappier-Mazur, in *La Comédie humaine*, ed. P.-G. Castex (Paris, 1977), 8:1207.

7. Stendhal, *The Red and the Black*, book 1, chapter 15.

8. *The Charterhouse of Parma*, chapter 25, trans. R. Howard, Modern Library paperback (New York, 2000), 433. [WEH: Quotation marks around "movement" have been added to suggest the point.]

9. Stendhal, *The Red and the Black*, book 2, chapter 19.

10. *Anna Karenina*, part 2, chapter 10–11 (Constance Garnett trans., adapted).

11. Maupassant, "Mots d'amour," in *Contes et Nouvelles*, ed. L. Forestier (Paris, 1974), 1:359.

12. Dante, *Inferno*, canto 5, 138.

13. L. Renzi, *Le Conseguenze di un bacio* (Bologna, 2007), esp. 106 and 132.

14. Manzoni, *The Betrothed*, chapter 10, trans. B. Penman, Penguin ed. (London, 1972), 206.

15. P. Verstraten, "L'ellipse, catalyseur au cinéma," in *Ellipses, Blancs, Silences*, ed. B. Rougé (Pau, 1992), 201.

16. Chapter 52 of the novel, in his *Œuvres*, ed. L. Guichard (Paris, 1970), 1:428–31.

17. P. Hériat, *Famille Boussardel*, chapter 20.

18. *Tristram Shandy*, passim.

19. *In Search of Lost Time*, vol. 1, *Swann's Way*, "Swann in Love," trans. C. K. Scott Moncrieff and T. Kilmartin, rev. by D. J. Enright (New York, 1992), 312.

20. Ibid., vol. 4, *Sodom and Gomorrah*, part 1, 6.

21. A. Pierron, *Dictionnaire des mots du sexe* (Paris, 2010).

22. E. Partridge, *Shakespeare's Bawdy: A Literary and Psychological Essay and a Comprehensive Glossary*, rev. ed. (London, 1955). [WEH: A PDF version is available online.]

23. Act 2, scene 3.

24. Act 2, scene 5.

25. Letter to Sutton Sharpe, March 23, 1828, in Stendhal, *Correspondance générale*, ed. V. Del Litto (Paris, 1999), 3:671.

26. Stendhal, *Œuvres romanesques complètes*, ed. Y. Ansel and P. Berthier (Paris, 2005), 1:89–90.

27. H. Martineau, introduction to *Armance* (Paris, 1950), 1.

28. Stendhal, *Œuvres romanesques*, 1:905, 907.

29. *Armance*, in Stendhal, *Œuvres romanesques*, 1:210. This aphorism reappears in *The Red and the Black*, where it is attributed to Gabriel Malagrida, an eighteenth-century Jesuit (book 1, chapter 22) and in Stendhal's *Courrier Anglais*, ed. H. Martineau (Paris, 1936), 4:346, where it is attributed to Talleyrand in a slightly different form: "The role of speech, this veteran diplomat said, is to conceal thought."

30. Stendhal, *Œuvres romanesques*, 1:895.

31. Ibid., 897 (and 101 for the corresponding text).

32. Letter to Sutton Sharpe, March 23, 1828, in Stendhal, *Correspondance générale*, 3:671.

33. Letter to Prosper Mérimée, December 23, 1826, in Stendhal, *Correspondance*, 3:598–601.

34. H. Martineau in his edition of *Armance*, 307n403.

35. P. Berthier, in Stendhal, *Œuvres romanesques*, 1:867.

36. J.-J. Hamm, *Armance, ou la Liberté de Stendhal* (Paris, 2009), 37.

37. N. Gardini, *Lacuna: Saggio sul non detto* (Turin, 2014), 212.

38. Stendhal, *Œuvres intimes*, ed. V. Del Litto (Paris, 1982), 2:412.

39. *La Vieille Fille* (*The Old Maid*) in Balzac, *La Comédie humaine*, 4:827.

40. Ibid., 830.

41. M. Le Yaouanc, "Le plaisir dans les récits balzaciens," *L'Année balzacienne* (1973): 209; N. Mozct, introduction to *La Vieille Fille*, in Balzac, *Comédie*, 4:797–98, with notes, 1490.

42. P.-G. Castex, *H. de Balzac: La Vieille Fille* (Paris, 1957), vii.

43. *Le Père Goriot*, in Balzac, *Comédie*, 3:260 (apropos of the care lavished on Père Goriot during his illness, care that the novelist refrains from describing in detail).

44. N. Mozet, in Balzac, *Comédie*, 4:795.

45. *La Vieille Fille*, in Balzac, *Comédie*, 4:935.

46. *Échantillon de causerie française*, ed. R. Pierrot, in Balzac, *Comédie* (Paris, 1981), 12:480–82.

47. T. Billard, *Félix Faure* (Paris, 1995), 901–34.

48. A. Lanoux, *Madame Steinheil ou "la connaissance du Président"* (Paris, 1983).

49. Since I was not able to consult this issue of the *Journal du peuple*, I cite this remark as found in A.-C. Ambroise-Rendu, "La mort de Félix Faure: autopsie d'un scandale," in *Presse à scandale, scandale de presse*, ed. C. Delporte, M. Palmer, and D. Ruellan (Paris, 2001), 51.

50. P. Morand, *Tais-Toi*, repr. (Paris, 2002), 21–22.

Chapter 8

1. A. Finkielkraut, *Le Mécontemporain: Péguy, lecteur du monde moderne* (Paris, 1991).

2. *"Il ne faut pas dire" (posthume)*, in Charles Péguy, *Œuvres en prose complètes*, ed. R. Burac (Paris, 1988), 2:572.

3. See the website http://rene.pommier .free.fr.

4. *Iliad* 9.312–13 (Lattimore translation); Philostratus, *Lives of the Sophists* 1.25.10, available in the Loeb Classical Library, Philostratus, vol. 4, trans. W. C. Wright (Cambridge, MA, 1921).

5. Demetrius, *On Style* 296–98; available in the Loeb Classical Library, trans. D. C. Innes (Cambridge, MA, 1995), in the vol. Aristotle, *Poetics*.

6. Quintilian, *The Orator's Education* 9.2.79; available in the Loeb Classical

Library, trans. D. A. Russell (Cambridge, MA, 2001).

7. Seneca the Elder, *Controversiae* 2.1.39; available in the Loeb Classical Library, trans. M. Winterbottom (Cambridge, MA, 1974) [here slightly modified, W.F.H: "aiebat illum acta in aurem legere"].

8. Ibid., 10, preface, 10 (adapted).

9. Quintilian 5.10.70; 9.2.69; Pseudo-Dionysius of Halicarnassus, *On Figured Speeches* 2.1; Julius Rufinianus, *On the Figures of Thought*, in *Rhetores Latini minores*, ed. R. Halm (Leipzig, 1863), 60.

10. Molière, *The Forced Marriage*, scene 4.

11. See chapter 7, p. 99, this volume.

12. Plutarch, "How to Tell a Flatterer from a Friend," 25; available in the Loeb Classical Library. Plutarch, *Moralia*, vol. 1, trans. F. C. Babbitt (Cambridge, MA, 1927).

13. Fronto, *Ad M. Caes.* 3.15; available in the Loeb Classical Library, *The Correspondence of Marcus Cornelius Fronto*, trans. C. R. Haines (Cambridge, MA, 1919), 1:100–101.

14. C. Carlos, "Techniques of Bold Speaking, Safely, in Bossuet's 'Sermon sur la prédication évangélique' (1662)," *Rhetorica* 28 (2010): 197–221.

15. *Iliad* 2.212ff.

16. *Le Nez du général Suif*, in G. Courteline, *Coco, Coco et Toto* (Paris, 1905), 63–65.

17. J. Starobinski, *Jean-Jacques Rousseau, Transparency and Obstruction*, English trans. by A. Goldhammer (Chicago, 1988).

18. Sterne, *A Sentimental Journey Through France and Italy*, conclusion of "The Rose. Paris."

19. I have been unable to find the exact reference for this oft-cited aphorism.

20. *Précis de décomposition*, in *Œuvres*, ed. Y. Peyré (Paris, 1995), 675. Available as *A Short History of Decay* in English trans. by R. Howard (New York, 1975/2012).

21. T. Adorno, *Minima Moralia*, French trans. by É. Kaufhoilz, J.-R. Ladmiral (Paris, 2003), 43.

22. C. Kerbrat-Orecchioni, *L'Implicite* (Paris, 1998), 5.

23. *Rhetoric to Herennius* 4.48–50; available in the Loeb Classical Library, Cicero, vol. 1, trans. H. Caplan (Cambridge, MA, 1954).

24. Quintilian 9.2.27–28.

25. Publication under the direction of F. Ewald and A. Fontana, ed. F. Gros:

L'Herméneutique du sujet: Cours au Collège de France (1981–1982) (Paris, 2001); *Le Gouvernement de soi et des autres: Cours au Collège de France (1982–1983)* (Paris, 2008); *Le Courage de la vérité: Le Gouvernement de soi et des autres II. Cours au Collège de France (1983–1984)* (Paris, 2009). A version of the courses, bearing on the same topic, but much more succinct, given in English at UC Berkeley in the autumn of 1983, had been published earlier under the title *Discourse and Truth: The Problematization of Parrhesia*, ed. J. Pearson (Evanston, IL, 1985). All three Paris courses are now available in English translation by Graham Burchell, as specified in notes below. They also appear in a later edition, *Fearless Speech*, ed. Joseph Pearson (Los Angeles, 2001).

26. In the first volume of the lectures, the word *parrhêsia* appears transcribed with an *h*, reflecting the aspirated *r* of ancient Greek, the letter rho, while, inexplicably, the word is printed without the aspiration in the succeeding two volumes. This has unfortunately led to a tendency to spell it in modern languages without the aspiration, which is absolutely incorrect, as incorrect as writing in English "retoric" or "rombus." One must write *parrhêsia* with an *h*.

27. Quintilian 9.2.27.

28. Pseudo-Dionysius of Halicarnassus, *Figured Speeches* 1.3–4; 2.3, 7; Pseudo-Hermogenes, *On Invention* 4.13.4; Syrianus, Sopater, and Marcellinus, *Scholia on Hermogenes*, in *Rhetores Graeci*, ed. C. Walz (Stuttgart, 1833), 4:103.

29. *L'Ordre du discours*, in M. Foucault, *Œuvres*, ed. F. Gros (Paris, 2015), 2:232. Available in English as an appendix in *The Archaeology of Knowledge and the Discourse on Language*, trans. A. M. Sheridan Smith (New York, 1972), 215–37.

30. Ibid., 252.

31. *L'Usage des plaisirs*, in Foucault, *Œuvres*, 2:746. Available in English trans. as vol. 2 of *The History of Sexuality, the Use of Pleasure* (Penguin, 1985).

32. *The Government of Self and Others*, trans. G. Burchell (New York, 2010), 41.

33. *The Courage of Truth*, trans. G. Burchell (New York, 2011), 2–3.

34. Ibid., 3.

35. *The Hermeneutics of the Subject*, trans. G. Burchell (New York, 2005), 2–3.

36. *Courage of Truth*, 5–6.

37. L. Spina, *Il cittadino alla tribuna: Diritto e libertà di parola nell'Atene democratica* (Naples, 1986).

38. *Government*, 131ff.

39. Ibid., 193.

40. Ibid., 45–46.

41. I summarize here *Government*, 52ff, and *Hermeneutics of the Subject*, 371ff.

42. *Government*, 188.

43. Ibid., 346.

44. Ibid., 229.

45. *Courage of Truth*, 165ff., 172, 174.

46. Ibid., 234.

47. *Government*, 45.

48. *Courage*, 316.

49. *Government*, 69–70.

50. *Courage*, 177ff., 283ff., note on 303.

51. F. Gros, "Situation du cours," postscript to *Le Gouvernement de soi et des autres*, 359n39.

52. "Interview de Michel Foucault," in Foucault, *Dits et écrits*, ed. D. Defert and F. Ewald (Paris, 2001), 2:1509.

53. S. C. Jarratt, "Untimely Historiography? Foucault's 'Greco-Latin Trip,'" *Rhetoric Society Quarterly* 44 (2014): 220–33.

54. *Government*, 47ff, 174ff.

55. *Hermeneutics*, 373, 381ff., 403; *Government*, 53, 134, 229, 236, 303ff., 357ff.; *Courage*, 13–14; "La Parrêsia," lecture given by Foucault in May 1982, at the University of Grenoble, *Anabases* 16 (2012): 166.

56. C. Lévy, "From Politics to Philosophy and Theology: Some Remarks about Foucault's Interpretation of *Parrêsia* in Two Recently Published Seminars," *Philosophy and Rhetoric* 42 (2009): 313–25; M. Möller, "Am Nullpunkt der Rhetorik? Michel Foucault und die parrhesiastische Rede," in *Parrhesia: Foucault und der Mut zur Wahrheit*, ed. P. Gehring and A. Gelhard (Zurich, 2012), 106–14; A. E. Walzer, "*Parrêsia*, Foucault, and the Classical Rhetorical Tradition," *Rhetoric Society Quarterly* 43 (2013): 1–21.

57. *Courage*, 198, 253, 275–78. See chapter 5, pp. 60–61, this volume.

58. *Britannicus*, act 1, scene 2.

Chapter 9

1. Aelius Aristides, *Oration* 2 (*Defense of Rhetoric*), 346–49; available in the Loeb Classical Library, Aristides, vol. 1, trans. M. Trapp (Cambridge, MA, 2017); Pseudo-Dionysius of Halicarnassus, *On Figured Speeches* 2.6.

2. *Persecution and the Art of Writing* (Glencoe, IL, 1952; reissued Chicago, 1988), 23–24.

3. *Oration* 1 (*Panathenaicus*), 332, 335 (available in the Loeb, vol. 1).

4. I am indebted to Luc Fraisse for having alerted me to these passages.

5. M. Proust, *The Guermantes Way, In Search of Lost Time*, vol. 3, trans. C. K. Scott Moncrieff and T. Kilmartin, rev. by D. J. Enright (New York, 1992), part 2, chapter 2, 544.

6. M. M. Magill, *Répertoire des références aux arts et à la littérature dans À la recherche du temps perdu de Marcel Proust* (Birmingham, AL, 1991), 227.

7. *La Jalousie* (Paris, 1957), 101. Available in English as *Jealousy*, trans. Richard Howard (New York, 1978).

8. B. Morrissette, *Les Romans de Robbe-Grillet* (Paris, 1963), 125 (with a discussion on the thrust of the passage); C. Michel and L. Verdier, *Robbe-Grillet, Les Gommes, La Jalousie* (Neuilly, 2010), 129. [Translator's Note: It is worth observing that Robbe-Grillet employs similar devices in his films, notably *Last Year at Marienbad*, where, in addition to repeated scenes, the repeated shots and camera pans along with repetitions of voice-over narration at the film's start suggest both the baroque splendor of the hotel setting and the mysteries and deceptions lying beneath those facades.] For *mise en abyme*, see chapter 3, pp. 32–33, this volume.

9. Quintilian, *Education of the Orator* 9.2.75, available in the Loeb Classical Library, vol. 4, trans. D. A. Russell (Cambridge, MA, 2001).

10. Quintilian, 9.2.93–95.

11. Pseudo-Dionysius of Halicarnassus, *Figured Speeches* 2.5, 14.

12. A. Billy, *Vie de Balzac* (Paris, 1944), 2:12–13.

13. *Le Canard enchaîné*, June 29, 2016.

14. M. Fumaroli, "*Les Contes* de Perrault et leur sens second: L'éloge de la modernité du siècle de Louis le Grand," *Revue d'histoire littéraire de la France* 114 (2014): 775–96, esp. 777–79.

15. Esp. Demetrius, *On Style* 8–9, 102, 241, available in the Loeb Classical Library, trans. D. C. Innes (Cambridge, MA, 1995), included in the vol. Aristotle, *Poetics*; Tryphon, *On Tropes*, in *Rhetores Graeci*, ed. L. Spengel (Leipzig, 1856), 3:202.

16. W. Empson, *Seven Types of Ambiguity* (New York, 1966), 134–35.

17. C. Kerbrat-Orecchioni, *La connotation* (Lyons, 1977), 58–65.

18. *Oedipus Tyrannos* 927–28.

19. P. N. Papageorgius, *Scholia in Sophoclis tragoedias vetera* (Leipzig, 1888), 199.

20. O. Longo, *Scholia Byzantina in Sophoclis Oedipum tyrannum* (Padua, 1971), 59, 237; Syrianus, in *Syriani in Hermogenem commentaria*, ed. H. Rabe (Leipzig, 1892), 1:37 (=Anonymus, *Scholia on Hermogenes*, in *Rhetores Graeci*, ed. C. Walz (Stuttgart, 1834), 7:950.

21. Quintilian 9.2.70.

22. Pseudo-Hermogenes, *On Invention* 4.13.18–19.

23. S. Bern, *Piques et Répliques de l'Histoire* (Paris, 2017), 191.

24. Freud, *Le Trait d'esprit et sa relation à l'inconscient*, in *Œuvres complètes: Psychanalyse*, (Paris, 2014), 7:135. Available in English as *Jokes and Their Relation to the Unconscious*, trans. James Strachey (New York, 1960).

25. J. Borges, *Evaristo Carriego*, section 6; available in English, trans. N. T. di Giovanni (New York, 1984). Cf. P. Odifreddi, *C'era una volta un paradosso: Storie di illusioni e verità rovesciate* (Turin, 2001), 133.

26. *The Dawn of the Day*, Aphorism 273 [WEH: from the original German]. There is an English trans. of *Dawn* by J. M. Kennedy (London, 1924) available online.

27. Ibid., Aphorism 228, Kennedy trans. adapted.

28. *Beyond Good and Evil*, trans. M. Faber (Oxford, 1998), Aphorism 283.

29. *Human, All Too Human*, trans. R. J. Hollingdale (Cambridge, UK, 1996), Aphorism 360.

30. Alfred de Musset, *Il faut qu'une porte soit ouverte ou fermée*, in *Théâtre complet*, ed. S. Jeune (Paris, 1990), 451.

31. Thucydides, *Peloponnesian War* 1.80–85; Demosthenes, *Oration* 14 (*On the Symmories*): texts analyzed by Pseudo-Dionysius of Halicarnassus, *Figured Speeches* 1.7.

32. The speech is reprinted in C. Boutin, *Les Grands Discours du XXe siècle* (Paris, 2009), 336–42.

33. An expression of G. Leduc, "Quelques chemins de traverse rhétoriques empruntés par des Anglaises de la Renaissance: entre

34. Homer, *Odyssey* 2.89–110.

35. A. Romeo, *Orfeo in Ovidio: La creazione di un nuovo epos* (Soveria Mannelli, 2012), 146.

36. Heliodorus, *Aethiopica* 1.22–23. An English trans. is available online.

37. Xenophon of Ephesus, *The Ephesian Tale (Ephesiaca)* 2.13. An English trans. is available online.

38. Balzac, *La Duchesse de Langeais*, ed. R. Fortassier, chap. 2, in *La Comédie humaine*, ed. P.-G. Castex (Paris, 1977), 5:972.

39. Gospel according to St. Matthew, 5:37 (AV).

40. Borges, *Evaristo*, section 7, in *Œuvres completes*, ed. J.-P. Bernès (Paris, 2010), 151.

41. C. Kerbrat-Orecchioni, *L'Implicite* (Paris, 1986), 73.

42. Menander Rhetor, 2 (*On Epideictic Orations*), 379–80, in *Menander Rhetor*, ed. D. A. Russell and N. G. Wilson (Oxford, 1981), 96–101.

43. P. Fontanier, *Les Figures du discours* (Paris, 1968).

44. See chapter 2, p. 15, this volume.

45. Fontanier, *Les Figures du discours*, 114, 116.

46. See chapter 1, pp. 12–13, this volume.

47. Fontanier, *Les Figures du discours*, 125.

48. See chapter 6, pp. 82–83, this volume.

49. Fontanier, *Les Figures du discours*, 265.

50. Ibid., 371.

51. Alexander and Herodian (authors of treatises on the figures), in *Rhetores Graeci*, ed. L. Spengel (Leipzig, 1856), 3:24, 96, referring to Homer, *Iliad* 2.284ff.

52. Phoibammon, in Spengel, *Rhetores Graeci*, 354.

53. Fontanier, *Les Figures du discours*, 266.

54. B. Dupriez, *Gradus: Les procédés littéraires (Dictionnaire)* (Paris, 1980), 205.

55. Fontanier, *Les Figures du discours*, 123.

56. See chapter 1, p. 1, this volume.

57. Aelius Aristides, *Oration 26 (Encomium of Rome)*, 60. An English trans. is available in Aelius Aristides, *Complete Works*, ed. C. A. Behr (Leiden, 1981–1986).

58. Fontanier, *Les Figures du discours*, 447.

59. See chapter 8, p. 112, this volume.

60. Fontanier, *Les Figures du discours*, 133.

61. Corneille, *Le Cid*, act 3, scene 4.

62. Fontanier, *Les Figures du discours*, 143.

63. See chapter 5, p. 68, this volume.

64. Fontanier, *Les Figures du discours*, 404, 427, 375, respectively.

65. See chapter 5, pp. 59–62, this volume.

66. Fontanier, *Les Figures du discours*, 135.

67. See chapter 5, p. 68, and chapter 7, pp. 94–95, this volume.

68. Fontanier, *Les Figures du discours*, 79, 87, 99.

69. See chapter 3, p. 33; chapter 5, p. 65; chapter 6, p. 75; and chapter 7, pp. 96–97, this volume.

70. E. Lavric, "Rencontres avec le Dit et le Non-dit tout au long d'une vie de linguiste," in *Le Dit et le Non-dit: Langage(s) et traduction*, ed. S. Berbinski (Frankfurt, 2016), 51–52.

71. J. Scott, *Domination and the Arts of Resistance: Hidden Transcripts* (New Haven, 1990).

72. Ibid., 183.

73. Ibid.

74. Ibid., 136ff.

75. Ibid., 138, 184–92, 203.

76. W. Knight, *MIT Technology Review*, July 26, 2016, https://www.technologyreview.com/s/601949/yahoo-has-a-tool-that-can-catch-online-abuse-surprisingly-well.

77. L. Ferry, "Les trois visages de l'intelligence artificielle," *Le Figaro*, April 5, 2018, 15.

78. Notably, not to go back too far in time: P. Hamon, *L'Ironie littéraire: Essai sur les formes de l'écriture oblique* (Paris, 1996); E. Behler, *Irony and the Discourse of Modernity* (Seattle, 1990); P. Schoentjes, *Poétique de l'ironie* (Paris, 2001); *L'Ironie aujourd'hui: lectures d'un discours oblique*, ed. M. Trabelsi (Clermont-Ferrand, 2006).

79. Fontanier, *Les Figures du discours*, 145–46.

80. See chapter 2, p. 19, this volume.

81. Quintilian 9.2.65, 87, 89.

82. Demetrius, *Style*, 291; Hermogenes, *The Stylistic Categories of Speech* 2.8.9–13; Pseudo-Dionysius of Halicarnassus, *Figured Speeches* 2.1; Quintilian 9.2.97.

83. W. Empson, *Seven Types*, 192ff.; J. Haffenden, *William Empson* (Oxford, 2005), 1:211.

84. D. Thouard, *Le Partage des idées: Études sur la forme de la philosophie* (Paris, 2007).

85. J. Laplanche, J.-B. Pontalis, *Vocabulaire de la psychanalyse*, ed. D. Lagache (Paris, 1967), "(Dé)négation," 112–14.

86. Molière, *The Misanthrope*, act 1, scene 2.

87. Empson, *Seven Types*, 205ff.

88. Scott, "Dans le dos du pouvoir," an interview pub. in French in *Vacarme* 42 (Winter 2007/8), reprinted in the French trans. of *Domination* (Paris, 2008), 248.

89. See *Forbes*, September 29, 2016, https://www.forbes.com/sites/robertpearl/2016/09/29/what-the-presidential-candidates-left-unsaid-in-the-debate-three-winning-solutions-for-healthcare/#4db8c408193e.

90. See *New York Times*, June 9, 2017, https://www.nytimes.com/video/us/politics/100000005152876/what-comey-left-unsaid-and-what-it-means.html.

91. I. A. López, *Dog Whistle Politics: How Coded Racial Appeals Have Reinvented Racism and Wrecked the Middle Class* (Oxford, 2014), 4.

92. E. Wheeler, *Tested Sentences That Sell* (1937), ed. R. C. Worstell (Midwest Journal Press, 2014), 37.

93. Ibid., 24–25.

94. Ibid., 96, 109, 104–5.

95. G. Roudière, *Traquer le non-dit: Une sémantique au quotidien* (Issy-les-Moulineaux, 2002), 152.

96. P. Levillain, "Quelle place pour l'implicite dans l'analyse de la proposition interro-négative en anglais?" in *Autour des formes implicites*, ed. S. Anquetil, J. Elie-Deschamps, and C. Lefebvre-Scodeller (Rennes, 2017), 76.

97. Marcus Aurelius, *Meditations* 1.10.

98. J.-L. Vix, *Alexandros de Cotiaeon: Fragments* (Paris, 2018), lxv–lxix.

99. Y. Guégan, *Les Ruses éducatives: Agir en stratège pour mobiliser les élèves*, 5th ed. (Paris, 2016), 82.

100. Macrobius, *Saturnalia* 7.3, available in the Loeb Classical Library, Macrobius, ed. R. A. Kaster (Cambridge, MA, 2011), 3:162–75.

101. Ibid. (Kaster's Loeb trans., modified: *salsamenta vendebas*); and 2.3.10, Kaster's trans., Loeb Macrobius (Cambridge, MA, 2011), 1:342–43, with note 43 on a difficulty in interpretation, which there is no need to go into here.

102. E. Hemingway, *Death in the Afternoon* (New York, 1932), chapter 16, conclusion.

103. E. Hemingway, *A Moveable Feast* (New York, 1964), "Hunger Was Good Discipline," 75. Cf. P. Smith, "Hemingway's Early Manuscripts: The Theory and Practice of Omission," *Journal of Modern Literature* 10 (1983): 268–88.

104. C. Baker, *Ernest Hemingway: A Life Story* (New York, 1969), 3.14.

105. Corneille, *Le Cid*, act 1, scene 3.

106. Racine, *Phèdre*, act 2, scene 5.

107. Gregory of Corinth, *Scholia on Hermogenes*, in *Rhetores Graeci*, ed. C. Walz (Stuttgart, 1834), 7:1287, 1289 = Planudes, *Scholia on Hermogenes*, in Walz (1833), 5:569.

108. See chapter 2, pp. 22–23, this volume.

109. Apsines, *On Figured Problems*, 6–13; Syrianus, Sopater, and Marcellinus, *Scholia on Hermogenes*, in Walz, *Rhetores* (1833), 4:122 = H. Rabe, *Prolegomenon Sylloge* (Leipzig, 1931), 211.

110. Servius, *Commentary on the Aeneid*, at 5.687, in *Servii grammatici qui feruntur in Vergilii carmina commentarii*, ed. G. Thilo (Leipzig, 1881), 1:641.

111. Servius, at 10.617, in Thilo (1884), 2:453.

112. Ovid, *Metamorphoses* 2.279–81.

113. Schiller, *Die Räuber* (*The Robbers*), act 2, scene 3.

114. Heliodorus, *Aethiopica* 10.16, with the analysis of J. R. Morgan, "Un discours figuré chez Héliodore: 'comment, en disant l'inverse de ce qu'on veut, on peut accomplir ce qu'on veut sans sembler dire l'inverse de ce qu'on veut'" [A figured speech in Heliodorus: "how, by saying the opposite of what one wants, one can accomplish what one wants without seeming to say the opposite of what one wants"], in *Discours et Débats dans l'ancien roman*, ed. B. Pouderon, J. Peigney, and C. Bost-Pouderon (Lyons, 2006), 51–62.

A Final Word

1. This expression, in Latin, *"fandi cuniculi,"* is from the encyclopedist Martianus Capella, apropos of the "oblique" conduct of speech, *Wedding of Mercury and Philology* 5.470, in the edition of J. Willis, *De nuptiis Mercurii et Philologiae* (Leipzig, 1983), 165.

2. These instances have been met before, pp. 9, 44, 58, 73, 81–82, 91, 133, this volume.

3. Cf. Theophrastus, cited by Demetrius, *On Style* 222; Quintilian 9.2.65, 71–72; J. Paulhan, *Entretien sur les faits divers*, in *Œuvres*, 2:124; W. Empson, *Seven Types of Ambiguity* (New York, 1966), 23.

4. Aragon, *Cette vie à nous*, in *Le Roman inachevé* (*Œuvres poétiques complètes*, ed. O. Barbarant [Paris, 2007]), 2:225.

5. See p. x and p. 138, this volume.

Index

1984 (Orwell), 4, 89–90
2048: The End of the World (Sansal), 4

acting, 5–6
Adorno, Theodor, 111
Aelius Aristides
    city names in encomia, 65
    encomium of Athens (*Panathenaicus*),
        119–20
    Encomium of Rome, 63–66, 68–69, 153n34
    figured speech, 54–55
    Greek identity, 54
    health issues, 62
    spiritual superiority beliefs, 62–63
Aeneid (Vergil), 139–40
Aeschines of Sphettos, 42
Aeschylus, 70
Aethiopica (Heliodorus), 127
Agamemmnon (Aeschylus), 70
allegory, 12–13, 17, 129
allusion
    aesthetics, 31
    after-the-fact, 41–42, 88
    Aragon's smuggled poetry, 72–73, 75–76,
        79
    Fontanier's definition, 129
    intertextual, 32
    to names, 65–67, 76
    sexual subtexts, 103
    Soviet bloc writers, 80
ambiguity typologies, 33–34
Animal Farm (Orwell), 3–4, 45
Anna Karenina (Tolstoy), 94
antifiguration (*antiskhêmatismenos*), 121
antiphrasis, 129

apostrophe, 129
Aragon, Louis
    biography, 71, 73
    on Mayakovsky, Vladimir, 142
    secrecy, 73
    wife Elsa Triolet, 71–72, 74–76
    See also smuggled poetry
Aristotle, 46–47, 59
Armance (Stendhal), 98–101, 103–4, 133
art, 26–27, 35–36
artificial intelligence, 132–33
asking for death, 138–40
Aspasius of Byblos, 149n5
L'Assommoir (Zola), 38
attenuation, 19, 60–61, 84
authorial intent, 44, 101
authoritarian regimes, 87–90
    See also Greek pretenses about Rome;
        Roman Empire; smuggled poetry;
        the Soviet bloc; totalitarianism

Balzac, Honoré de
    Chouans, Les, 93
    Duchesse de Langeais, La, 127
    and Dumas, 121
    the French language, x
    half of language as subtext, 143
    Human Comedy, The, 46, 104
    Old Maid, The (La Vieille Fille), 101–3
    sexorama term, 92, 156n3
    and Stendhal, 101, 104
Barthes, Roland, 31–32
Baudelaire, Charles, 43
beauty and ugliness, 26–27
Bern, Stéphane, 3

Betrothed, The (Manzoni), 86–87, 95
Beyle, Marie-Henri. *See* Stendhal
Blacks, The (Genet), 68
Blanchot, Maurice, 51
Boileau, Nicolas, 30
boldness, 112
Borges, Jorge Luis, 127–28
Bourdieu, Pierre, 2
Boussardel, Les (Hériat), 96
Brecht, Berthold, 82
Bruni, Carla, 8

Caillois, Roger, 35–36
Calpurnius Flaccus, 149n17
Carrinas Secundus, 55
Carroll, Lewis, 86
Castex, P.-G., 103
censorship, 79–82, 85
ceremonies, 1
character substitution, 59
Charterhouse of Parma, The (Stendhal), 94
Chateaubriand, François-René de, 82
China, 81–82
Chirac, Jacques, 41, 43
Chouans, Les (Balzac), 93
Cicero, 25, 41–42, 137
Cid, Le, 130, 138–39
Ciliga, Ante, 90
Cinderella, 122
Cioran, Emil, 111
classroom correction methods, 136–37
Clemenceau, Georges, 105–6
Clérambault, Gaëtan Gatien de, 40
Clérambault syndrome, 40–41
Coco (Courteline), 111
coded novels, 3–5
collusion, 47–50
Confessions (Rousseau), 43
connotation, 27–28, 48
conspiracy theories, 14, 134
context, 46–47, 51, 107
contrebande. *See* smuggled poetry
Cornély, Jules, 107
Courrier Anglais (Stendhal), 156n29
Courteline, Georges, 111
Crucible, The (Miller), 5
cynicism, 115–16

damnatio memoriae, 65, 67
Daniel, Arnaud, 74
Dante, 94–95
Darnton, Robert, 79, 81
Death in the Afternoon (Hemingway), 138
declamations, 22, 109
    See also figured declamation

declarations of war, 126
decoding in literary criticism, 31–32
Delacroix, Eugène, 12
della Casa, Giovanni, 1
Demetrius, 16, 24
democracy, 91
Demosthenes, 139
denegation, 134
diagonal coherences, 35–36
dictionaries of sexual innuendo, 97
Dio Chrysostum, 54–55, 61–62, 69
    See also *Discourses on Kingship*
Diogenes, 115, 117–18
"Dionysius at Corinth" phrase, 122
Dionysius of Halicarnassus. *See*
    Pseudo-Dionysius
Dio of Prusa. *See* Dio Chrysostum
diplomatic function of subtext, 142
direct speech. *See* frankness
Discourses on Kingship (Dio Chrysostum)
    overview, 55–56, 68–69
    contexts, 61
    figured speech, 60–61
    Foucault's use of, 118
    generalization, 57–58
    good king qualities, 55
    paratextual introduction, 57–58
    prosopopoeia, 130
    purposes, 61
    simplicity emphasis, 57
    third party use, 59–60
distinction, 2–3
dog whistle politics, 135
Domitian, 55–58, 61
double-meaning abuses, 109
double-talk, 83–85
Draghi, Mario, 7
Duchesse de Langeais, La (Balzac), 127
Ducrot, Oswald, 150n11
Dumas, Alexandre, 121

Eco, Umberto, 44
L'Écornifleur (Renard), 95–96
egg-texts, 32
ellipses in sexual subtext, 93–95
Empson, William, 33–34, 133
encomia, 58, 61, 63, 66–67, 69
    See also *Discourses on Kingship*
encomium of Athens (Aelius Aristides),
    119–20
Encomium of Rome (Aelius Aristides), 63–66,
    68–69, 153n34
Enduring Love (McEwan), 40
enigmas, 9, 17
epitexts, 45

erotomania, 40
ethopoeia, 59, 130
etiquette, 1–2
   See also polite speech
eulogies, 43, 106–7
euphemism, 129

fables, 9
fairy tales, 121–22
the fantastic, 35–36
Farewell Address (Gregory of Nazianzus), 42
Faure, Félix, 104–7
Ferry, Luc, 132
fictitious dialogue, 130
figured declamations
   overview, 22
   asking for death, 139
   criticisms of, 109
   double meaning abuses, 109
   St. Jerome, 42
   textual collections, 22, 149n17
   topics commonly used, 22–23
   use of pauses, 123
figured sarcasm, 137–38
figured speech
   overview, 15, 17
   Aelius Aristides, 54–55
   attenuation, 19, 60–61, 84
   the contrary, 133
   criticisms of, 109–10
   Dio Chrysostum, 60–61
   Heliodorus, 161n114
   hinting, 19–21, 61
   inversion, 19–20, 61, 84
   versus linguistics, 28–29
   literary criticism, 25
   persuasion techniques, 17
   quoting third parties technique, 59
   reasons for using, 18
   relation to styled figures, 16–17, 149n7
   smuggled poetry similarities, 73–74
   texts on, 15–17, 149n5
   theoretical development, 15–16
   typology, 19–21
   use contexts, 23–25
   See also figured declamations
figures of speech, 128–31
Finkielkraut, Alain, 108
Flaubert, 46
Flies, The (Sartre), 5
Fontanier, Pierre, 128–29, 133
Fortunatianus, 16
Foucault, Michel, 113–18
Fraisse, Luc, 32
France, Anatole, 3, 66–67

frankness
   boldness, 112
   Foucault's research, 118
   occasions calling for, 110
   paradox of, 118
   parrhêsia, 113–18, 158n26
   perils, 111
   philosophical, 115
   political freedom of speech, 114, 116
   preaching, 110–11
   versus subtext, 118
Freud, Sigmund, 27, 29, 124
friendship, 110
Fumaroli, Marc, 82, 121–22

gastronomastics, 131
Gaulle, Charles de, vii
generalization, 58
Genet, Jean, 68
Genette, Gérard, 32, 45, 128
German occupation of France, 76
   See also smuggled poetry
Gide, André, 32–33
Giscard d'Estaing, Valéry, 8
Glucksmann, André, 31
Gone with the Wind (film), 95
Greek myths, 13, 126–27
Greek oligarchs, 82–83
Greek pretenses about Rome
   games of disguises, 59–62
   identity issues, 52–54, 69
   omissions, 63–65
   pretense as weapon, 54
   silence, 67–69
   simplicity, 56–57
   sophistic milieus, 54–55
   speaking generally, 57–58
   See also Aelius Aristides; Dio Chrysostum
Greenspan, Alan, 7
Gregory of Nazianzus, 42
"grey song" (Verlaine), 30–31, 91
Grice, Paul, 27
Guermantes Way, The (Proust), 120

Hadot, Pierre, 11
Haraszti, Miklós, 81
Heliodorus, 127, 140, 161n114
Hemingway, Ernest, 138, 143
Heraclitus, 11–12
Hériat, Philippe, 96
hermeneutics of suspicion
   overview, 26–27
   ambiguity typology, 33–34
   diagonal coherences, 35–36
   linguistic connotation, 27–29

Index

hermeneutics of suspicion (*continued*)
    literary criticism and decoding, 31–33
    poetics, 30–31
    psychoanalysis, 29–30
Hermogenes. *See* Pseudo-Hermogenes
Hermogenes of Tarsus, 55
Herodes Atticus, 55
Herzl, Theodor, 6–7
hidden clues, 119–20
hinting, 19–21, 61
historical analogy, 82–83
Hollande, François, 121
Homer
    Iliad, 19–20, 109, 111, 133
    Odyssey, 126–27
Horace, 43
humorous function of subtext, 143
Hungary, 81
hyperbole, 130
hypocoristic function of subtext, 143

iceberg theory, the, 138
Iliad (Homer), 19–20, 109, 111, 133
L'Illusion délirante d'être aimé (*Attachment*)
    (Noiville), 40
implication, 27, 150n11
impotence in literature, 97–104
indecency. *See* sexual subtext
indirection, 70–73
Inferno (Dante), 94–95
infrapolitics, 132
In Search of Lost Time (Proust), 37–38, 43,
    96–97, 120
intention, 27
interpretation risks and safeguards, 42–45
    collusion, 47–50
    context, 46–48, 51
    one word for another, 50–51
    overinterpretation, 38–42
    paratexts, 45–46, 51
    slippery eels, 42–45
    subtexts missed by message recipients,
        37–38
    textual criteria, 48–50
intertextuality, 32
inversion, 19–20, 61, 84
irony, 17, 133–34, 137
Isaac, Jules, 82–83
Isocrates, 16, 44

Jarratt, Susan, 117
Jealousy (Robbe-Grillet), 120
St. Jerome, 42
Johnson, Boris, 154n1
Junius Otho the Elder, 149n5

Jupiter (god), 139–40

Kapuściński, Ryszard, 80
Kerbrat-Orecchioni, Catherine, 27–28, 128,
    150n5
Ketman (secret dissimulation), 80–81
"kill me" expression, 138–40
Klemperer, Victor, 87–91

Laberius, 137–38
Lacan, Jacques, 40
La Fontaine, Jean de, 87
Language of the Third Reich, The (*LTI*)
    (Klemperer), 88–90
La Rochelle, Drieu, 76
Lasso de la Vega, 21
L'Assommoir (Zola), 38
Lavric, Eva, 131
leading questions, 135–36
Learned Ladies, The (Molière), 38–39
Le Duc, Léozon, 106
"left unsaid" expression, 134–35
Lemaître, Frédérick, 123
Lenin, Vladimir, 82
Le Tellier, Hervé, 41
Libanius, 24, 149n17
license, 130
    See also boldness; *parrhêsia*
lies, 85, 90–91, 143
linguistics, 27–29, 48
lip service, 124–25
listeners creating subtext, 49
literary criticism
    debates over textual interpretation, 44
    decoding, 31–32, 109
    Empson's ambiguity typology, 33–34
    figured speech, 25
    intertextuality, 32
    School of Constance, 47
    self-reflexivity, 32–33
literature
    coded novels, 3–5
    modern, 26–27
    self-reflexive, 32–33
    See also poetry; *individual works by title*
litotes (understatement), 130
Londres, Albert, 90
LTI (*Language of the Third Reich, The*)
    (Klemperer), 88–90

Maalouf, Amin, 67
Machiavelli, Niccolò, 42
Macrobius, 137
Madame de Sévigné, 45
Mademoiselle de Belle-Isle (Dumas), 121

Mallarmé, Stéphane, 31, 66, 97
Mandrake, The (Machiavelli), 42
Manzoni, Alessandro, 86–87, 95
Marcus Aurelius, 55, 136
Marion, Paul, 79
Martianus Capella, 16
Martyrs, The (Chateaubriand), 82
Maternus, 55
Mayakovsky, Vladimir, 142
McEwan, Ian, 40
messages, 35, 124
metaphors
    allegory, 12–13, 17, 129
    ambiguous, 33–34
    censorship, 79
    comparison tropes, 130–31
    euphemism, 129
    political correctness, 91
    self-reflexivity, 32
    sexual, 92, 96–97
    synecdoches, 65, 130–31
Middle Ages, the, 74
Miller, Arthur, 5
Miłosz, Czesław, 80–81
Misanthrope, The (Molière), 134
mise en abyme, 33, 120
Mitterrand, François, 8, 41
modernity, 26–27
Moi et François Mitterrand (Le Tellier), 41
Molière
    Amphitryon, 42–43
    comedy, 5, 38
    generalization, 58
    Learned Ladies, The, 38–39
    Misanthrope, The, 134
    speech and thought, 110
    Tartuffe, 5, 43
monetary policy officials, 7
Montaigne, Michel de, 49, 67–68
Montherland, Henry de, 74
Morand, Paul, 107
Moveable Feast, A (Hemingway), 138
Much Ado About Nothing (Shakespeare), 39
mysteries (religious), 11–12
myths, 13, 126–27

names, 65–67, 76
nature's secrets, 10–12, 14
Nazi regime, 88–90
negation, 134
Neoplatonism, 47–48
Nerva, 55, 61
Nerval, Gérard de, 35–36
Nietzsche, Friedrich, 27, 124–25
Noiville, Florence, 40

Nunez, Laurent, 43

Odyssey (Homer), 126–27
Oedipus Tyrannos (Sophocles), 122–23
Old Maid, The (*La Vieille Fille*, Balzac), 101–3
oligarchs, 82–83
Oligarques, Les (Isaac), 82–83
omission, 63–66, 68–69, 138
one word for another, 50–51
On Style (Demetrius), 16
Order of Discourse, The (Foucault), 113–14
Orwell, George, 3–4, 33, 45, 89–91
Otho, Junius, 109
Out of Season (Hemingway), 138
overinterpretation, 38–42
Ovid, 140

parables, 47
paralipsis, 68
paratexts, 45–46, 51, 99–101
parrhêsia, 113–18, 158n26
Partridge, Eric, 97
Pascal, Blaise, 38, 44
St. Paul, 13
Paulhan, Jean, 9–10, 48, 71
pauses in oration, 123
Péguy, Charles, 108
Penelope (Greek myth), 126–27
Penguin Island (France), 3
Pensées (Pascal), 38, 151n5
Perec, Georges, 4–5
Perrault, Charles, 121–22
"Persecution and the Art of Writing"
    (Strauss), 49
Phèdre (Racine), 139
Philip of Macedon, 122
Philo of Alexandria, 13
Philostratus, 149n17
Pierron, Agnès, 97
plague, 86–87
Plato, 11, 49–50, 115
playing the devil's advocate, 21
pleading the false, 21
Pliny the Younger, 56
poetic and philosophic function of subtext,
    142–43
poetics, 30–31, 74
poetry, 9–10, 33–34
    See also smuggled poetry
Poland, 80–81
polemical function of subtext, 143
polite speech, 1–3
    See also attenuation
political correctness, 91
politics, 6–8

Pommier, René, 109
Port of Shadows (*Quai des ombres*, Prévert), 40
power, 85–86
 See also authoritarian regimes
pragmatics (linguistics), 27
praise, 124–25, 128, 137
 See also encomia
pretense, 52
 See also Greek pretenses about Rome
preterition, 130
Prévert, Jacques, 40
Prince, The (Machiavelli), 42
procrastination, 126–27
Promessi Sposi, I (Manzoni), 86–87, 95
prosodic acts, 122
prosopopoeia, 130
Proust, Marcel, 37–38, 43, 96–97, 120
proverbs, 10
Pseudo-Aristotle, 92
Pseudo-Dionysius (Dionysius of Halicarnassus), 16–17, 19, 21, 24–25
Pseudo-Hermogenes, 15–16, 19, 21
psychoanalysis, 29–30, 65, 134

questions, 135–36
Quinault, Philippe, 67
Quintilian
 arranged will case, 73
 boldness, 112
 figured speech theory, 15–18, 24, 153n10
 figured topics, 149n17
 irony, 133
 subtext responses, 121

Racine, Jean, 6, 118, 139
readers creating subtext, 49–50
Red and the Black, The (Stendhal), 93–94, 156n29
religion, 11–13
Renard, Jules, 95–96
restaurant menus, 131
reticence, 68, 130
Retz, Cardinal de, 111
rhetoric
 antifiguration (*antiskhêmatismenos*), 121
 audience emphasis, 46–47
 boldness, 112
 classes, 23
 contemporary, ix, 28–29, 148n1
 declamation, 22
 figures of silence, 17
 hidden clues, 119
 irony, 133
 versus linguistics, 28–29

literary roots, 21–22
parrhêsia connection, 117
persuasive goals, 17
quantitative figures, 17
styled figures, 16–17, 58
 See also figured declamations; figured speech
Rhetoric (Aristotle), 46–47
rhetorical encomia. *See encomia*
Rhetoric to Herennius, 112
Richards, I. A., 33, 133
Ricœur, Paul, 27
riddles, 9
Robbe-Grillet, Alain, 20, 159n8
Robbers, The (Schiller), 140
role-playing. *See* acting
Roman Empire
 Domitian, 55–58, 61
 governance strategies, 52–53
 Marcus Aurelius, 55, 136
 Nerva, 55, 61
 provincial governors, 128
 sophist persecution, 55
 Trajan, 55–58, 60–62
 word meanings, changing of, 86
 See also Greek pretenses about Rome
Rousseau, Jean-Jacques, 43, 111

Sadoul, Georges, 71
sales techniques, 136
Sansal, Boualem, 4
Sanskrit epics, 45
sarcasm, 137–38
Sarkozy, Nicolas, 8, 121
Sarraute, Nathalie, 26
Sartre, Jean-Paul, 5, 31, 92
Schiller, Frederich von, 140
School of Constance, 47
Scott, James, 131–32
Seghers, Pierre, 76
self-denunciation, 22–23, 139
self-reflexivity, 32–33
Seneca the Elder, 149n17
Septimius Severus Pertinax, 66
serious games, 61
Servius, 139
Seven Types of Ambiguity (Empson), 33–34
sexual subtext
 overview, 92–93
 death of Félix Faure, 104–7
 ellipses, 93–95
 half-rapes, 95–96
 impotence, 97–104
 metaphors, 96–97
Shakespeare, 39, 97

silence, 17, 67–68
Silence of the Sea, The (Vercors), 68
smuggled poetry (Aragon)
    overview, 70–71
    allusions, 72–73, 75–76, 79
    broad appeal and popularity, 76
    censorship avoidance, 78–79
    closed invention, 74
    coding practices, 77
    contextual complexities, 76–77
    decoding challenges, 77–78
    figured speech similarities, 73–74
    poetic influences, 74
    resistance themes, 75
    women, 74–75, 154n14
    See also smuggled poetry (works
        discussed)
smuggled poetry (works discussed)
    "Art poétique," 78
    Crève-cœur collection, 71–75
    Elsa's Eyes collection, 75
    Grévin Museum, The, 77, 86
    "La terre...ne mentira plus," 75–76
    Leçon de Ribérac ou l'Europe française,
        La, 74
    "Le criminel azur d'un rêve de Crimée,"
        75
    "Le Temps des mots croisés," 72, 78
    "Nymphée," 79, 155n31
    "Plus belle que les larmes," 75
    "Pour un chant national," 75
    "Prière pour faire pleuvoir," 75
    "Romance du temps qu'il fait," 71
    "Rose and the Reseda, The," 78–79
    "Twenty Years Later," 77–78
social niceties. *See* etiquette
Socrates, 115, 117
Socratic irony, 133
Solzhenitsyn, Aleksandr, 90–91
Sopater, 149n17
sophists, 54–55, 128
    See also Aelius Aristides; Dio Chrysostum
Sophocles, 122–23
Soviet bloc, the, 80–82, 90–91
Spartans, the, 67–68, 122
Spina, Luigi, 114
Sponger, The (Renard), 95–96
Steinheil, Marguerite, 105–6
Stendhal
    Armance, 98–101, 103–4, 133
    and Balzac, 101, 104
    Charterhouse of Parma, The, 94
    Courrier Anglais, 156n29
    impossibilities of love, 97
    Red and the Black, The, 93–94, 156n29

Sterne, Laurence, 111
Strauss, Leo
    allusive literature, ix–x
    biography, 48
    hidden clues, 119
    resistance by the intellectual elite, 132
    textual criteria, 48–49
subordinated groups, 131–32
subtexts
    overview, vii–viii, 142
    advantages, 110
    billiards metaphor, 142–43
    criticisms, 108–10
    dynamism, 142
    versus frankness, 118
    functions, 142–43
    morality, 143
    responses, 120–21
    scope of the problem, 141–42
    semiotics, vii–viii
    translation difficulties, 44–45
subtext thinking, 10–12
Suetonius, 153nn10–11
suspicion. *See* hermeneutics of suspicion
sweetening speech, 1–2
synecdoches, 65, 130–31

Tacitus, 86
talking turkey, 110–12
Tardieu, Jean, 50–51
teaching, 136–37
textual criteria, 48–50
theater, 5–6
Theophrastus, 82–83
Thibault, François-Anatole. *See* France,
    Anatole
third party creation, 59, 130
Thompson, Mark, 6
Thouard, Denis, 133
Thucydides, 86
Tiberius, 59
time and timing, 126–28
Tolstoy, Leo, 39–40, 94
totalitarianism, 4, 87–91
    See also authoritarian regimes
Trajan, 55–58, 60–62
Triolet, Elsa, 71–72, 74–76
tropes, 130–31
truth-telling, 124

understatement, 130
Un mot pour un autre (Tardieu), 50–51

Valéry, Paul, 43, 66–67
veiled discourse, 12

Vercors, 68
Vergil, 12, 139–40
Verlaine, Paul, 30–31, 91
Vigny, Alfred de, 33
Villepin, Dominique de, 126

W, or the Memory of Childhood (Perec), 4–5
War and Peace (Tolstoy), 39–40
Wheeler, Elmer, 136
women
    Aragon's smuggled poetry, 74–75, 154n14
    in impotence literature, 97–104
    procrastination uses, 126–27

words
    changing the meaning of, 85–86, 88–89
    substituting, 86–87

Xenophon of Ephesus, 127

"yes" and "no," 127

Zink, Michel, 74
Zola, Émile, 38

CPSIA information can be obtained
at www.ICGtesting.com
Printed in the USA
BVHW040522280223
659342BV00001B/3